WISDOM AND ✳ KNOWLEDGE
✳ ✳ SHALL BE THE ✳ ✳
STABILITY OF THY TIMES

INSIGHT GUIDES

Created and Directed by Hans Höfer

NewYorkCity

Edited and Produced by Martha Ellen Zenfell
Update Editor: Divya Symmers
Principal Photography: Catherine Karnow

Editorial Director: Brian Bell

April, 2000

Het was een echte vakantie,
dank je wel!
Zal er nog heel vaak aan
terugdenken,

Liefs, Joss

Houghton Mifflin

APA PUBLICATIONS

Automobile magnate Henry Ford once observed: "New York is a different country. Maybe it ought to have a separate government. Everybody thinks differently and even acts differently."

Putting together a book on New York City posed quite a few questions. How best to give insight into a place which claims such an assortment of identities? How to document the energy and the animosity, the chaos and the great charm of New York, without resorting to clichés?

Such challenges are nothing new to the *Insight Guides* series, created in 1970 by **Hans Höfer**, founder of Apa Publications and still the company's driving force. Like the other 190 titles, *Insight Guide: New York City* encourages readers to celebrate the essence of a place rather than try to tailor it to their expectations and is edited in the belief that, without insight into people's character and culture, travel can narrow the mind rather than broaden it.

The task of compiling the book fell to project editor **Martha Ellen Zenfell**, editor-in-chief of Apa Publications' North American titles. A native of the American South now based in London, Zenfell knew from having project edited *Insight Guides* to New Orleans, the Greek Islands and Bermuda that Apa's award-winning formula of hard-hitting text and superb photographs would give scope for in-depth coverage.

Zenfell's own New York adventures were varied – everything from attending a lavish cocktail party at a penthouse overlooking Central Park, with red, white and blue firecrackers exploding at eye level, to being thrown out of Grand Central Station along with several other homeless people at 2 am and being forced to seek refuge in a Times Square flophouse. Story ideas rapidly began to take shape.

Putting together a team of contributors was relatively straightforward, for, in the words of Edmund Love in *Subways are for Sleeping*, "New York attracts the most talented people in the world in the arts and professions. It also attracts them in other fields. Even the bums are talented."

Helping Zenfell assemble the cast was assistant editor **Divya Symmers**, a freelance writer who has contributed to the *New York Post,* the *New York Daily News* and *Travel Holiday.* Symmers alternated traveling the world with living in the Village and in Midtown, next door to Greta Garbo; writing a column about lower Manhattan provided the basis for her research into the downtown area of this book's "Places" section. Symmers' savvy for city living, plus her unerring eye for detail, proved to be invaluable contributions to the book.

Also early to be recruited was **John Gattuso**, who majored in English and anthropology in college. These useful subjects were brought to bear, not only on the editing of his own books (*Insight Guides* to *Native America* and *Philadelphia* and two volumes on National Parks), but also when applied to the history, the places and the immigrants of New York.

A former associate editor of *Ebony Magazine,* and past president of the New York Association of Black Journalists, **A. Peter Bailey** lived and worked in Harlem for over 20 years. Bailey was a natural when it came to tackling the culture of this little-known and often-misunderstood neighborhood.

"Everyone should experience New York City at least once," says contributor **John Wilcock**, who, along with **John Strausbaugh** of the *New York Press,* assembled the Travel Tips section. Wilcock's New York experience

Höfer

Zenfell

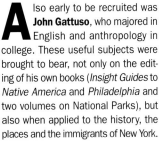

Symmers

Gattuso

Bailey

Wilcock

lasted 30 years, during which time he helped found *The Village Voice* and Andy Warhol's *Interview* (you can see his portrait by Warhol on page 74), among other projects. Wilcock "lived in the Village when it was still a village; TriBeCa when it was just warehouses; and Hell's Kitchen when it was heaven." He now lives in Los Angeles and is the project editor of several *Insight Guides* to California.

The essays in this book were contributed by a variety of experts and enthusiasts. **Michele Abruzzi**, ("Culture in the City") covered the New York Film Festival and Rolling Stones concerts while features editor at Reuters news agency.

Abruzzi

Michael Shapiro, a native of Brooklyn and a freelance contributor to *Esquire*, *The New York Times Magazine*, and *The Village Voice*, toured the Times Square area around midnight to pen the piece called "Eight Hours in a Police Car."

Shapiro

After 10 years as a New York radio broadcaster, **Kathy Novak** is now a magazine columnist and an executive producer for Public Television. This multi-media career led to her article on Manhattan's media.

Novak

Tim Harper, who relocated to London via New York and the Midwest, writes about economics for publications like *Time* and the *International Herald Tribune*. He is the project editor of *Insight Guide: Chicago*, and, for this book, trained his eye on New York's corporate culture.

Two contributors offered important guidance along the (occasionally rocky) way. **J. P. MacBean**, author of *New York: Heart of the City* and this book's "Regards to Broadway," answered what seemed like a million questions while serving as vice-president of the New York Convention & Visitors Bureau. **Clay Edmunds** drew on years of

Harper

success on Madison Avenue to write the piece on advertising, and, along with **Rona**, provided revealing insights into city life with their generosity and parties at One Fifth Avenue.

Samuel G. Freedman ("Metropolis of the Mind") and **Daniel Goleman** ("Super Achievers") are both veterans of *The New York Times*. These essays originally appeared in *The New York Times World of New York* by A. M. Rosenthal and Arthur Gelb, and are reprinted here with permission. **Anita Peltonen**, of New York, London and Finland, interrupted her travels to pen two short pieces.

As American cities go, New York is one of the most photogenic, but also one which is surprisingly difficult to photograph. Soaring buildings and people on the run are not easy targets to capture, and Zenfell looked through several thousand slides, gathered from eight different countries, before selecting some of the 320 images reproduced here.

Still not satisfied, she called on **Catherine Karnow**, whose witty, sympathetic portraits feature in many *Insight Guides*, to produce a series of stunning double-page spreads. Acknowledgement must also go to other first-class photographers, notably **Douglas Corrance**, **Bill Wassman**, **Carl Purcell** and **Gerard Sioen**.

Karnow

Thanks, too, to **Brook Hersey** and **Stacy Cochran**, for their choice words about various NY areas. **Sgt Edward Burns** of the New York Police Department recommended restaurants and smoothed our reporter's way while doing the cop story. **Tony Clark** proofread the manuscript in New York while **Dorothy Stannard** did the same, plus indexing, in London. **David Whelan** helped with the non-stop NY research and the initial picture edit.

CONTENTS

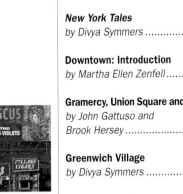

Maps

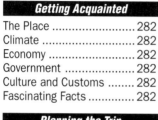

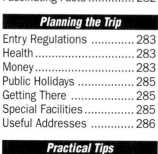

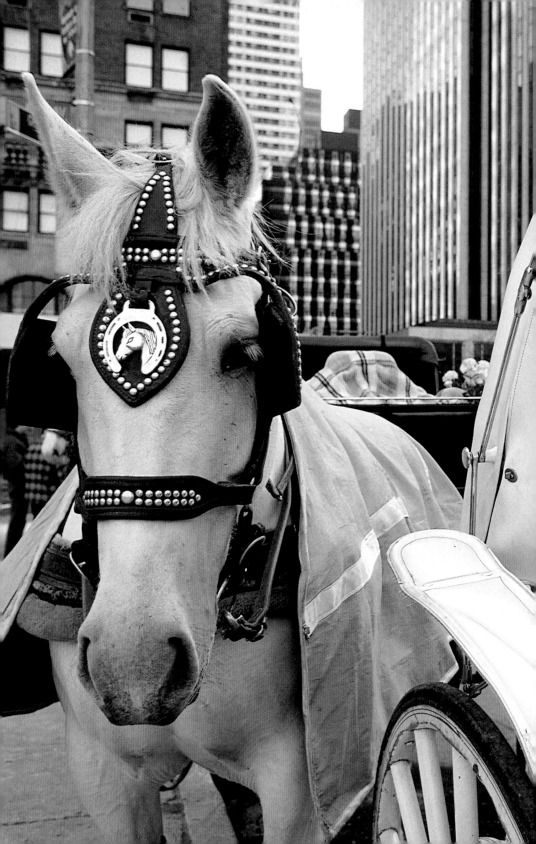

THE SIDEWALKS OF NEW YORK

"What is barely hinted at in other American cities is condensed and enlarged in New York," the writer Saul Bellow has at times been quoted as saying.

True words, undoubtedly. Since its purchase by the Dutch in 1626, through its growth as a maritime hub, fueled by cheap immigrant labor, to its contemporary position as, arguably, the cultural and retail center of the world, New York has become a city that can't be ignored.

The figures speak for themselves: there are more than 700 museums, exhibition spaces and galleries in New York. Four of the seven largest banks in America have their headquarters here, as do four of the half-dozen prominent insurance companies. The city supports more than a dozen official sports organizations, and generates at least $3 billion annually from both the film and TV industries.

There is a reason why famous recluses of our time, like Jacqueline Onassis and Greta Garbo, settled in New York City. It's the same reason why Janet James of Atlanta, or Marco Sabbadin from Rome, might pack their bags and head here some day. New York is the place where ordinary people can become stars, by performing in Washington Square Park, or by making it big in industry, and the place where real stars can walk down the street totally unnoticed. Or so we are led to believe: New York is the city of myths, and making them is a part of it.

New Yorkers play their own role in all this. In the quest to be the biggest and the boldest, this sometimes works to their disadvantage. Crime, for instance, although scary and tangible, is not the all-prevailing madness newspapers suggest. According to statistics released by the Federal Bureau of Investigation, the city recently ranked only 22nd in the country in the total number of crimes committed, well below "safe" cities like Seattle, or Boston. Plenty of people walk the streets around midnight, and live to tell the tale.

New York attracts the brightest and the best; beauty and the beast; the serious, the insane, and the just plain silly. The people who live here, and the 24 million people each year who visit here, wouldn't have it any other way.

Preceding pages: Rockefeller Center detail; the flip side of the city; twin grins; top-hatted transportation; skyline security force; shopping in Bloomingdale's. Left, tongue twister.

Mare glaciale.

IRCVL⁹ ARCTIC⁹

AM

Caput de bo na ventura

zipan gri īs iula

CVINOE

Spagnola

Isabella

OCCEANVS OCCIDENTALIS

Terra incognita

monte fregol

Allag

rio de indias 330 340 350 360

0 Z 60 Z 70 Z 80 Z 90 Z 00 Z 10 Z 20 Z 30

90°

vnus q̄d⁹ continet miliar..6.

Anthropologists say that people use mythology to imagine their own beginnings. It seems fitting, then, that according to local myth New York City began not with a divine urge to create but with a real-estate deal – and a swindle at that. In 1626, a Dutch official by the name of Peter Minuit bought Manhattan Island from the Indians for a box of trinkets worth 60 guilders, or about $24. Today in downtown Manhattan, $24 buys less than one square inch of office space.

Native Americans: The Indians Minuit did business with were of Algonquin stock, a family of loosely associated tribes ranging along the northeast coast. They led fairly settled lives, moving seasonally within tribal territory and making their livelihoods from hunting, fishing and planting.

Despite occasional skirmishes, their relations with Europeans in the first years of contact were cordial, if not exactly friendly. But when the Dutch set up house for good in Manhattan, the peace deteriorated. Theft, murder and squabbles over land rapidly escalated into a cycle of revenge that kept both Indians and colonists in a constant state of fear. At its worst, in 1643, a detachment of Dutch soldiers fell on two Indian camps, savagely murdering about 120 men, women and children, and then, two years later, massacred 1,000 more in villages north of Manhattan. In 1655 the Indians launched the so-called Peach War to avenge the murder of an Indian woman caught stealing from an orchard. Two thousand warriors terrorized the town for three days, killing 100 colonists, setting fire to houses and slaughtering cattle. In the end, however, the Algonquin were overwhelmed. Outnumbered by the well-armed Dutch, under constant threat of attack from the neighboring Iroquois, and riddled with European diseases, the tribes were muscled out of their own territory.

It was perhaps inevitable that the Indians would be pushed off their land from the first

Preceding pages: detail from map, *circa* 1507. **Left**, statue of early settler, St Patrick's Cathedral.

moment that Europeans set eyes on it. In 1524 Giovanni da Verrazano sailed into the Lower Bay and remarked on its "commodiousness and beauty" which he believed was "not without some properties of value." Verrazano took glowing descriptions back to his patrons in France, but no one in Europe paid much attention to the new land until 1609, when Henry Hudson sailed into New York Harbor flying a Dutch flag.

English by birth, Hudson was hired by a Dutch trading company to discover the elusive Northwest Passage to India. Although he didn't have much luck finding the legendary short-cut, he did stumble into the Upper Bay and agreed with Verrazano that "this was a very good land to fall with and a pleasant land to see." After tangling with a group of Indians, he pointed his ship, the *Half Moon*, up the river that would later bear his name, and sailed to the site of Albany before realizing he wasn't headed for the Pacific Ocean. The voyage wasn't a total loss, though. Along the way, he discovered a woodland that was brimming with commercial possiblities. He was especially interested in the pelts worn by local Indians. Fur meant big money in a cold country like the Netherlands, so he sent samples back to his trading company, explaining there was plenty more where they came from.

Hudson's employers were not impressed. But when word of his discovery leaked out, independent merchants sailed for the New World determined to bring back a fortune in pelts. One corporation in particular – the Dutch West India Company – pulled ahead of its competitors, and in 1621 acquired exclusive trading rights to the whole of New Netherland, a territory stretching from Cape May (New Jersey) well into New England – a land grab that made the English particularly nervous. To seal its claim, the company built trading posts along the coast and rivers, and sent a boat load of French-speaking Protestants known as Walloons to occupy them. In the summer of 1623, Dutch ships dropped off about 50 Walloons on tiny

Nut Island (Governor's Island) just off the tip of Manhattan. Within a few months, late arrivals crowded the camp, and the group decided to move to Manhattan. They planted their new settlement at the southern end of the island, naming it New Amsterdam.

Among the first men appointed by the company to govern the small village was Peter Minuit, who arrived in 1626 and immediately made his fateful deal with the Indians at the site of Bowling Green, plunking down a chest of beads, knives and hatchets in exchange for the entire island. Unfamiliar with the European notion of private property, the Indians probably didn't

town itself was little more than a cluster of wood houses and mud streets huddled around a rude fortification. In its first few years, the Walloons and Dutch were joined by a motley collection of convicts, slaves, religious zealots, profiteers, a variety of ne'er-do-wells and outcasts who had nowhere else to go, as well as an occasional group of Indians wandering in to trade. In all, the people of New Amsterdam represented four continents, at least eight nationalities, and spoke as many as 15 languages. It was an explosive mix, made all the more volatile by the short-sightedness of Dutch leadership. After Peter Minuit was ousted on charges of

understand what they were giving away. On the other hand, it's been argued that Minuit didn't understand the division of tribal territory and may have paid off a group of sachems that had no particular claim to Manhattan in the first place.

Life in tiny New Amsterdam was tumultuous, to say the least. There were Indian raids to worry about, and rumors concerning the English, who made no secret about their imperialist ambitions in the New World. Drinking seems to have been a favorite pastime among the lustier sorts, with boozy knife-fights finishing a close second. The

corruption, a parade of incompetents followed in the governor's seat, the worst of whom, Willem Kieft (known as Willem the Testy), provoked an Indian war, imposed unfair taxes, and dipped into public funds.

In 1647 the company decided to put New Amsterdam back on the straight and narrow, and they knew just the man to do it. Peter Stuyvesant was a hard-bitten soldier who had formerly served as the governor of Curaçao, where he lost his right leg in a tussle with the Portuguese. Upon arriving in New Amsterdam, "Peg Leg" Pete made no bones about his intention to rule with an iron hand.

He quickly cracked down on the smuggling and tax evasion, and made much frequent use of the whip and branding iron on the town's rowdier citizens.

Stuyvesant made few friends in New Amsterdam, but he got things done. During his 17-year rule, he established the town's first hospital, prison, school and post office. In order to keep both the English and Indians at arm's length, he fortified the town and built a wood barricade from river to river at the present site of Wall Street (hence the name). He was so successful at attracting settlers that New Amsterdam doubled in population to about 1,500 people.

and glad for the opportunity to get out from under Stuyvesant's rule. Without firing a single shot, the English raised the Union Jack over Fort Amsterdam and renamed the town New York in honor of the King's brother. The Dutch recaptured the town about 10 years later during the Second Anglo-Dutch War, but a quick deal at the negotiating table put it back in British hands, all without shedding a single drop of blood.

The British didn't fare much better than the Dutch at keeping a lid on their new possession. In 1689 a merchant by the name of William Leisler led a confused anti-Catholic rebellion against the governor and

But Stuyvesant's success provided no defense against intervention. Wedged into the North American coast with the English on either side, it was only a matter of time before the Dutch got squeezed out. In 1664, King Charles II dispatched Colonel Richard Nicholls to New Amsterdam with four warships and instructions to seize the town. Stuyvesant was ready to start a war, but the townspeople refused to fight. They were hopelessly outnumbered by Nicholls' men,

Left, French colonialists greeting Indians. **Above**, lower Manhattan in the 1730s.

took over New York for two stormy years before being hanged for treason. In 1712, a group of slaves set fire to a house and killed nine whites who rushed to put it out. Six of the would-be revolutionaries committed suicide rather than face the cruel colonial court. Others were banished, burned alive or tortured to death. Apprehension over the incident lingered until 1741, when a series of mysterious fires touched off a shameful anti-slave hysteria. Fearing what they thought was a bizarre black-Catholic conspiracy, white New Yorkers executed more than 30 slaves and banished many more.

The British were also having a difficult time keeping a handle on their increasingly independent subjects. Despite efforts to control trade between the mother country and the colonies, pirates and smugglers – including the infamous Captain Kidd – swarmed to New York in order to fence their ill-gotten merchandise and avoid paying hefty customs taxes. Meanwhile, in the political arena, a young publisher by the name of John Peter Zenger was making a career of lampooning government figures in his *New-York Weekly Journal*, only to get tossed into jail for slander in 1734. Zenger continued dictating his scathing diatribes from prison and after a long and riveting trial was acquitted, establishing precedent for the principle of freedom of the press.

But the real test of New York's independence came in 1765 with passage of the Stamp Act. After a 100-year struggle for supremacy in North America, the English decided it was time to show the colonies who was boss. King George III launched a battery of legislation designed to assert his authority over colonial affairs and fill the royal coffers. The new laws prohibited colonial currency, curtailed trade, and, in accordance with the Stamp Act, levied a heavy tax on everything from tobacco to playing cards.

To the feisty colonials, these restrictions were worse than the old Navigation Acts and smacked of the same arbitrary use of power. The rallying cry went out, "No taxation without representation" – and New Yorkers hit the streets. Spurred on by a group of agitators known as the Sons of Liberty, angry mobs stormed Fort James and terrorized government officials. By the time the stamps actually arrived in New York, there wasn't a bureaucrat in town who was brave enough to distribute them. Pressured by a colonial boycott, the British finally relented, and the Stamp Act was repealed.

But King George wasn't a man who took defeat lightly. In 1767 his new prime minister, Charles Townshend, lashed out with a new tax on imported items like paper, lead and tea. This time the King sent along an extra contingent of redcoats.

The Sons of Liberty despised the soldiers and took every opportunity to make their lives miserable. They erected a symbolic Liberty Pole and taunted soldiers. The year-long battle of nerves finally exploded in January 1770, when rebels and redcoats faced off at the Battle of Golden Hill.

Following the example of their Boston cousins, New Yorkers protested the hated Tea Tax by staging their own "Tea Party." On April 22, 1774, a mob of angry citizens boarded an English cargo ship and dumped the tea into the harbor. One year later, the "shot heard 'round the world" was fired at Lexington, Massachusetts, and the American Revolution was off and running. When the Declaration of Independence was read to crowds in New York, a mob raced down Broadway to topple the statue of King George III in Bowling Green. According to legend, the statue was melted down into musket balls and fired at British troops.

Resounding defeat: After General George Washington chased the British out of Boston, he came down to New York for a rematch against General Howe, but this time he lost his shirt. British troops beat back Washington's fledgling army from Brooklyn, through Manhattan, to a resounding defeat at White Plains. The battle at Fort Washington was especially tragic. While Washington led his men across the Hudson River, a single regiment defended them from Washington Heights. But rather than follow the rest of the army, the commanding officer decided to dig in at Fort Washington and face the British head-on. It was a fatal error of judgment. Watching from New Jersey, General Washington wept at the sight of more than 5,000 men being slaughtered by the superior British force. They settled in for a brutal seven-year occupation.

When Washington returned to New York in 1785 it was to celebrate America's victory and to bid farewell to his officers. If the General had had his way he would have retired to Virginia, never to serve again. But four years later he was back in New York, his hand on a Bible, taking the oath of office at Federal Hall. For a single year, New York was the nation's capital.

Right, primitive painting by J. Califano of Washington en route to New York.

A GREAT FIRE

Tms florishing city bicame, on the 25 december 1855, a prey to the flames. The fire broke out at nine in the evening, in the high north-east wind; together with the intensity of the cold, having paralysed the effect of the pumps, nothing could stop the miles distance (12 or 13 leagues). It is impossible to describe the awful horrible sight and desolation which the return of day piers amounting to above 5000 men. Seventeen clusters of the most vast and rich buildings were devoured; from 1000 to 120 impossible to estimate the immense losses occasioned by this unfortunate event, which are valued to above 260 millions of fra dreadful fire plunged many families in misery. Fortunately the harbour was preserved; they have only to deplore the loss of th fire was consumed in an instant. The president of the bank, though ill, came from Philadephia to New-York, and upon th they may cover a part of the reimbursements to the insured victims.

METZ, (Mozel) : printed and published by DEMBOUR, Engra

est and richest part of the town. Ever since the great fire in Moscow, there has been no example of such disastrous an event. A
aud violence of the fire. It was a dreadful despairing night for this unfortunate city; the flames were perceived at 30 or 40
ill more sensible. The courage and endeavours of man proved fruitless, and likewise the labours of the beautiful corps pum-
burnt; storehouses in wgich were heaed quantities of goods, and other valuable objects were equally lost. It would be
t many people perished in the flames, and that part of the town, so handsome and élégant, is but a heap of ruins. This
cent ship, the PARIS, arrived since two days from China, with a cargo valued to 200,000 dollars, which having caught
curity of the burnt city, he ordered six millions of dollars to be advanced by the bank, to the directors of assurances, that

Lithographer, the successor of LACOUR and Cⁱ, of NANCY.

C.J.STANILAND

At the turn of the 19th century, New York was still a small town. The population stood at about 35,000 people, and although an outbreak of yellow fever scared some residents to the open spaces of Greenwich Village, most stayed where they were, huddled in the crooked lanes south of Canal Street.

Since the Revolution, there had been plenty to keep New Yorkers busy. A public debate raged over the new Constitution; a group of brokers hammered out the New York Stock Exchange in the shade of a buttonwood tree on Wall Street; five people were killed during a riot against Columbia University doctors who were robbing graves to supply their anatomy labs; and an occasional buffalo hunt was held in the city with animals shipped from the western territories.

Politically, the town was split between Democrats and Federalists, represented by the city's two most prominent lawyers: Aaron Burr, who would serve as Vice-president under Thomas Jefferson, and Alexander Hamilton, the nation's first Secretary of Treasury. After years of feuding, the two schemers finally had it out on the field of honor. In 1804, Burr shot and killed his rival in a duel at Weehawken, New Jersey.

But it wasn't until the opening of the Erie Canal in 1825 that the sparks really started to fly. The Erie Canal took 12 years to build, stretched over 350 miles from Buffalo to Lake Erie, and provided a vital link between New York and the ripe markets of the midwest. Almost overnight, New York was transformed into a maritime giant as ships from all over the world jammed into the East River Harbor (now South Street Seaport) carrying goods destined for the heartland. Fueled by cheap immigrant labor, the city became an industrial dynamo too. Business boomed, the population soared to 312,000 (1840), and real estate prices went through the roof. Wheeler-dealers like John Jacob

Astor and Cornelius Vanderbilt made a killing in real estate and shipping, and the banking industry rose to national prominence. In 1835 the city celebrated its new affluence by hosting the World's Fair at the magnificent, although short-lived, Crystal Palace.

Immigrant labor: But while wealthy businessmen were "lapping up the cream of commerce," the people who actually did the work – most of them poor immigrants from Germany and Ireland – were struggling to

keep their heads above water. Although a trickle of Irish immigrants had arrived in time to work on the Erie Canal, the floodgates didn't really open until the 1840s, when the Potato Blight in Ireland and the failed revolution in Germany sent thousands to the New World.

The immigrants piled into overcrowded tenements owned by slumlords like John Jacob Astor who grew fat (literally in Astor's case) on exorbitant rents. The dilapidated Five Points district – the largest Irish community outside Ireland – was particularly rancid, with frequent outbreaks of cholera

Preceding pages: The Great Fire. Left, etching of Jewish refugees arriving in New York Harbor. Right, a fashionable gentleman *circa* 1818.

and yellow fever, and gangs like the Bowery Boys and Plug Uglies marauding the streets.

So-called native Americans organized against foreigners, declaring that "Americans will never consent to allow the government established by our Revolutionary forefathers to pass into the hands of foreigners." The highly secretive nativists – whom newspaper editor Horace Greely called "know-nothings" because they responded to every question that was asked them with the stock answer, "I know nothing" – focused their bigotry on the Irish, who they linked with a trumped-up "Catholic conspiracy" against god-fearing Yankees.

By the 1850s, however, it seemed less likely that the country would be overrun by foreigners than split apart by domestic conflicts. Thanks largely to a Bostonian named William Lloyd Garrison, slavery was fast becoming the issue of the day. Disparaged as fanatics and demagogues, New York abolitionists tried to bring their message to the people only to find themselves facing angry bankers and businessmen who were heavily invested in Southern crops. "The city of New York belongs almost as much to the South as to the North," the *Evening Post* reported. Even Mayor Fernando Wood supported the "continuance of slave labor and the prosper-

The Irish weren't scorned by all New Yorkers, however. The Democratic politicos at Tammany Hall saw the Irish as a keg of electoral power just waiting to be tapped, and they went out of their way to recruit them. If an immigrant needed naturalization papers, a Tammany man was there to pull the right strings. If a poor Irish lad got himself arrested, a Tammany lawyer bailed him out. If an old widow couldn't make the rent, Tammany money came to the rescue. It was a simple enough deal, tit-for-tat. And all the Irish had to do to meet their end of the bargain was cast Democratic votes.

ity of the slave master." When civil war seemed inevitable, he proposed that New York City declare itself independent in order to protect its business with the South.

In February, 1860, a dark-horse candidate by the name of Abraham Lincoln spoke at Cooper Union, a free college established a year earlier by philanthropist Peter Cooper. Despite an ill-fitting suit, painfully tight shoes and an initial touch of stage fright, Lincoln's reasoned words and powerful delivery riveted the audience. Copies of the Cooper Union address were distributed throughout the country, and Lincoln himself recognized that it was a critical turning point in his bid for the presidency.

In November, Lincoln was elected without a single Southern electoral vote, and five months later Fort Sumter was bombarded by Confederate artillery. At the Plymouth Church of Brooklyn, abolitionist minister Henry Ward Beecher shrieked for "war redder than blood and fiercer than fire." And that's exactly what he got.

In April 1861, Lincoln called for volunteers to put down the rebellious Southerners and New York responded dutifully, producing 8,000 soldiers, including Irish and German regiments. Patriotism was suddenly in

was outrageous. When it was learned that wealthy young men could buy their way out of the army for $300, the city's poverty-stricken masses were unable to contain themselves. On a steamy July morning a mob of several thousand stormed the Third Avenue draft office, routed police, and set fire to the entire block. Their appetite for carnage whetted, the mob rampaged for three more days while what little was left of the civil guard tried to put the rebellion down. Apparently unsatisfied with beating policemen to death, the mob turned its attention to the few unlucky blacks who were unable to escape. An orphanage for black

vogue. Even local businesses got in on the act. Tiffany's started crafting military regalia, and Brooks Brothers churned out uniforms. As the war dragged on and hope of a speedy victory faded, however, New York's fighting spirit started to sag. Among the war-weary lower classes, defeatism turned to rage when Lincoln pushed for a conscription law in 1862. Bad enough that Lincoln had dragged them into a war. But a draft? That

Left, carriage-riding in Central Park in the mid-1800s. **Above**, New York sent 8,000 soldiers to the Civil War.

children was burned on Fifth Avenue, and, in all, 18 black men were caught and lynched, their mutilated bodies left hanging from lampposts. The Draft Riots were the most disgraceful and barbaric display of violence New York had ever seen. In the end, armed regiments had to be recalled from the Union Army in order to get the city under control. But by then more than 1,000 people had been killed, 8,000 wounded, and about 300 buildings damaged or destroyed.

The Civil War ended two years later. Within months, Abraham Lincoln's body lay in state at New York City Hall.

Historians put the founding of New York at 1625, when the Dutch first settled on lower Manhattan. But the New York most people envision – the financial giant bristling with skyscrapers, the dream-city of immigrants – *that* New York didn't really start until after the Civil War. The late 19th century was Manhattan's Big Bang, a time of explosive growth and wondrous achievements. The American Museum of Natural History was established in 1877, and the Metropolitan Museum of Art in 1880. The Metropolitan Opera opened in 1883, the same year as the Brooklyn Bridge opened (a few days after which a dozen people were trampled to death when someone got it in his head that the span of the bridge was about to collapse). Three years later, the Statue of Liberty was dedicated in New York Harbor.

Tenement city: Mass immigration continued after the Civil War, although most of the new arrivals were now coming from southern and eastern Europe as well as China. Italians – most from the southern provinces – crammed into the dilapidated tenements around Mulberry Street or in Greenwich Village. Jews forced out of Russia by anti-semitic pogroms flooded into the Lower East Side. And Chinese immigrants settled around Mott Street. In 1898, the unification of the five boroughs under a single city government brought New York's population to 3.4 million people – half foreign-born, and two-thirds living in tenements.

As far as politics was concerned, the city was run by Tammany Hall, and Tammany Hall was run by William Marcy Tweed. A 300-pounder of voracious appetites, "Boss" Tweed started out as a chairmaker, worked his way up the ranks of the Democratic machine, and then landed a position on the County Board of Supervisors. Within a few years, he was the most powerful politician in New York City, if not the entire state.

Preceding pages: Riverside Drive in 1896. **Left,** the Brooklyn Bridge. **Right,** detail from a poster of *Metropolis*.

Tweed established his influence the old-fashioned way – patronage, graft and kickbacks. The foundation of Tammany power was the loyalty of the lower classes, who saw Tweed as a sort of Robin Hood figure, stealing from the rich and cutting the poor in for a slice of the pie, however small. As one observer put it, "The government of the rich by the manipulation of the vote of the poor is a new phenomenon in the world."

Although Tweed did his share of do-

gooding for the poor, most of his energy was spent lining his own pocket. City contracts, for example, were commissioned on a simple percentage basis. Jobs were padded with extra funds, and a percentage of the total – sometimes the overwhelming percentage – wound up fattening Tweed's wallet. In one spectacular morning, Tweed and his cronies raked in a cool $5.5 million. Ironically, the contract in question was for the New York City Courthouse (a.k.a. the "Tweed Courthouse") immediately behind City Hall. As far as opposition went, Tweed simply bought off anyone who stood in his way. He kept the police department in his back pocket and had a number of judges on the payroll. And if money wasn't enough to cool the fires of reform, a visit from the police, health inspector or local Plug Uglies did the trick.

But after 17 years as New York's unofficial monarch, Tweed's reign came to an abrupt and desperate end. Oddly enough, the Boss's thunderous fall from power started with a cartoon. In 1869 Thomas Nast started publishing blistering caricatures of Tweed and his sidekicks in *Harper's Weekly*, making it plain even to the illiterate masses what the Tweed Ring was all about. Soon after, a couple of Tweed's disgruntled henchmen

away to Spain. He was recaptured, thrown back into jail, and died of pneumonia less than two years later.

Tweed's corrupt empire had little if any effect on the new breed of "social Darwinists" who seemed to be pulling in money hand over fist. Cornelius Vanderbilt consolidated his vast railroad empire; the Astor family continued to collect rents from hundreds of tenements, and financier Jay Gould cornered the gold market, precipitating the Panic of 1869. By the end of the century, J. P. Morgan was well on the way to creating the first American company to hit the billion dollar mark (US Steel); John D. Rockefeller

started feeding inside dope to *New York Times* publisher George Jones, who had been itching to get Tweed's head on a platter but didn't have any hard evidence to back himself up. Two years passed before the press had slung enough muck to get Tweed dragged in front of a judge, and after three years of litigation he was locked away in the Ludlow Street Prison – which, as luck would have it, he had been responsible for building. Tweed hardly led the life of a typical jailbird, though. During one of his frequent visits to his Madison Avenue brownstone, Tweed ducked out the back door and was spirited

struck pay dirt with Standard Oil, and Andrew Carnegie plunked down a tidy $2 million for a brand-new concert hall. He named it after himself, of course, and even managed to get Tchaikovsky to conduct at the opening gala.

Pushed out of their downtown haunts by immigrants, the upper crust began a 50-year march up fashionable Fifth Avenue, leaving a trail of extravagant mansions as they moved farther and farther uptown. It was at this time that the elite came to be known as the Four Hundred because of Mrs. Astor's habit of inviting 400 guests to her annual ball. "There are only about four hundred people in fashionable New York society," an insider explained. "If you go outside the number you strike people who are either not at ease in a ballroom or else make other people not at ease. See the point?"

While the Four Hundred gorged themselves on lavish parties, the downtown scene was as wretched as ever. Two thousand immigrants poured into the new Ellis Island Immigration Station every day, cramming tenements and sweat shops with more people than they could possibly handle. Despite the work of reformers like photo-journalist Jacob Riis, it wasn't until tragedy struck that

wept out loud as girls jumped from the eighth and ninth floors and thudded against the pavement. In all, the blaze only lasted about 10 minutes, but over 140 workers were killed, most of them women no more than 20 years old. Although the two men who owned the company were acquitted, the tragedy stimulated sweeping labor reforms.

Jazz Age: World War I came and went with minimal impact on New York City. Doughboys, as the US infantrymen became known, returned home to find business still booming, the population still growing, and an era of good feelings taking hold of the city. Prohibition kicked off the "Roaring Twen-

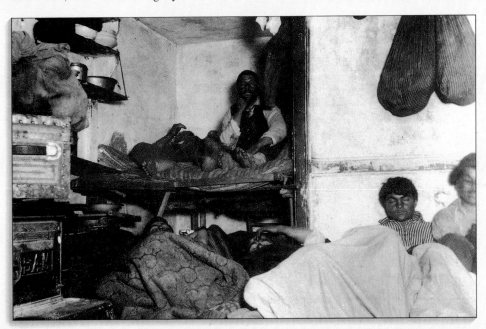

people took notice of the horrid conditions.

On March 25, 1911, just as the five o'clock bell sounded, a fire broke out on the top floors of the Triangle Shirtwaist Company, a garment industry sweatshop near Washington Square Park. There were about 600 workers crowded inside, most of them young Jewish and Italian women. With stairways locked or obstructed by flames and only a few slow elevators to take workers down, many were trapped inside. Spectators

Left, city junkman. **Above**, tenement life photographed by Jacob Riis.

ties" on a somewhat dreary note, but somehow the good times seemed better and the parties wilder now that drinking was taboo. In fact, Prohibition backfired in New York even more than in other cities. The liquor trade turned into a gold mine for organized crime, especially the *mafiosi* sinking roots into Mulberry Street. By some estimates there were twice as many speakeasies in New York after Prohibition as there were legitimate bars before. As a well-known madam is supposed to have said, "They might as well try to dry up the Atlantic with a post office blotter."

A Day in the Life of a Jewish Immigrant

The Lower East Side went by many names: the typhus ward, the suicide ward, the crooked ward, or simply Jewtown. It was the new world ghetto, an irregular rectangle of tenements and sweatshops crooked between the Bowery and the East River, an energetic Babel crammed with Russian, Polish and German Jews.

Between 1880 and 1920, more than 2 million Eastern European Jews came to the United States and over 500,000 settled in New York City, mostly on the Lower East Side. With 330,000 people per square mile, it was the most densely populated place in the world. Sanitation was primitive; yellow fever and cholera were a constant threat, and child labor and exploitation were regarded as everyday facts of New York life.

People occupied every available inch. It was not uncommon for families of six or seven to live in one small room, and then take on a boarder or two to help meet living expenses. Some lived in hallways, in basements, in alleyways – anywhere they could squeeze themselves in. And the rents they paid were extortionate.

Living and working quarters were often the same. A family slept, cooked and ate in the same room where they made their living, and from the youngest to the oldest, everyone did their part. The "needle trade" was the cornerstone of the economy, and tenement rooms were often cluttered with half-sewn clothes piled on the floor. Payment was made strictly on the basis of piecework. The more a person produced, the more he or she was paid. As a result, the hours were long and the pace grueling. The whine of sewing machines started no later than 6am and continued well into the night.

For those who toiled in the sweatshops, the situation was no better. Not only were working conditions appalling, but employees were charged for needles, thread and other supplies, billed for their lockers and chairs, and fined for material accidentally damaged at twice or three times its actual value. A working day could stretch anywhere from 10 to 14 hours.

In either case, wages were minimal – maybe $8 or $10 a week for a family of five or six, $14 or $15 for those getting along exceptionally well. With so little coming in, survival was often hand-to-mouth, with every penny counting.

As writer Michael Gold remembered, "On the East Side people buy their groceries a pinch at a time; three cents' worth of sugar, five cents' worth of butter, everything in penny fractions." There was no margin for any error. A family's survival could ride on a few cents.

Even compassion for one's friends was given at a personal cost. "In a world based on the law of competition," Gold noted, "kindness is a form of suicide."

The Hester Street market was the central fixture of the neighborhood, and of those Jews who did not enter the needle trade many worked as peddlers or

pushcart vendors selling meats, fish, produce or cheap clothing. As activist Jacob Riis explained, the area was nicknamed the Pig-market "probably in derision, for pork is the one ware that is not on sale."

Eastern European Jews placed a high value on learning and political organization, however, and among members of the community with left-wing leanings, there was a good deal of interest in the labor movement. Rudimentary unions were organized under the umbrella of the United Hebrew Trades, and immigrants launched several important strikes, often facing down "strike-busters" hired to intimidate them with threats and violence. Socialist and Zionist publications such as the *Jewish Daily Forward*, *Freiheit* and Emma Goldman's *Mother Earth* advocated for immigrant rights. Despite the efforts of Tammany Hall to recruit their votes for the Democratic Party, East Side socialists eventually saw their candidates reach Congress.

Meanwhile, organizations such as the Educational Alliance were sponsoring lectures and demanding libraries. A new Yiddish theater was blossoming on the stages of Second Avenue, and the traditional round of religious observances continued as it had in the old country.

Day after day, the people of the Lower East Side ground out a living – working, saving, moving slowly ahead – and created an enduring niche for themselves in the complex cultural and economic world of New York City. ∎

The free-spirited Twenties had its share of free-thinkers as well. Cheap rents and a certain "old quarter" atmosphere turned Greenwich Village into a hotbed of writers, artists and radicals, much to the chagrin of the Italian and Irish families that occupied the neighborhood. People like John Reed, Emma Goldman, Louise Bryant and Edna St Vincent Millay advocated everything from communism to free love. All the while Eugene O'Neill was knocking 'em back with his hoodlum buddies (the Hudson Dusters) at a speakeasy called the Hell Hole, and blowing the lid off the theater world at the Provincetown Playhouse.

Reigning over the festivities was the undisputed prince of Jazz-Age New York, Mayor James Walker. The wise-cracking, high-living playboy – a former Tin Pan Alley songwriter – was the perfect embodiment of the freewheeling Twenties. He was a gambler, a lady's man and a fashion plate, as loose with money as he was with Prohibition. Walker wasn't much of an administrator, though. He mostly acted as a figurehead and let the hacks at Tammany Hall take care of running the city. He played craps with reporters, hobnobbed with the stars, and flaunted his affair with a Broadway actress. When he raised his own salary by $10,000,

Uptown, the Jazz Age was true to its name. In the early years of the century, the black community started moving out of the West 30s and into the failed developments of Harlem. In the 1920s, a blossoming of black culture known as the Harlem Renaissance produced writers like Langston Hughes and Zora Neale Hurston, while jazz greats like Count Basie and Duke Ellington played to white audiences at the Cotton Club, Small's Paradise and other ritzy after-hours clubs.

Left, portrait by Jacob Riis. Above, Brooklyn Bridge footpath, 1923.

critics attacked his extravagance. The Mayor's reply was pure Jimmy Walker: "Think what it would cost if I worked full-time."

The city may have been going to Hell in a handbasket, but most New Yorkers kept right on partying. And they kept on spending too. In the 1920s the city went on a stock-buying binge that sent the daily numbers through the roof – and it didn't look like they were ever coming down. It didn't matter that stocks were being bought on credit. It didn't matter that the city was being bilked of millions by Tammany Hall. As long as the money kept rolling in, the lights still burned on Broadway, and Jimmy Walker was still smiling, everything seemed all right. As broadcaster Walter Winchell remembered, "In the 1920s the American people were hell-bent for prosperity and riches. And they wanted a politician who was hell-bent only for reelection… a man who would respect the national rush to get rich, who would accept greed, avarice and the lust for quick gain as a legitimate expression of the will of the people… Walker knew what the people wanted. And as mayor, he gave it to them."

But when the bottom fell out of the stock market on Black Thursday – October 24, 1929 – Walker's reign of good feelings came

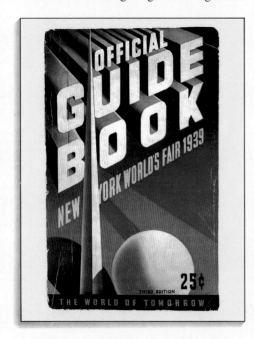

tumbling down with it. The Great Depression hit New York hard. Total income was slashed by more than half. Unemployment soared to 25 percent. People were robbed of their livelihoods, their homes and their dignity. Makeshift "Hoovervilles" sprang up in Central Park, and bread lines became common. As Groucho Marx put it, he knew the city was on the skids "when the pigeons started feeding the people in Central Park."

Before Walker could ride out his second term, his administration started to unravel. An investigation into city government uncovered a pile of corruption second only to

the Tweed Ring. Walker was hauled up to the town of Albany where Governor Franklin D. Roosevelt reviewed the charges against him. Walker knew there was no way he was going to walk away without a political, and personal, skinning. He resigned his office in 1932, and caught the first ship to Europe.

About a year later, a new mayor moved into City Hall. Fiorello LaGuardia was a small, rather plump man with an animated face and a penchant for rumpled suits. He had none of Walker's finesse, but he was quick-witted, savvy, and determind to whip the city back into its proper shape. He could be hard-nosed, almost ruthless, but still paternalistic and warm. The same man who ordered Lucky Luciano off the streets also read out the comics over the radio every Sunday. LaGuardia had his critics, but for a city ravaged by the Depression, he was the closest thing to a savior.

LaGuardia was elected in 1933 and immediately got on board Franklin Roosevelt's New Deal, launching massive relief and construction programs in an effort to revive the economy. His administration swung into action, building bridges, highways, parks, housing, even finding work for artists and writers with the Works Progress Administration. At the same time, large-scale projects that had been launched in the 1920s were nearing completion. Art Deco came gloriously into its own with the opening of the Chrysler Building in 1930, the Empire State Building and Waldorf-Astoria Hotel in 1931, and the Rockefeller Center in 1933.

Then, in 1941, the US entered World War II, and the city was swept into the war effort. German spies were arrested; Japanese families were locked up on Ellis Island, and blackouts were ordered – even the torch of the Statue of Liberty was turned off. In the basement of a Columbia University physics lab, Enrico Fermi and Leo Szilard were experimenting with atomic fission, laying down crucial groundwork for development of the atomic bomb, known later as the Manhattan Project.

Left, program from the 1939 World's Fair. <u>Right</u>, the emblematic Empire State Building was completed in 1931.

With the United Nations moving into the city in 1947, New Yorkers were flush with a sense of possibilities. World peace, a healthy economy, the riches of technology – they all seemed within reach. The glass-walled UN Secretariat Building brought a sleek look to midtown and kicked off the 1950s with a fitting sense of modernity. A new generation of glass-box skyscrapers multiplied on Park and Madison Avenues and eventually spread to the west side and financial district.

Goodbye to glory: But like many other northeastern cities, the post-war years brought an unexpected turn for the poorer in New York. The middle class began moving out to the suburbs, corporations relocated, and poor blacks and Hispanics flooded into the city. By the mid-1970s, the budget was so stressed the city teetered on the verge of bankruptcy. It seemed as if the glory days were gone for good.

The trouble started in 1946 when William O'Dwyer took over the mayor's office. Although never charged with any crime, O'Dwyer presided over an administration thick with underworld connections. A change had come over Tammany Hall by this time. After Fiorello LaGuardia broke the old Democratic machine, Tammany was infiltrated by members of organized crime – "Murder Inc." as the papers called it. The new Tammany politicos were heavily involved in gambling, prostitution and the "waterfront rackets," and they made substantial political in-roads, especially at the police department, in order to protect their interests. When the papers got wind of what was going on, it was clear that a major shake-up was in the works. A senate investigation into police corruption led directly to the top, but before O'Dwyer could be nailed down, he was rescued by President Harry Truman, who nominated him for Mexican Ambassador. Just a year into his second term,

Preceding pages: tickertape parade for *Apollo 11* astronauts. **Left**, King Kong visits Midtown. **Right**, Fiorello LaGuardia, mayor who changed the city.

O'Dwyer resigned his office and took off for Mexico. As one reporter noted, "The departure looks a touch peculiar."

In the 1950s, Mayor Robert Wagner oversaw a gradual political healing, but by then a social transformation was well under way that would have repercussions for the city right up to the present day. In the late 1940s a wave of Puerto Rican immigrants began arriving in New York and continued straight through the 1950s. Attracted by war-time

jobs, the black community also experienced a good deal of growth during and after World War II. Like the immigrants before them, the black and Hispanic communities faced a wall of opposition. Equality in jobs, housing, city services and education were denied them, and with the civil rights movement taking shape across the nation, they began to demand their slice of the pie.

As the black power and anti-war movements gained momentum in the 1960s, the situation grew more volatile. Intended to enhance the city's international reputation, the 1964 World's Fair became a staging ground for one demonstration after another. Bitter questions were raised over the segregation of New York schools. Police were accused of brutality against minorities, and demonstrators grew more militant. One sit-in at City Hall lasted 44 days before Mayor Wagner ordered the police to haul off the protestors, setting off a minor riot.

By the summer of 1964, the black communities of Harlem and Bedford-Stuyvesant (Brooklyn) were seething with anger and energized with a new spirit of activism. When a police officer shot a young black man under questionable circumstances, Harlem erupted. Two days after the killing,

Republican named John Lindsay tried to find progressive solutions to New York's problems, but with the tax base eroding and city services at an all-time high, the city was in a financial stranglehold. By 1975, New York was on the verge of bankruptcy.

In 1976, Edward Koch was elected mayor and an effort was launched to buoy the city budget with massive borrowing. A resurgence of corporate development injected new capital into the economy, and the city gradually got back on its feet. Evidence of re-investment seemed to be popping up everywhere. Half-empty since it was opened in 1973, the World Trade Center's Twin Tow-

on July 18, 1964, a mob of several thousand assaulted the 123rd Street Police Station. Molotov cocktails exploded in the street, shots were fired into the sky, and tear gas floated through the air. For six days, rioters raged through Harlem, setting fire to white-owned buildings, looting stores that refused to hire blacks, and assaulting unfortunate passers-by. All the while Mayor Wagner tried to assure black New Yorkers that "Law and order are the Negro's best friend."

Although the Harlem riots passed, the bitterness behind them was never resolved. In the late 1960s and early 1970s, a liberal

ers sprang to life, to be followed by the development of Battery Park City and the South Street Seaport. In Midtown, the Citicorp Building opened in 1977, and stimulated the development of One UN Plaza, the AT&T (now Sony) and IBM buildings, and several other skyscrapers.

Life in the neighborhoods started looking up too. By the 1980s, the transformation of SoHo from an industrial wasteland to an artistic mecca was in full swing. Even the crime-ridden streets of the Upper West Side were being flooded by "young urban professionals" opening businesses.

But the city's good fortune wasn't shared by everybody. While gentrification swept through the neighborhoods and corporate America built glass-plated skyscrapers, the underclass grew more entrenched. Apparently, Ronald Reagan's "trickle-down" economics didn't trickle quite far enough. People at the lowest rungs of the economic ladder were slipping through the cracks, and the fall-out was painfully obvious. The legacy of homelessness is evident today on every street corner and subway station. To make matters worse, Aids and drug abuse pushed health care systems beyond their capacity to serve; and racial conflicts

incident," violent crime or drug bust while a supporting cast of characters – from Leona Helmsley to Cardinal O'Conner – made a habit of dropping bombshells on the press. As always, keeping up with the news was like watching a three-ring circus.

In the 1990s, under Mayor Rudolph Giuliani, New York again travels a troubled path. And yet, without the problems – without crime, traffic, crowding and racial tension – this would be an entirely different place. There would be no exhilaration, no enlivening sense of frenzy. It might sound trite, but New York is a place where absolutely anything can happen. It's a rollicking

erupted with disturbing regularity. All the while, super-rich moguls like Donald Trump and Harry Helmsley were gobbling up New York real estate as if it were squares on a Monopoly board. The disparity between rich and poor became enormous.

In 1989, David Dinkins became the first black man elected mayor of New York, and as usual, the city found itself in the throes of transition. Every week, it seemed, the newspapers raved about the latest scandal, "racial

Left and above, the city is addressing serious modern problems.

testimony to the creative powers of chaos.

There are a few things you can always count on, though: world-class museums and art galleries, a wild variety of food and shopping, earth-shaking business deals, stunning architecture, great entertainment, immigrants from every corner of the world.

In the end, this is a city about living and change, excitement and struggle, joy and ambition. There are opportunities at every turn, realities no one suspected. And that's what makes it such an interesting place. As soon as you understand New York, your understanding is obsolete.

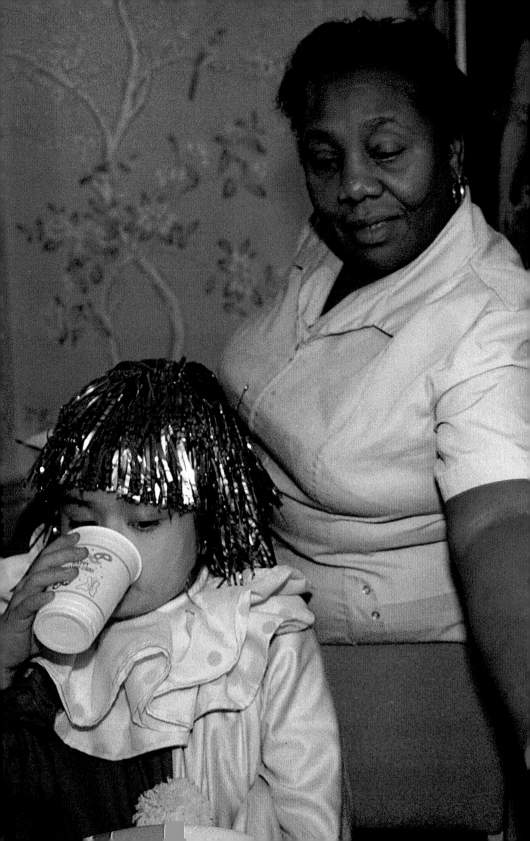

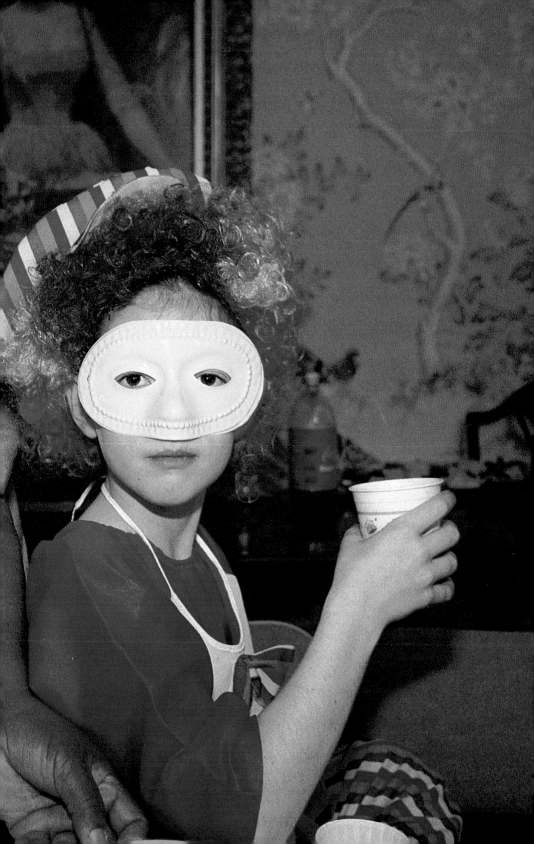

METROPOLIS OF THE MIND

A beggar staggers up the aisle of a Broadway local subway and into the next car. In his wake sits a woman reading *One Hundred Years of Solitude* by Gabriel García Márquez, the Colombian Nobel laureate. On a sidewalk off Times Square, near a *souvlaki* stand and a pornographic bookstore, 10 men bend over five chessboards. A window is thrown open on a warm night and the sound of someone playing the English horn wafts in. It is impossible to know its source – lights burn in dozens of nearby apartments. And in a sense, that sound has no single origin; it is born out of New York itself.

Snapshots: These are scenes – snapshots, if you will – of the intellectual life of a city, New York City. This life of the mind is not a graft on the metropolitan body; it is something organically, naturally, often anonymously part of the constitution of New York. It is the contrast, or perhaps the coexistence, between life ascendant and life descendant: chess next to pornography, a book and a beggar. It is that English horn music, moving on the air like a transparent streamer, as much a part of the sophisticated urban atmosphere as oxygen.

Certainly, there is a public face to intellectual accomplishment in this city. The intellectual life here has its rituals, like museum openings, and its venues, like Elio's Restaurant. There are professional philosophers and critics who by their presence give definition to the proper noun New York Intellectual. But those people, places, and events represent only the surface stratum of something deeper.

Intellectual life in New York is not a cerebral speakeasy where a panel slides open in a door and you whisper "Kierkegaard sent me." Rather, it is a range of mental endeavor – Sinology and sculpture, poetry and particle physics – and it is a rich and polyglot marketplace of lectures, galleries, museums, plays, concerts, libraries, films and, of course, din-

Preceding pages: Manhattan mystique. **Right,** facing the city head-on.

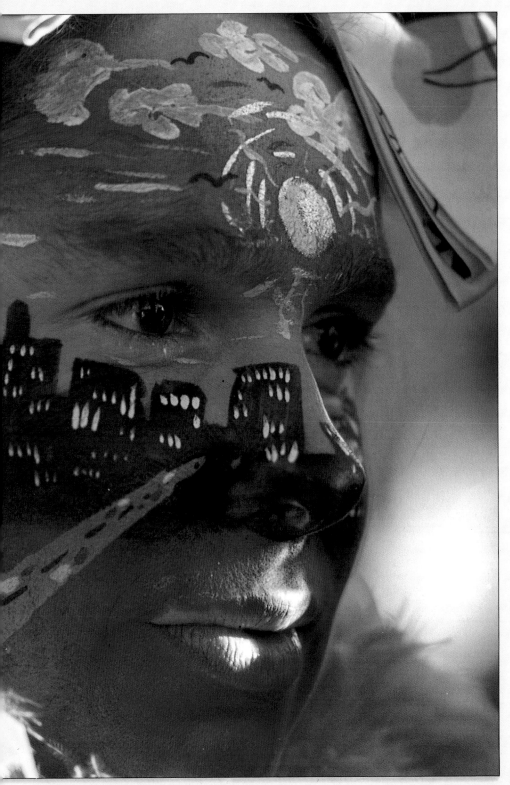

ner parties. It is the casual way great minds have always moved through the landscape: Thomas Wolfe stalking the streets of Brooklyn, Sonny Rollins practicing his saxophone on the Williamsburg Bridge. It is a painter named Mizue Sawano, who has gone to the Brooklyn Botanic Garden once a week for several years to sit with her easel beside the Lily Pools. The lily pads there remind her of Monet's lily pads, she says, and they inspire her own art.

All this amounts to a kind of aura. Stephen Tim, director of scientific affairs at the Brooklyn Botanic Garden, found an analogy in his studies. "The process is osmosis," he

Steinberg, whose famous cover for *The New Yorker* suggests an earth largely occupied by Manhattan.

Alexander Alland, Jnr, the former chairman of the anthropology department at Columbia University, puts the myth into words: "The intellectual life is why I am a New Yorker. It's why I stay here. I spend my summers in Europe, and when they ask me if I'm an American, I say, 'No, I'm a New Yorker.' I don't know about everyone else, but for me that's a positive statement."

New York began its rise to intellectual primacy in the 1850s. It is easy now to forget that throughout the colonial era and the early

explained. "You absorb the intellectual life, the culture. Without even consciously learning from it, you are stimulated by it. It is almost a passive thing that happens. You cannot stop it."

Culture and intellect not only transform the individual, they give identity to the mass, to the city as a whole. In his book *The Art of the City: Views and Versions of New York*, Peter Conrad writes, "Every city requires its own myth to justify its presumption of centrality," and he then goes on to cite artistic annotators of New York, from the songwriter George M. Cohan to the painter Saul

19th century New York was at best the third city of the nation, behind Boston and Philadelphia. What shifted the gravity was the migration of the publishing industry to New York from Boston. Initially, the publishers were simply seeking more customers – New York had the largest population – but their relocation set off a chain reaction that altered the city. With publishing houses came writers and editors and illustrators.

Meanwhile, the city had begun to change in other ways. At the top of the New York economic scale, the captains of commerce and industry began to endow museums and to support individual artists; at the bottom, each wave of immigrants enriched and diversified the intellectual community. City College, established in 1849, acted as the great pedagogue for those without wealth and later came to be known as "the poor man's Harvard."

As more creative people lived in New York, even more were drawn to it. Scale is the key word: the number of college graduates living in New York City today collectively would constitute the 11th-largest city in the United States.

With size comes sustenance for all sorts of specialized intellectual communities.

record of his era appeared decades later in the striking album *Harlem on My Mind*.

New York supports a museum of pianos and two museums of African art; it supports Yiddish theater and a Haitian newspaper. The Cathedral of St John the Divine maintains a poets' corner, and the staff of Montefiore Hospital Medical Center has even included a philosopher-in-residence.

The whole notion of pop culture versus high culture is rendered almost meaningless, because the esoteric can enjoy a mass audience: such demanding playwrights and composers as Tom Stoppard and Stephen Sondheim can have hit plays on Broadway,

Greenwich Village became an urban version of the artists' colony, a home to creators of all stripes, the neighborhood that gave Eugene O'Neill a stage in the 1920s (at the Provincetown Playhouse) and Bob Dylan a bandstand in the 1960s (at Folk City). Miles uptown, Harlem has been home in this century to a black intelligentsia that has included the writers Langston Hughes, James Weldon Johnson, James Baldwin, and Ralph Ellison, the political theorist W.E.B. Du Bois, and the photographer James Van Der Zee, whose

Left, drawing a veil. <u>Above</u>, sight-seeing.

while a gospel-music version of *Oedipus at Colonus* – could anything seem more unlikely? – can be a sell-out at the Brooklyn Academy of Music.

Intellectual life also interacts with political life. From A. Okey Hall, the hack figurehead for Boss Tweed, to Edward I. Koch, New York's mayors have often doubled as authors. Former governor Mario Cuomo, a native of Queens, is a published author who spices his speeches with knowing references to Thomas More and Teilhard de Chardin. Before Senator Daniel Patrick Moynihan became a politician, he was a respected and provocative academic. A debate on an issue now decades old – whether or not Julius and Ethel Rosenberg were Soviet spies – still fills Town Hall and is argued with ferocity.

Like politics, religion in New York is a matter not only of passion or rote, but also of intellectual rigor. There are almost a dozen Roman Catholic colleges in the city; there is an Islamic Seminary on Queens Boulevard. And in the *shtibels* – the houses of study – of Crown Heights and Flatbush and the Upper West Side, Hasidim gather to carry on theological debates that are centuries old. The Society of Ethical Culture and Fieldston, its affiliated school in Riverdale, similarly pro-

vide education, advocacy, and a sense of community for nonbelievers.

The intellectual force of New York sends ripples far beyond the city. The principal network news in the United States originates not from the nation's capital but from New York. Two major news magazines, *Time* and *Newsweek*, and two national newspapers, *The New York Times* and *The Wall Street Journal*, are published here. Most of the leading critics of theater, film, art, dance, and music make their pronouncements from Manhattan.

And from the time Walt Whitman pub-

lished *Leaves of Grass* in 1855, artists have been bards of New York. Whitman is the common ancestor in an artistic family that includes novelist Theodore Dreiser and photographer Alfred Stieglitz, painter Ben Shahn and poet Delmore Schwartz, composer Duke Ellington and film maker Woody Allen, Diane Arbus, photographer of the bizarre, and Martin Scorsese, director of *Mean Streets*, *Taxi Driver*, and *New York, New York*. These artists have drawn on New York for subject matter, and their work, in turn, has informed the world's impression of the city.

But the point here is not name-dropping. Without any of those figures, important as they are, intellectual life in New York would proceed with just as much vigor. It is, remember, largely a private and a personal affair. Manifested in individual taste and style, at its heart it has very little to do with either celebrity or vogue.

"When I see a movie like *Manhattan*," says anthropologist Alexander Alland, "that's not my world. I don't know if such people really exist, and if they do I'm not interested in them except as some curious sort of aborigines." For Alland, intellectual life means spending every Friday at the Metropolitan Museum of Art. For his wife, Sonia, it means playing flute in an amateur orchestra that performs every other Sunday in the couple's Chelsea loft. There is a difference, Alland points out, between a scholar and an intellectual. One is a brilliant specialist, sealed inside a single discipline; the other is eclectic, a searcher.

The intellectual sweep of New York allows almost unparalleled opportunities for eclecticism, for search and discovery. Flora Roberts, for instance, is a literary agent. Her clients have included Stephen Sondheim, Maya Angelou, and Tina Howe, and her work situates her at high levels of the literary and theatrical worlds. "For me there are two great thrills," she says. "One is going to Carnegie Hall to hear Marilyn Horne doing Rossini. The other is looking at a Goya. I grew up in New York, and I remember when I first heard Laurence Olivier scream in *Oedipus*. I think of the audience at *Death of a Salesman* leaping up out of their seats to try to keep Lee J. Cobb from killing himself. In New York, there's this marriage of feeling."

There is also a marriage of ideas. A thinker need not remain in solitude; there are circles and networks to challenge assumptions and hypotheses while supporting the act on inquiry. Dr Bruce Yaffe's is a characteristic story. During the 1980s, Dr Yaffe realised that he never got to talk about politics with knowledgeable people the same way he could talk about, oh, ulcer disease with his fellow digestive-tract specialists. So he placed a want ad in the *New York Review of Books*, looking for partners in a discussion group. And from then on, Dr Yaffe and his

people – a record for their living room – for a discussion of the Falkland Islands war. They brought Soviet diplomats and exiled Soviet dissidents to the same symposium on internal problems in Russia, which predictably raised the decibel level. At a session on United States policy in Central America, a writer from a conservative magazine opined that Fidel Castro sought to export revolution throughout the region. "And then," Dr Yaffe recalls, "some 60-year-old Cuban businessman in the corner said, 'My dear, that's wrong. When Fidel and I were considering our plans in the hills of Cuba that was the farthest thing from our minds'."

wife, Karen, held frequent seminars in their Upper East Side apartment.

Topics ranged from Sino-Soviet relations to evaluating public education, and in the course of collecting ammunition for the debates, the Yaffes took subscriptions to 150 magazines. "The mailman came up to our apartment once," Dr Yaffe says. "He said he wanted to see who we were."

In the Yaffe apartment the going often gets, let us say, spirited. The couple had 43

Left, a wedding at St Patrick's Cathedral. <u>Above</u>, Gay Lib's Day.

A more public hub of intellectual activity is a great bookstore, and in New York the Strand is arguably the best. Occupying a former clothing store at Broadway and East 12th Street in Manhattan, the Strand carries some two million volumes, of such vast variety that on a single table the tomes range from *The Sonata Since Beethoven* to *Civil Aircraft of the World*. Over the years, the Strand has counted among its regular customers writers Anaïs Nin and Saul Bellow; Senator Mark Hatfield; David Hockney, the painter; and the late William J. Casey, former director of the CIA.

Zero Mostel, the comedian, once extemporized in the rare-book department on the relative artistic merits of the Mexican painters Diego Rivera and David Siqueiros. Fred Bass, the Strand's owner, recalls eavesdropping on an argument between two customers about whether Douglas R. Hofstadter's *Gödel, Escher, Bach* or Martin Heidegger's *Being and Time* was more difficult to read. His employees, typically writers or musicians, have included poet Tom Weatherly (Americana aisle) and poet/rock singer Patti Smith (typist). "I always consider that after graduating from Columbia," says Craig Anderson, a supervisor in the rare-book de-

district along the Avenue of the Americas recognise Miss Graves, when she comes to buy dried vegetables, as an artist who has had several national exhibitions. Nor do the shopkeepers in Chinatown, her source for lotus roots and fans, or the cashiers at Balducci's, where she gets brussel sprouts. These are not the makings of dinner or some sort of talisman; they are among the organic bits of New York that Miss Graves uses in the direct casting for her sculptures.

She has also drawn on the industrial resources of the city – the foundry that casts her work – and on its academic sector. When she made a film about the moon as a personal art

partment, "the Strand is where I really got my education."

Energy and hostility: Nancy Graves pursued her education at Vassar and Yale and her studies in painting in Paris and Florence. For all that, her move to New York in 1966 was to affect her art profoundly. "I couldn't sleep for my first two weeks here," she recalls. "I remember the energy and the hostility. The chaos. I enjoy it. The anonymity, even. You may have a career and be somewhat visible in your field and yet have the sense of a private life."

Certainly few of the vendors in the flower

project, she studied the fossil collections at the American Museum of Natural History. And, again, there are the circles: Miss Graves numbers many dancers among her friends; she has served on the board of the Mabou Mines theater troupe. "The fact of being in New York allows people to contact you," she says. "It's not just artists reaching out, but others reaching in."

In fact, artists tend to define the resurgent neighborhoods of the city. When Ms Graves first moved to SoHo years ago, "it was hard to get cabs to go there." Now the neighborhood is established and expensive, so much so that she often longs for some place a little more "ethnic and sociological."

Younger artists have already advanced on a new set of frontiers. They have moved to the area variously referred to as Alphabetland, Alphabetville, or Alphabet City (Avenues A, B, C, and so forth on the Lower East Side of Manhattan), across the Hudson to Hoboken and Jersey City, across the East River to Greenpoint and Williamsburg, and to a part of Brooklyn they simply call DUMBO, for Down Under Manhattan Bridge Overpass. Trendy Haagen-Dazs ice-cream stores cannot be far off.

If artists define much of the New York

ate Faculty of Political and Social Science) as a graduate school to be staffed by European scholars who escaped the Nazi regime. The international dynamic continues today, with the Soviet Jews of Brighton Beach, with the West Indians of Jamaica, with the Southeast Asians of Elmhurst, with Iranians like Bahman Maghsoudlou.

Until 1979, when he went into self-exile from the theocracy of the Ayatollah Ruhollah Khomeini, Mr Maghsoudlou was a leading film scholar in Iran. Now he is one of perhaps 4,000 Iranians living in New York; Mr Maghsoudlou's own estimate is that 90 percent of Iran's artists have fled the nation

landscape, geographically and intellectually, then so, emphatically, do immigrants and refugees. The German influx of 1848, the Irish flight from famine, migrations of Jews, Italians, Greeks, Chinese, Koreans, and Vietnamese – all have brought knowledge and culture from abroad to New York, making an American city cosmopolitan. In 1933, the New School for Social Research acknowledged that rich resource by founding the University in Exile (now the Gradu-

in the years since the Iranian revolution.

His words are a reminder of what America and New York still mean. "It is a country of dreams, a city of dreams, to everybody all over the world," Mr Maghsoudlou says. "Whatever happens anywhere in the world – if it is violent revolution, if it is radical change, if it is disaster – people of those countries rush to America. In our own countries, we cannot paint, write, put on a play. Here you have freedom of expression. You can lecture. You can say what you want."

Left, over 75,000 people are homeless in New York. **Above**, food for thought.

Predictably, life for Iranians has not been entirely easy here. Mr Maghsoudlou has done fairly well for himself, operating a film-distribution company, studying at Columbia, writing a book on Iranian cinema. However, he also knows a film director who is driving a cab and other intellectuals who are working as doormen.

The same process occurred, too, with the Polish intellectuals who clustered in New York after martial law was declared back in their homeland in December 1981. Janusz Glowacki is a journalist, novelist, and playwright whose Kafkaesque tragicomedy *Cinders* was mounted by the New York Shakespeare Festival. Like Mr Maghsoudlou, Mr Glowacki grappled with the mix of freedom

and foreignness. No longer was he writing with the fear of censorship; but on the other hand, New York's world of agents and grant applications is a strange one. And crime, particularly a murder in his apartment building, was shocking.

But Mr Glowacki had his circle of expatriate Polish writers and professors. And his apartment building has been the home to other Poles as well – an actress, a stage designer, various Solidarity sympathizers. Mr Glowacki calls the building an *akademia* (Polish for academy). "The first task of a man when he is in exile," he says, "is to survive. I am starting from the beginning again. I worry, will my book sell, will I make any money. Different world. All of it. But maybe this *akademia* will replace some of what we had in Poland."

Sounded by sin: That Broadway local subway, the one with the beggar and the woman reading *One Hundred Years of Solitude*, ran to South Ferry in lower Manhattan. Not far from there, wedged in amid the towers of Wall Street, sits Our Lady of Victory Church, where Father George Rutler was once a priest. He has now transferred to a Midtown parish, but remembers his time in there vividly. Although he ministered to the men and women of the financial district, he himself rejected the consumer society they serve when he chose the collar.

He is, moreover, someone who might have good reasons to abhor New York. A man of faith and ideas, who reads Greek and Hebrew, who speaks French and Italian and Latin, who talks knowingly of the writings of C.S. Lewis and G.K. Chesterton, he is surrounded by sin. He has gazed out of his window to see cocaine being sold in the alley below; if some New Yorkers can pooh-pooh such commerce, it deeply disturbs Father Rutler. New York, he says, puts a tangible face on the theological idea of Satan.

But, as much as Janusz Glowacki or Nancy Graves, Father Rutler finds intellectual stimulation in the city, finds his circles; in the Roman Catholic theological body Opus Dei or in conversation with a fellow Dartmouth graduate who stops in occasionally to discuss St Augustine – in French.

And there are times, in the evenings and on weekends when much of the city is deserted, when Father Rutler takes his daily hour of meditation in the form of a solitary run around the empty streets. And in the silence, paradoxically, New York becomes a stimulating and catalytic place. "When you see all the misery of this city," Father Rutler says, "it makes the grandeur of it stand out in greater relief. When you see the skyline of New York at night, it's the closest we've invented to the medieval depictions of the heavenly Jerusalem."

Left and right, life in the city.

Manhattan is home to cultural legends at every possible level and under every possible definition of the word "culture." Here are Broadway, Radio City, Lincoln Center and Carnegie Hall, major venues which have launched big names in music, theater, stage and cinema. Here also, on every street corner, are dreamers – talented students performing chamber music, an Ecuadorian folk band or a Caribbean musician playing Bach on steel drums, hoping for the big-time. But that leap is not easily made, as one sidewalk violinist found out: he had such a local following that he was able to raise funds for a recital in Avery Fisher Hall, where he was less popular with the critics.

Some New Yorkers stick to the mainstream theater for their culture, never going below 42nd Street. Others shun Broadway's extravagance or just can't afford it. But even if you don't actually pay for a seat, there's still a chance of bumping into a star: you could sit next to Madonna or John Kennedy Jr at the Public Theater on dingy Lafayette Street one day and the next day you might even see your favorite film star splurging on caviar at the Russian Tea Room next to Carnegie Hall.

There are some who get their cultural enrichment vicariously, from the closeness of stars, even going star-spotting at celebrity funerals. One *aficionado* who had the *chutzpah* to stroll in to pop icon Andy Warhol's funeral described it as "a cultural, historical event."

Not all New York's culture has a hefty price tag. There are free operas and concerts on Central Park's Great Lawn all summer. A picnic and an outdoor performance of the Philharmonic or of Shakespeare in the Park are popular forms of fresh air and free culture. Shakespeare means waiting in line for the free tickets and, though the cast is always star-studded, the production may not be all

Preceding pages: Santa Claus is coming to town.
Left, *Brief Fling* **choreographed by Twyla Tharp.**
Right, **Lincoln Center.**

that it should. But queues are quintessential New York, as Woody Allen showed in his classic film *Annie Hall*. And if the picnic is from Zabar's (Broadway and 80th Street), there's one more line, in this case for the best deli food in the city and some amusing patter.

Theater: Broadway, dubbed the Great White Way in 1901 for its electric street signs, is not really just one street, but takes in Seventh Avenue and several side streets. The district's heyday was before the advent

of talking pictures, in 1927, and long before television. It has deteriorated alarmingly since then, but, love it or hate it, Broadway is still unique. It's also one of the seediest places in America. The art on its stages is matched by the drugs, pornography and prostitution on its streets, patrolled by hundreds of police. (Talk of "cleaning up Times Square" has ebbed and flowed, but is now actually happening.)

Broadway has emerged from a long slump with excellent new American dramas and musicals. The closing of *A Chorus Line* in 1990 after 6,137 performances marked the end of a New York theatrical institution which had come to represent Broadway. Millions of people had seen Broadway's longest-running musical; some claimed they'd gone as many as 35 times.

Each of the old-time theaters has its own personality and story. The Shubert Theatre, where *A Chorus Line* played, opened in 1913 between Broadway and Eighth, separated by an alley from the Hotel Astor. Originally a private passage for the Shubert brothers, who built dozens of theaters, the thoroughfare is still famous as Shubert Alley. During the Depression years, the Shubert and Booth theaters had their stage doors on the alley and

a priest – though he was said not to live like one. After his death, actors and backstage personnel claimed he haunted the theater, but according to the *New York Times* several years ago, the ghost has not been seen since the controversial nude review *Oh! Calcutta* in the 1970s. Apparently this was too much for "the Bishop".

Off-Broadway venues throughout Manhattan have become both the feeding ground for Broadway stages and a strong cultural center in their own right, offering greater diversity at lower prices. Off-Broadway dates from the days following World War I, when Eugene O'Neill was presenting his

during intermissions audiences could see the cast go out for fresh air, popsicles and soda.

The Palace, on West 47th Street, had a rocky start but Sarah Bernhardt's 1913 appearance saved the house from disaster, and it went on to become the world's foremost theater devoted to vaudeville from 1910 to the 1930s. Nowadays it's a prime venue for lavish musicals.

The Belasco Theatre, between Broadway and Sixth Avenue, was founded by flamboyant playwright-actor-director David Belasco in 1907. Belasco was known as the bishop of Broadway because he dressed like

early one-act plays at the Provincetown Playhouse (both the one on Cape Cod and the one downtown in Greenwich Village). It came into its own in the late 1940s and early 1950s, when Geraldine Page appeared in an unforgettable production of Tennessee Williams' *Summer and Smoke* and Jose Quintero directed a stunning production of O'Neill's *The Iceman Cometh*.

Downtown today, Circle Rep or the Cherry Lane Theatre in the Village are doing their bit for off-Broadway. In the less pictur-

Times Square's theater discount ticket booth.

REGARDS TO BROADWAY

The New York theater, like Miss Jean Brodie, is going through a prime period. Broadway is selling more than 8 million tickets annually, earning a record $356 million in sales.

The megahits – *Miss Saigon*, *Les Misérables*, *Cats* – have dominated the headlines in the past decade, but dramas and comedies (often lumped together as "straight plays") are also being produced with regularity. In an average season of 35 new productions, roughly half will be new plays.

Critics may complain that this is a far cry from the early part of the 20th century, when over 100 new plays were staged each season. Playwrights and composers such as Eugene O'Neill, Lillian Hellman, Cole Porter, Irving Berlin, Rodgers and Hart, Arthur Miller and Tennesee Williams all made their names in New York, and their work is often revived. Only time will tell whether the present crop of playwrights, which includes August Wilson, Wendy Wasserstein, Craig Lucas, John Guare and Aaron Sorkin, will also be flattered by revivals. Occasionally a playwright who achieved fame in New York will bypass Broadway entirely in favor of smaller venues: Alfred Uhrey's *Driving Miss Daisy* sped directly from a tiny theater on far-West 42nd Street to the hills of Hollywood.

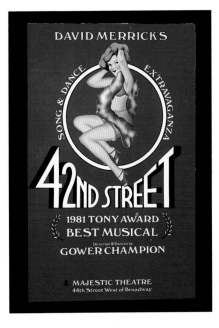

Today there are 35 so-called Broadway theaters but only a handful are actually on Broadway, including the Broadway Theatre, the Marquis, the Palace and the Winter Garden. The rest are on the side streets around Broadway and 41st Street as far north as 65th Street. Roughly half of them are owned by the Shubert Organization; the Nederlander Organization is also a major owner.

One of the oldest theaters, as well as one of the most beautiful, is the Lyceum (1903), a neo-baroque beauty. Even older is the Victory Theatre on 42nd Street. Built by Oscar Hammerstein in 1890, it later housed porno movies but, in keeping with the Times Square area's recent resurgence, has now been recast as the New Victory, a venue for productions aimed at young audiences.

Broadway may make the headlines, but off-Broadway is considered by many critics to be the true soul of New York theater. At the time of its inception, off-Broadway was a cautious producer's way of staging plays that were considered to be too avant garde or unsuitable for the mainstream theaters of Broadway.

Off-Broadway theaters are still havens for the avant garde, but they now also serve a major economic function. Plays and musicals which, in the past, would have appeared on Broadway itself cannot be mounted there today due to rising costs. A hit in an off-Broadway theater provides the confidence backers need in order to move uptown. Those plays which have successfully made the transition from off- to on-Broadway – and subsequently the world – include *Torch Song Trilogy* and *A Chorus Line*. Occasionally, however, the initial backers resist the temptation to move to Broadway.

The reasons are sound: costs are less prohibitive, runs are likely to be longer and audiences often prefer the greater sense of intimacy that a smaller house can provide. *Steel Magnolias*, *Forbidden Broadway* and *Other People's Money* were plays that remained resolutely off-Broadway.

Anyone intending to go to see something on the New York stage should not get too obsessed with seeing a specific show at a specific time. It is recommended that you have several options in mind and to pick the one that offers the best tickets.

Don't be afraid to play a hunch and try something you've never heard of. All actors and actresses start at the bottom. If you'd been a theatergoer in past years you might have caught Meryl Streep in *Alice*, William Hurt and Jeff Daniels in the *Fifth of July*, Al Pacino in *Camino Real*. Even today, established stars return to off-Broadway to refresh their acting skills.

Sometimes the drama extends beyond the stage, as when someone committed suicide by leaping from the top balcony of the Metropolitan Opera during the intermission of Verdi's *Macbeth*. Theatergoers recall the occasion when Katharine Hepburn had a patron ejected for popping a flash bulb right in her face. Or the time when an enraged member of the audience mounted the stage to protest against the abuse being given to the female lead of John Osborne's *Look Back in Anger*. ∎

esque but dynamic East Village, the Public Theater offers experimental, quality theater and P.S. 122 on First Avenue is among the ultra-casual spots for performance art.

Not all new material is deadly serious. Comedy clubs all around town highlight the top comics and, if you're lucky, you may see Robin Williams, Rita Rudner or Joan Rivers working out new material at some of them, on certain nights. Among the best known venues are Caroline's, the New York Comedy Club, and the Comic Strip.

Dance: The dance boom began in the 1960s, with an infusion of funding and the excitement over the defection of Russian

music of Stravinsky. This mercurial genius had a widely known preference for tall ballerinas and even chose what he considered as appropriate perfumes for them. It is said he could often tell which ballerina had preceded him when he took the elevator up to his office in the morning.

Balanchine, who died in 1983, designed much of the performance space at the New York State Theater, including a basket-weave dance floor to provide elasticity and minimize injury. Peter Martins, one of Balanchine's tall, elegant *danseurs nobles*, succeeded him as ballet master after being groomed for the job, but Balanchine's dis-

superstars Rudolf Nureyev, Mikhail Baryshnikov and Natalia Makarova. These days dance is still "in" but some fans feel the fanaticism and ovations that went on forever are a thing of the past. The technical expertise is still there but not the stars.

The legendary George Balanchine, one of the artistic giants of the century, created the New York City Ballet, a company of hand-picked dancers put through almost super-human training. "Dancers are like race-horses; they need a jockey on their backs," was a favorite saying of "Mr B," who choreographed a large repertory of works to the

tinctive imprint on the company remains.

The American Ballet Theater (ABT), which performs at the Met, has a more classical repertory than the New York City Ballet. *Dancing On My Grave*, a revealing autobiography by dazzling ex-ABT ballerina Gelsey Kirkland, shocked the theatrical world with tales of drug use and her stormy relationship with Baryshnikov, the celebrated defector and phenomenal jumper who was the artistic director of the company for several years. Under Baryshnikov, ABT branched out from its classical repertory – to its artistic detriment, critics said at the time.

Visual arts: Recent publicity about prices paid at Sotheby's and Christie's auctions have opened the art world to unprecedented attention. In the early 1990s a Renoir fetched $78.1 million at Sotheby's and a Van Gogh sold for a record $82.5 million at Christie's (Van Gogh once wrote that he wished his paintings were worth what he had spent on the paint).

At the time, downtown art experts felt the auction frenzy was an aberration. The sales had stimulated a wider interest in the galleries but prices remained more realistic than at auction. And the major New York museums, unlike the Getty Museum in California, don't have the megabucks to enter the auction fray. The last time the Metropolitan Museum of Art purchased a "major painting" was in 1970, when it acquired a Diego Velázquez portrait of Juan de Pareja for roughly $5 million.

"Museum Mile" along Fifth Avenue between 82nd and 104th Streets includes the Metropolitan, Guggenheim, Jewish Museum and International Center of Photography. And at the end of the "mile," through the Central Park gate at 105th Street, there is a pair of beautiful formal gardens.

The Metropolitan and the Museum of Modern Art are the biggest and the best. The Frick, in a once-private Fifth Avenue mansion with a courtyard, has an excellent collection of Rembrandts, Vermeers and Fragonards. Even the huge New York Public Library has excellent exhibits in a majestic setting. The reading room has been an "office" for many well-known writers.

And, if TV is your idea of art, classic episodes of *Star Trek* and *I Love Lucy* are all safely stored at the Museum of Television & Radio, along with thousands of other landmark television shows.

Cultural centers: Lincoln Center was built on the site of former tenements in the 1960s as a comprehensive arts center; it helped revitalize the Upper West Side. Besides being the center of dance, it is, of course, also home to great music: the Metropolitan Opera and New York City Opera, the Philharmonic

and various chamber music concerts and recitals in Avery Fisher Hall and Alice Tully Hall. Excellent theatrical productions can be seen here, and each September, the distinguished New York Film festival kicks off. Directors like Martin Scorsese and Jean-Luc Godard gained valuable early exposure here.

Even visitors with no interest in classical music or dance should visit the Lincoln Center for the Performing Arts, especially at night when the elegant fountain is lit and the drapes that protect the huge Chagalls from the sun are sure to be open. The fountain, which has become one of the great meeting places of the West Side, is highly intricate

and controlled by a computer which adjusts the water supply according to the wind velocity to keep people from being soaked.

The Lincoln Center's cultural multiplicity is matched by that of Carnegie Hall, now over 100 years old, which has provided a stage for a diverse range of performers, from Frank Sinatra, the Beatles and Judy Garland to Vladimir Horowitz, Luciano Pavarotti and Maria Callas to Albert Einstein, Amelia Earhart and Winston Churchill. In the late 1950s, the hall was sold to developers who wanted to demolish it and erect a large office building. With violinist Isaac Stern as

<u>Left</u>, East Village theater group imitates life. <u>Right</u>, Julliard music student.

spokesman, a group of outraged citizens managed to save it. Many say that its acoustics are still the best.

Carnegie is famous for more than just music: Charles Dana Gibson drew the Gibson Girls and established the first *Life* magazine in his studio on the premises, and Isadora Duncan was the first dancer to actually live at the hall. The Guggenheim Foundation was established in Studio 1011–12 after the Baroness Hilla von Rebay convinced Solomon Guggenheim to aid struggling artists. Alexander Calder and Wassily Kandinsky were among the artists who received checks for $10, $25 or $50 for paint

and supplies. The baroness's paintings became the nucleus of the Guggenheim Museum collection, which is now housed in the famous and controversial Frank Lloyd Wright building.

Live music: The bohemian parts of town, most of which are downtown, all have great jazz clubs. Of particular note are Bradley's, the Blue Note, the Village Vanguard and Sweet Basil. Rock music is a perpetually changing scene that is pinned down most successfully in *Village Voice*.

The Bottom Line offers terrific, mainstream groups, while CBGB's in the Bowery

is a dark cave that has long been the mecca for groups like Talking Heads and the Ramones. The Knitting Factory in SoHo has come on as a place for the avant garde, while Village standbys like the Bottom Line are still going strong. Sounds of Brazil on Varick Street is the place for world music.

Moving pictures: Manhattan is a film lover's paradise with scores of cinemas, including a bevy of revival houses that show only old films.

Once upon a time in history, Radio City Music Hall on Sixth Avenue was to cinema what Lincoln Center is to dance and music. Nowadays it's something of a throwback – albeit a spectacular Art Deco one. Even the ladies' powder room is something worth seeing. The building was designed by S.L. "Roxy" Rothafel, a showman known for the excesses of his silent film theaters, and opened as a vaudeville house in 1932. Its concept reportedly came out of a dream Roxy had while he was standing on the deck of an ocean liner watching the sun rise.

Many of its concerts and events, such as Easter and Christmas shows with the Rockettes, hold little interest for sophisticated New Yorkers but it's still the most exciting place to see a film, although it now only screens openings and special events.

Space is precious in the city and many cinemas have expanded by multiplying the number and reducing the sizes of screens, which can make movie-going like watching television away from the comforts of home. The best place for movies is the Angelika Film Center on the SoHo–Greenwich Village border. Located in a Stanford White building, it has six screens and a massive espresso bar with a fine café atmosphere.

Movie lines are a way of life in Manhattan. It will seem strange to see two-block-long queues but it's a common sight, partly due to the annoying practice of movie houses to stage "exclusive engagements." Lines do provide great potential for eavesdropping and people watching, however. And who knows, that unobtrusive guy just ahead of you might even be Woody Allen.

Left, *Insight Guide* contributor John Wilcock, by Andy Warhol. <u>Right</u>, *Bauhaus Stairway*, 1932.

New Yorkers differ from one another in a multitude of ways, but so many share the same autobiographical tale that it has become almost mythic. With countless variations and nuances, the story goes something like this:

An able young man (or woman) feels the need to leave home. Perhaps he feels misunderstood and unappreciated, surrounded by what playwright Eugene O'Neill called "spiritual middle-classers." He yearns to escape these small-town minds and to be among people with broader vision. Perhaps he simply wants to reinvent himself by shedding the identities and labels of his childhood and youth. Or perhaps he has a dream, an aspiration too great to be realized at home. He feels imprisoned, be it in Iowa or the Bronx. He believes that only in a great urban center like Manhattan will he find people who can understand his strivings and applaud who he is and what he has to offer.

So he comes here, and whether or not his dreams are realized even partially, he eventually feels the city has spoiled for him any other place in the world. Despite the pressure, the pace, and the grime of New York, he has a tremendous sense of being alive. In his heart he has come to agree with the unabashed sentiment of ex-mayor Jimmy Walker: "I'd rather be a lamppost in New York than the mayor of Chicago."

Alternative possibilities: In reality, of course, it is possible in some degree to find in other places what New York City offers. Certainly, excellence in medicine, art, the law, entertainment, business, and education can be found elsewhere. But the New York striver has come to believe that nowhere else in the world is there a city with such a profusion of excellence and genius, such an abundance of alternatives and possibilities. And so for him success in New York symbolizes the success of successes.

Preceding pages: TV awards only the best with Emmys. Left, fashion designer Issac Mizrahi: sought-after and successful.

In *From Death to Morning*, the writer Thomas Wolfe tried to capture in print the magic of this quest: "The great vision of the city is burning your heart in all its enchanted colors just as it did when you were twelve years old and thought about it. You think that some glorious happiness of fortune, fame and triumph will be yours at any minute, that you are about to take your place among great men and lovely women in a life more fortunate and happy than any you have ever known – that it is all here, somehow, waiting for you..."

Many New Yorkers harbor the memory of a single, vivid episode that stands out as the epitome of just what is in the city somehow waiting for them. To the psychoanalyst, such moments from the past are known as "screen memories," episodes in life that are striking because they carry a special meaning.

Take, for example, the episode recalled by Dr Gerald Fogel, who has been a training and supervising analyst at the Columbia University Psychoanalytic Center. "I grew up in Detroit and came to New York the summer just after I graduated from high school," he says. "I remember the first weekend I spent in New York as a 16-year-old, with my friends. We arrived on a Sunday evening, checked into a Midtown hotel, and then went walking around town. And there, a few blocks away at a jazz club, was Dave Brubeck, playing on a Sunday night. And I could walk in off the street and see him at midnight on a Sunday. Sunday at midnight! I couldn't conceive of such a thing – it was like heaven.

"When I look at myself now, I realize my interest in jazz as an adolescent stood for other kinds of aspirations. The idea of jazz, James Dean, Marlon Brando, and all that signified a freedom, social and sexual, from the kinds of deep inhibitions that all shy adolescents feel.

"New York meant all that. It was the place where the action was. It had all of it: the sophistication and freedom, the underside of life, the vitality. It had all the seductive allure of a place you could do things you could not do anywhere else."

It is that allure, in one form or another, that draws people to the city in what is typically a radical break from home and past.

Exotic attraction: Psychiatrists say that the move away from home is a key step in psychological development. It marks the break between the person one has been as a child and the person one will become as an adult. "The classic psychoanalytic notion is that to express your autonomy, to become your own person, you have to leave home, if only psychologically," Dr Fogel says. "Home, in this sense, stands for that part of

the self that keeps you inhibited and limited. Some people have to go far away to make the break. To become someone else, they seek out people unlike members of their own family. That is why some people marry out of their religion or social class – they feel they can be sexually freer with someone who does not belong to their own group. For a person from a small town or another part of the world, New York may have that same exotic attraction."

Dr Ethel Person, among other notable jobs, has been director of the Columbia University Psychoanalytic Center, one of New York's principal institutions for training psychoanalysts. When she was a 12-year-old in Kentucky, she decided that she was meant to live in New York City even though she had never been there. "Leaving home lets you reinvent yourself," Dr Person says. "For me, the quintessential New Yorker is someone who came to Manhattan – or stays here – by choice, to do just that.

"I like to be with people who don't know who I was when I was 17 years old. In New York you have that lovely double thing: the anonymity to experiment with new identities and the chance to tie in with people who share those interests. Those people are your truer family. New York is the city *par excellence* of invented families. A lot of people leave for New York because their particular gifts or way of being in the world makes them misfits where they are.

"In my generation, which grew up in the 1950s, it was the women who didn't want to follow the traditional role of just being a wife and homemaker, who wanted a career of her own. A more contemporary equivalent might be a woman who wants to be a mother, but who does not want to be married. That would be no picnic among people with small-town attitudes, but there would be more support for it here in the city."

Fast lane: But why should someone be drawn to New York rather than another city?

"Every city has its personality, its unique style that will attract its own to it," says Dr James Hillman, a well-known Jungian analyst who for many years was director of training at the C.G. Jung Institute in Zurich. In keeping with Jungian thought, which deals freely in archetype and myth, Dr Hillman sees the pull of the city in terms of a larger psychological dimension.

"Dallas, where I lived for a while, is for people in the fast lane, people concerned with consuming," Dr Hillman says. "It pulls to those who are already Dallas types. Whether they be in Illinois or Pennsylvania, they are meant for Dallas. Likewise, New York draws the cosmopolite, the person who wants to be challenged the most, who needs the most varied and rich stimulation. It is the person who is full of possibilities, but who needs New York to draw them out of him.

You come to New York to find the ambience that will evoke your best. You do not necessarily know precisely what that might be, but you come to New York to discover it.

"If there were a god of New York it would be the Greeks' Hermes, the Romans' Mercury. He embodies New York qualities: the quick exchange, the fastness of language and style, craftiness, the mixing of people and crossing of borders, imagination.

"New York is the city of rampant creativity, of abundant imagination, whether you are in advertising or the theater or the stock market. They are all fields built on imagination, the spinning of ideas and creations, of

person who fits the syndrome is, archetypally, someone who is exhilarated by the intensity of the city's challenges, who is invigorated rather than defeated by them.

"New York is a city that loves what has been called the 'Type A' personality: always feeling the press of time, aggressive and competitive, a workaholic, dedicated to achievement," says Dr Anthony Zito, a psychiatrist who numbers among his patients many artists and performers.

"This is the Type A's town," says Dr Zito, who is also engaged in research on the mechanism of stress. "There is a common breed here who prefer that intense level of

fantasy becoming reality. It is everything. Any syndrome that might characterize another city is found in New York: manic energy, depression and hopelessness, the extreme excitement of the hysteric, the anger of the paranoid. Psychologically, New York is the complete city."

There are many – too many – who are drawn to the city only to end up depressed by it, hating it, even destroyed by it. But the

Left, high achieving = high blood pressure. **Above**, Donald Trump with ex-wife Ivana and *Playboy's* Christie Hefner.

stimulation, who seek the greater challenge. For them, it's not stressful – it's the level of action they prefer. They are unhappy without it. That need is a defining quality of the New Yorker."

The Type A pattern was first identified as an indicator of susceptibility to heart disease. The original research suggested that while it might make people highly successful, it could also kill them. Subsequent studies, however, have focused on determining what makes some people with this hard-driving pattern more hardy, and thus able to thrive under pressure that might make others more prone to coronary disease. It is important, Dr Zito observes, that people match their preferred level of activity with their environment.

"Because of its pace, this city offers more of a challenge to the person who takes it on," Dr Zito says. "He knows that if he fails, he will get plowed under. That kind of risky challenge appeals particularly to the person who seeks to define himself through his achievements."

Why come to compete in New York City rather than settle for success in a smaller venue? In the view of those psychotherapists who are familiar with the syndrome, the

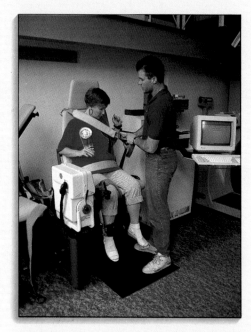

intense drive to compete and succeed on the grandest scale is of primary importance. From the clinical perspective, that kind of person falls in the category of "narcissist." The negative connotations the term holds in lay understanding are unfortunate, psychologists say, because to some degree a streak of narcissism is essential for mental well-being and is necessary for success.

Healthy narcissism: "The concept of narcissism, to put it simply, refers to self-love, or self-esteem," says Dr Robert Michels, over the years a chairman of the department of psychiatry at Cornell University Medical College and psychiatrist-in-chief at the Payne Whitney Clinic. "Its origins are linked in early development with parental regard and approval, the desire to be the kind of person you believe your parents like and approve of. As you grow up, that becomes an internal psychological reality rather than an interpersonal one. You desire to be the kind of person you yourself hold in high regard. In its healthy form, that can lead you to many accomplishments. Take the case of someone in a small town who recognizes he has great talents. The person with a healthy dose of narcissism would seek the environment that would allow him to maximize his potential, and so may leave for a city like New York.

"The boundary between normal and pathologic depends on whether one's pursuit of success actually leads to enhanced performance or simply is the service of a psychological hunger that can never be gratified," Dr Michels says. "People who are hungry for applause are never satisfied with the reality of their feats. They feel an ever-present yearning: the praise they receive is never enough to appease what is, unconsciously, a craving for the total approval from the infant's mother.

"Still, you have to have a bit of narcissism to succeed. To some extent healthy narcissism is one of the key motives in achievement. In order to achieve, one has to work, one has to pride oneself, to put off gratifications. All those things require a strong, healthy narcissistic pleasure in the rewards of success, and a willingness to pay the multiple prices to get that success."

As Dr Michels suggests, a related ingredient for success is the capacity to work, and to work hard. Lionel Trilling once noted how, in past centuries, people were thought to be driven by pleasure, while in modern times people seem to be more driven by a sense of self-worth, for which they will forgo all kinds of pleasures. If any city epitomizes that ethic, it is New York.

From the psychoanalytic perspective, this drive for a higher satisfaction entails some degree of masochism, not in the sexual sense, but in the psychological meaning of the term: the taking of pleasure from painful sacrifice and intense work.

"The need for mastery requires great pain and sacrifice, but it offers another order of satisfaction, not what we ordinarily think of as pleasure," says Dr Arnold Cooper, a psychoanalyst who has written extensively about the psychodynamics of this variety of masochism and how it interacts with masochism. "It is like a person who runs a marathon and feels great pleasure in the achievement afterward, while putting up with great pain during it.

"Bertrand Russell said toward the end of his life that the writing of his great treatise, the *Principia Mathematica*, had permanently damaged his brain. Whether apocry-

aspirations. They work harder, push themselves a bit more, take fewer vacations. And finally there are the narcissists who really aspire to be great. Some of them really do have talent, and it makes sense for them to aim that high. But some of them actually just want people to declare them great. They have no intention of doing the hard work that greatness takes. That is where pathological narcissism begins."

Thus, the New York striver is usually the kind of person who is drawn to the city because it gives him the opportunity to make himself over in terms of excellence. And then there is the school of thought that holds

phal or not, the point is that he was not at all sorry he had done it. The process was painful and excruciating, but one he and the world would say was worth it.

"The urge to be great is within the spectrum of healthy narcissism. That spectrum includes those who simply do their thing well and live productive lives. They don't dream they will write the Great American Novel; they are satisfied just doing their work. There is another group with higher

that city life may be good for the soul.

"The city, in its mythic aspect, has traditionally been maligned as crushing the soul," says Dr Hillman, the Jungian analyst. "I don't agree. I believe the city is good for the soul. In fact, it is as if there were a human need to have cities to manifest the richness, including the darkness, of human nature. In nature there is no human past, no trace of man's unique stamp, of his creativity. But the city, as Lewis Mumford puts it, is a living work of art. It manifests the human imagination. The alive, pulsing city is the greatest artistic achievement of humankind."

<u>Left</u>, the New York City syndrome. <u>Above</u>, the ultimate super achiever.

"A map of the city, colored to designate nationalities, would show more stripes than on the skin of a zebra and more colors than any rainbow." Jacob Riis wrote these words in the early 1900s at the very peak of the great tide of immigration that swept into the United States – and especially into New York – between 1840 and 1925. More than half a century has passed since that time, during which the city's immigrant population gradually decreased. That is, until the past 10 years or so, when immigrants started flooding back into the city, bringing with them an exotic melange of cultures, cuisines and languages. Today, New York is once again a city of immigrants.

Averaging about 30 percent of the city's population, the percentage of foreign-born residents is somewhat less than it was at the turn of the century, although the total number is actually slightly higher – somewhere in the 2½ to 3 million range, possibly more depending on one's estimate of undocumented aliens. Despite the predictable grumbling concerning immigrants moving into "the old neighborhood," or new foreign workers driving down the wages, it's a situation New Yorkers seem to be remarkably comfortable with.

Minorities rule: Never closely associated with the American mainstream, New York is one of the few American cities where minorities (including American-born blacks, Hispanics and Asians) comprise the majority of the population. Multiculturalism and multiracialism have long been New York traditions. They are an integral part of the city's color, complexity and problems, and in general the people of New York have learned to be accepting, if not always enthusiastic, about the difficulties and responsibilities that a large immigrant community inevitably entails.

Public schools offer bilingual instruction in seven languages and supplemental pro-

grams in eight others. Traffic signs, advertisements and subway signs are commonly printed in two or three languages depending on the neighborhood, but most often in Spanish or Chinese, the city's unofficial second and third languages. There are at least a dozen non-English newspapers published in the city itself and countless others imported from their countries of origin. Immigrants can take driving tests in five languages, and can do business at 200 foreign banks. As one

sociologist recently observed, even some automatic cash machines "talk" to users in Spanish or Chinese.

Although there are cities in the US (Miami and Los Angeles) that have a higher percentage of foreign-born residents, none can match the diversity of New York's ethnic communities or the cultural depth of even the smallest groups. A quick run-down of nationalities in the city makes it quite clear that New York is the home-away-from-home for people from every continent. As demographers are fond of pointing out, there are more Greeks in New York than in any city but

Preceding pages: Hasidic Jews inside the *schul*. **Left**, a portrait in color. **Right**, lox optional.

Athens; more Dominicans than in any city but Santo Domingo. And that only scratches the surface.

There are more Russians here than anywhere outside the Soviet Union, more Jamaicans here than anywhere outside Jamaica, and, although they are technically American citizens, more Puerto Ricans live here than anywhere but Puerto Rico. In fact, some people have suggested – and only half-facetiously – that there are more Puerto Ricans in the entire New York metropolitan area (the five boroughs, New Jersey, southern Connecticut and western Long Island) than in there are in Puerto Rico itself. All of

While New Yorkers are often aware of the ethnic variety of white immigrants – which include everyone from Russian Jews to Italian Catholics – they are, generally speaking, far less aware of differences within the other groups. The fact is, however, that there's as much diversity within categories as there is between them, and it's often the social and political differences within a particular group that are the most bitterly divisive.

A random sampling of Asians, for example, is as likely to turn up a rich Hong Kong financier or an Indian professional as it is a Cambodian refugee left destitute and homeless by the Cambodian holocaust. There's a

which is to say that the diversity of the city's immigrants is matched by the size of individual communities. As one contemporary observer wryly commented, "the city has more Ethiopian residents than several states have black people."

Trying to put New York's cultural mishmash into some kind of comprehensible order has given a king-sized headache to city planners, whose standard four-part categories – white, black, Hispanic, Asian – are at best inadequate, and at worst irrelevant, to the kaleidoscope of cultures, races and nationalities that they are trying to understand.

similar tendency to lump foreign-born blacks together with American blacks, which, considering that black immigrants include French-speaking Haitians, English-speaking Barbadians and Jamaicans as well as an increasing number of Africans, is obviously a mistaken assumption. Even Hispanics, who are bound together by a common language, are often divided by apparently insurmountable national, racial and class differences.

Arguments between Argentinians and Chileans, Cubans and Puerto Ricans are pursued with as much vigor in the neighborhoods as they are back home in South America. Little wonder, then, that Hispanics, numbering about 2 million people and easily the city's largest ethnic group, have yet to consolidate their political power into a single, unified voice.

Ellis Island museum: For travelers, the upshot of this ethnic mix-and-match is a sort of geographical shorthand that can turn any tour of the city into a first-hand survey of world cultures. A good place to begin is the Ellis Island museum, not far from the Statue of Liberty. The buildings through which millions of immigrants passed during the peak years 1898 to 1924, have been salvaged

passes through the Hasidic and West Indian enclaves of Crown Heights and Bedford-Stuyvesant to the Russian Jews of Brighton Beach, known by locals as "Little Odessa by the Sea." The same goes for the Bronx and Manhattan, from the Cubans and Domenicans in Washington Heights to the Hungarians, Czechs and Germans in Yorkville on the Upper East Side and "Little India" in Kips Bay.

Predictably, the city's ethnic grab-bag has created any number of oddball couplings: Jews and Puerto Ricans rub elbows on the Lower East Side; Colombians and Koreans maintain an uneasy truce in Flushing; Ital-

in order to tell the often wrenching stories of those en route to new lives in the New World.

A more contemporary survey can be achieved by subway. A 20-minute ride through Queens, for instance, takes you from the heart of "Little Athens" in Astoria, through "Little Bogota" in Jackson Heights, to a hodge-podge of Asians in Flushing that includes Indians, Pakistanis, Koreans and Chinese, among others.

In Brooklyn the same 20-minute ride

Left, the Ellis Island Museum. **Above**, "all good, all chef-special," claims this restaurant.

ians and Chinese dwell side-by-side in downtown Manhattan.

Foreigners settling into these neighborhoods hardly find themselves surrounded by mainstream America, which may be partly why the city is still such an attractive immigrant destination. Despite the hardships that come with living in New York (overcrowding, high cost of living, substandard housing, etc.), it's comforting to know that you are not alone. In a city of immigrants, no one is really an outsider. There are always other people in exactly the same situation, even if they come from other countries or speak different languages. In fact, it's one of the ironies of New York – and a clear testament to the city's cultural distance from the rest of the country – that an American tourist is more readily identified as an out-of-towner than an immigrant "just off the boat."

The other big attraction for immigrants, of course, is that New York remains a land of opportunity. Some variation of the American dream is still alive here, and immigrants seem eager to hop aboard. It's become a truism that once an immigrant group gets its hooks into a line of work, others follow in the same trade. Thus, Koreans seem to dominate the grocery business; Chinese workers have

flooded the garment industry, and Greek coffee shops and Hispanic bodegas are virtually New York icons.

The stereotypes are only half-true, of course, failing as they do to account for people who pursue non-typical careers and assuming that all immigrants start off at the bottom of the economic ladder. The recent influx of Japanese professionals, Hong Kong businessmen and the high-rolling "Eurobrats" from France, Germany and Italy are hardly Emma Lazarus's "huddled masses yearning to breathe free." Most come to New York to shelter their money from the

unfavorable political climate back home, not to mention the bigger returns they can realize on American investments.

In the end, it doesn't matter why they come. The fact is that they are here and more are arriving every day. People have argued that New York is the least American city in the country, perhaps because the process known as the "melting pot," a melding of cultures and attitudes into a uniquely American hybrid hasn't happened as noticeably in the city as elsewhere.

New York's immigrants aren't being boiled down into a homogenous cultural stew; they are hanging on to their identities and languages, and building institutions and alliances along ethnic lines.

Nor, as has been suggested by some people, is New York an example of pluralism – a multi-ethnic society where everyone has an equal say. The image of that tag is much too static. It doesn't account for the dynamism of the situation or the many possibilities for powerful conflict.

The proper term for New York's cultural mix is probably syncretism, a continuous state of cultural collision, conflict, blending and overlapping, a system in which groups and individuals are continually influencing each other and creating something new. It's like a jigsaw puzzle whose pieces are constantly reshaped and put back together in novel and surprising ways.

New York is a city of immigrants. It always has been. From the very beginning, when the Dutch shared the town with English, French and Scandinavian settlers as well as with African slaves and nearby Indians, it was the give-and-take – and frequently the push-and-shove – between cultures that gave the city an extraordinary, explosive vitality and a certain rough-cut worldliness.

Today, although immigrants come from much farther afield and speak languages never heard by New Yorkers 300 years ago, the same explosive energy runs through the city's ethnic communities. New York is a place that the entire world can call home.

Left, New York was founded by the Dutch. **Right**, home thoughts from abroad.

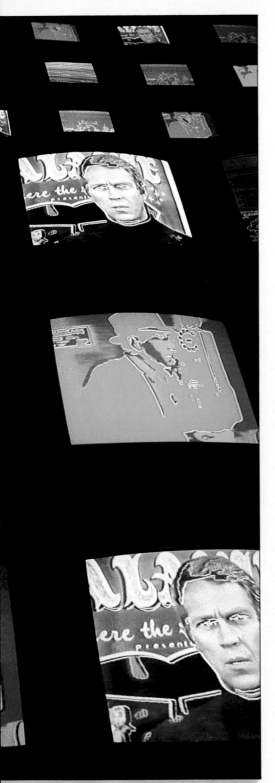

The media in New York is a physical force, not a concept. People are driven by the sheer intensity of their addiction to information. Who you are is not nearly as important as what you know. If a New Yorker wants to get ahead, knowledge is power.

When Frank Sinatra sings "I want to wake up in a city that never sleeps…" the lyrics have a hidden agenda: those who aren't sleeping are switching compulsively from one TV channel to another, obsessed by an appetite for stimulation.

E.B. White once wrote: "No one should come to New York to live unless he is willing to be lucky." For today's New Yorker, that should read willing and able to be bombarded by information. The average Manhattan apartment is capable of receiving around 50 radio stations, at least 70 television stations, several daily newspapers, hundreds of magazines and periodicals, plus all the bills that go with them.

A logical question might be: "Is it humanly possible to process all this information?" Nose buried in newsprint, a *bona fide* media-maniac answers back: "Yes!"

Literary layers: The first literary layer is of newspapers. (New York boasts the oldest continuously published daily newspaper in the country, *The New York Post*.) Following on, a voracious reader might be drawn to any number of weekly or monthly publications, ranging from *Cat Fancy* to *Parakeet Weekly*, *Guitar World* to *Sky and Telescope*, *Surfer* to *The Law Journal*, *The Jerusalem Post* to *Paris Vogue*, *International Currency Review* to *Workbench*, *Herbal Gram* to *Darkroom Techniques*, *Muscle and Fitness* to *The Teddy Bear Review*.

Most of the aforementioned are among thousands of titles stocked in the Eastern Newsstand in the Met Life Building above Grand Central Station. Magazines can be seen all over town: in lobbies, in doctors' offices, at grocery store counters, hanging

Left, switched-on New Yorkers can receive at least 70 television channels.

out of briefcases, on the rack of stationary bicycles at the health club, under the heating lamp at the hair salon, and, of course, there is the obligatory stack in the lavatory.

It goes without saying that a savvy New Yorker wants to be seen carrying the right sort of magazine – rather like wearing the right clothes. The most impressive all-purpose magazines are *New York* or the *New Yorker*, demonstrating a commitment to "being on top of things."

In publishing terms, it seems like New York must be where every book in the country originates – or at least the place where best-selling authors come to attend meet-

Broadway, or the cozily comfortable like the Gotham Book Mart on West 47th Street.

Simultaneous function: Reading or listening to the radio remain the most accessible ways of staying informed. Readers and listeners are friendly relatives, both being attracted to words written or spoken. Radio lends itself to bustling city life because listeners can do more than one thing at a time, important for New Yorkers.

Radio is a highly competitive product. At any given time of the day or night, a New York radio can be tuned to close to 50 commercial and non-commercial stations. It was radio that first introduced single-theme pro-

ings. Despite the fact that there are well over 500 listings under "Publishers" in the Manhattan *Yellow Pages*, the industry maintains a certain degree of glamour. The late Jacqueline Kennedy Onassis, for instance, was an editor at Doubleday.

And there are crossover moguls like S.I. Newhouse of Random House/*New Yorker*/ *Vogue* fame and Rupert Murdoch, once a full-time publisher with several city ventures, who is now a major television mogul.

Bookstores are great havens for kindred spirits, whether they are supermarket like Coliseum Books at the corner of 57th and

gramming, a concept that now extends to cable TV. In the early 1960s, a rock 'n' roll music station changed overnight to an all-news format. WINS, whose slogan "You Give Us 22 Minutes, We'll Give You the World" sounded ambitious at first, but it was soon copied by other stations.

Both WCBS and WINS remain two of the most successful radio stations in the New York market. All-sports radio arrived a couple of years ago with the call letters WFAN. It was the first radio station in the country to go round-the-clock jock. Call-in radio shows are big hits, too, especially if the host happens to be an expert in insulting his audience. Angry and abusive radio may be a reactionary trend to easy listening, but it does have a large working-class following.

Classical, heavy metal, rock, jazz, country, new age… all forms of music have found their home on the FM radio dial over the years, and each corresponding notch has a permanent setting on New York car radios. When taxicabs line up at traffic lights on Columbus Avenue early on a hot summer morning, their open windows emit the outrageous humor of Howard Stern, or the indomitable Don Imus can be heard, between sound-bites of traffic reports from one of the

appropriate. Whether alone or with friends, the most expedient user of tube-time makes sure the remote zapper is no more than an arm's length away. If *Late Show with David Letterman* goes to commercials, there are many options for alternative viewing. Within reach of the other arm will be stacks of publications in case things really slow down: the *New York Daily News*, the *Village Voice*, *Women's Wear Daily*, the *New York Observer*, *Vanity Fair*, or the Book Review section from the Sunday *New York Times* – the list is as endless as the supply of reading material inside their covers.

Mainstream media appetites get their

all-news stations' morning programs.

Radio's link to TV is through sports. Some New York fans are so finicky that if they don't like the TV announcer who is calling a ball game, they'll turn the sound right down on the television and get the play-by-play from their preferred radio sportscaster. This practice is known as simulcasting: a media-maniac's heaven.

When it comes to TV etiquette, remote channel zapping is now considered perfectly

Left, street wise. **Above**, broadcasting legend Walter Cronkite and his cover collection.

minimum daily requirement from commercial TV and its prime-time fare of morning shows (*Today*, *Good Morning America*, and the local *Good Day New York*), plus, at sunset the relative newcomers, the quasi-news shows.

It could well be argued that Ted Turner is the man responsible for the creation of media-maniacs. A decade after the founding of Cable News Network, the system was on offer in 90 countries. The station's brazen coverage of the 1991 Gulf War, the first war to be transmitted live on TV, probably pushed these figures even higher. There are even plans for a CNN Newsreel which could provide a two-minute program of news features for screening by movie houses.

CNN spawned FNN (Financial News Network), which carries a talking head delivering the latest in the world of business, with simultaneous lower-third screen stock-price video ticker-tape. Then there's C-Span, with its live proceedings of the US Congress and shooting matches between world leaders.

Cable offerings range beyond news to nostalgia channels like TNT and TBS (both Ted Turner-owned) which show colorized versions of films that were originally released in black and white. Re-runs on another station, Nickelodeon, of popular American sitcoms, like *Dobie Gillis* and *Mr Ed*, are attracting a new generation of followers 30 years later.

Most talkradio in town has always featured a call-in capability allowing the audience to know the opinions of other listeners. This kind of "interactive" media has now spread to television. Many of the issue-based shows on CNN provide viewers with a national telephone number they can call to vote on such pro/con questions as gun control or capital punishment. Another phenomena appeared in Public Television where New York's Channel 13 offered a local news-discussion program that allowed the audience to talk to the host and panel in the course of 30 minutes.

When it comes to narrowcasting, however, there are instances when the cable industry has gone too far. Anyone who has watched the Home Shoppers' Network or the Weather Channel for more than five minutes knows the risk of monotony inherent in such ventures. For real entertainment, New York's best-kept cable secrets reside in the land of Public Access.

Forbidden land: Here are the citizen-driven, home-grown programs featuring un-telegenic astrologers or numerologists who answer phone calls from viewers. Here is the forbidden land of cable-porn like *Midnite Blue* and Robyn Byrd's video strip-show.

Add to the mix a guy singing old show tunes by request at an upright piano complete with Liberace candelabra, and that's the gamut of public access, much of which has acquired cult chic. According to reports from a recent National Cable TV Association Convention, one vendor was offering a bingo-players' network. Satellite bingo?

The late Marshall MacLuhan, media guru, saw television replacing fireplaces in the home which now stand in for lamps, shrines, video light to read by. This is the global village that television has produced. How did things get to such a feverish media pitch, and are New York's media-maniacs any different from those found in other parts of the literate world?

It begins with the basic premise that New Yorkers need to know things before anyone else. A premise which led to the establishment of New York-1, a cable television station devoted exclusively to nonstop news *only* about New York – twenty-four hours a day, seven days a week. Add this need-to-know-first with the multiplication of media sources and there it is: the formula for obsessive-compulsive behavior.

Gone are the old days of 12 television channels, the daily newspaper and the evening newscast. Everything changed with the advent of CNN, the dawn of the FM radio fad and the proliferation of special interest magazines. Each stage of media development has confirmed New York's media imprint more indelibly.

Did you know, have you heard, what I saw and what he read either on page six of *The New York Post* or on "The Intelligencer" page of *New York* magazine? If you didn't read it or see it, you might catch up with it at New York's Museum of Television & Radio, whose TV archives are complete enough to satisfy the most dedicated media-maniac.

New Yorkers have fulfilled Alvin Toffler's forecast in *Future Shock*: "The mass media instantly and persuasively disseminate new images, and ordinary individuals, seeking help in coping with an ever more complex social environment, attempt to keep up... Racing swiftly past our attention screen, they wash out old images and generate new ones."

What will New Yorkers be keeping track of in the year 2010?

97

BROAD   F:NANCIAL   CENTER

In 1986, Steve Hindy, a young journalist, and Tom Potter, a young banker, were neighbors in Brooklyn Heights who liked to get together to watch the Mets on television when they were babysitting their children. Like most New Yorkers, their dreams were not far from the surface, and they got to talking about what they wanted out of life.

Within a few months, they had quit their jobs, mortgaged everything they had, borrowed everything they could, and announced that they were opening a microbrewery. Today Potter is chief executive officer, Hindy is president and they are partners in the Brooklyn Brewery, which makes Brooklyn Lager, one of the trendy "boutique" beers that have become popular in both neighborhood Brooklyn taverns and swank Manhattan watering spots.

Hindy and Potter are typical of the tens of thousands of small-business success stories that make up New York. To them, and to most of America, the unofficial motto of New York is not "I ♥ NY" but "NY Means Business." And while New York is known for its major corporations – more than 100 of the *Fortune* 500, the listing of the largest US corporations, are based in the city or its suburbs – it is really small companies like the 20-employee Brooklyn Brewery that make up the economic backbone of New York. Recent figures showed that while the 301 square miles that make up New York City are home to more than 4,000 companies with more than 100 employees, it is also home to at least 200,000 employing between one and 99 workers.

Wall Street: Like the figures that are so commonly tossed around – millions and billions of dollars, the power and influence of New York City business are difficult for many people to grasp. Peering down the crooked little lane that is marked Wall Street, visitors invariably look around to see if the sign has been misplaced, if someone is playing a joke. Can this be where a million bankers, lawyers, investors and other financial players make the decisions that affect the world? Yes, indeed. It is estimated that half the world's capital has come from investments out of New York. Small wonder that they say, "When Wall Street sneezes, the rest of the world catches a cold."

One of the lovely ironies of the modern financial world is that while all the other leading money centers are moving toward

computerized, screen-based electronic trading, where deals are made by pushing buttons on keyboards from offices where the dealers never see each other, the New York Stock Exchange is resolutely sticking to its open-outcry, face-to-face, shoulder-to-shoulder, littered-floor system. And tourists can still look down from the visitors' gallery and try imagining how the shouting and scurrying will ultimately affect their lives.

The diversity of New York – the "rag trade" of Seventh Avenue, the advertising of Madison Avenue, the retail of Fifth Avenue, the money of Wall Street and the small

Preceding pages: the sharper image. Left, mirror of the world. Right, dining in the stars.

businesses everywhere – are one reason for the city's economic resilience. New York does not suffer like Houston when oil prices drop or Detroit when auto sales slump or Seattle when government aerospace contracts run out. New York dominates its industries, rather than the other way around.

Better mousetraps may be invented, great books may be written and great food may be grown in small towns like Peoria or Paducah, but the people behind new ideas and products and services are unlikely to profit without the stamp of approval from New York City. Such is the scope of economic influence that it is New York, not Paris, that rules

the wine markets and in effect determines the prices year to year.

Even on the street, the business of New York is business. Panhandlers pay tuition to organized "begging schools" to sharpen their techniques. Drug dealers oversee their businesses with mobile phones and faxes. Cab drivers sell for $200,000 the city-issued medallions that make yellow cabs legal. When it rains, it's only a matter of seconds from the moment the first drop hisses onto the pavement until young men are breaking open boxes of cheap umbrellas.

Four of America's seven largest banks are based in New York City, along with four of the six largest insurance companies. One-quarter of America's international passenger travel is in and out of the New York area, along with almost half the import-export trade. More than twenty million people live within 60 miles of Manhattan, making it the center of American retail and distribution networks. The center for US publishing since surpassing Boston in the 19th century, New York is the undisputed media capital of the world.

Not everyone in New York, of course, is as affected by the entrepreneurial spirit as Steve Hindy and Tom Potter. New Yorkers might try to deny it, but many of them represent the American version of the Japanese "salaryman," the faceless office worker whose devotion to his company goes beyond allegiance to home, family or even his own personal betterment.

And that's the big difference in New York. Although New Yorkers may let their jobs become more important than home, family or other personal concerns, they never let their employers, their companies, become more important than their own careers.

People work hard in New York, often extraordinarily hard. That's not to say, however, that the "thirtysomething" workers who fill the skyscraper offices – there is more than 380 million square feet of office space in Manhattan alone – do not depend on their corporate employers for the routines of daily life. In the financial world, in law, in marketing, in advertising and public relations, in publishing, in communications, they start their days reading the newspaper at their desks, sipping coffee and nibbling Danish from the office trolley. They "schmooze" with co-workers at the water fountain, hold discreet telephone conversations and make distant eye contact with love-or-lust interests sitting at desks across the trading room or the newsroom.

As they gather information or make persuasive arguments over the phone, they stick out their feet so their shoes can be polished by little men who carry their shine kits from desk to desk. They eat lunch in the company cafeteria. They take extra suits along on business trips to have them dry-cleaned at company expense. They drink beer, go to dinner, jog around Central Park, compare acquisitions and swap aspirations with the men and women at the next desk or down the hall. Often they get together and buy or rent holiday homes in upstate New York or way out on Long Island. In New York, the people you work with are usually the people you play with.

In the big companies, the big bosses are typically suburban family types who take the trains out to New Jersey or Connecticut at 6.33 or 7.14 every night. They may literally rub shoulders, twice, each commuting day with the unwashed rabble, but in the office

the first baby comes along, both keeping jobs and paying $20,000 a year for child care. But as the family grows many follow their bosses to the suburbs and become Sitcoms – single income, two children, outrageous mortgage.

Those, of course, are the survivors. Many find themselves going back to the small towns they came from, or lowering their career goals and making "quality of life" decisions in favor of Phoenix or Sacramento or Springfield.

The changes imposed on the corporate culture, both from the outside and from the inside, have made New York a harder place to make it – and harder still to keep it.

they are the power centers, the managers and the rainmakers who are ultimately responsible for keeping the business growing.

On the other hand, the work centers, the people responsible for getting things done, are typically young singles or couples ranging in age from their late twenties to early forties. Of course they're all yuppies, but the classifications have long gone beyond. Dinkies, for example, are dual-income, no kids. Some try to stick it out in the city after

Left and above, New York supports around 200,000 small businesses.

The world stock market crash of October 19, 1987, hit New York harder than anywhere else. But then, why not? It was New York's booming financial services industry that had swaggered through the 1980s, inventing a host of new financial "products" such as junk bonds, creating a million new jobs and bringing about the very overheated, over-extended economic and fiscal conditions that triggered the market collapse.

In the end, takeover fever claimed many victims: companies that couldn't cover their debts, and dealmakers who found that no one wanted their kind of deals any more. In New

York, tens of thousands of people lost financial services jobs on or near Wall Street. Teamed with cash problems among the faceless parent companies that had taken over many New York retailers at the cost of huge debts, the inevitable consumer-buying slump brought an economic recession that extended into the 1990s.

Landmark stores such as B. Altman, Macy's, Fifth Avenue and Bloomingdales either went out of business or had a very shaky time with creditors. Banks and investment houses that are tightening their belts do not spend millions for new brochures, and department stores in bankruptcy procedures

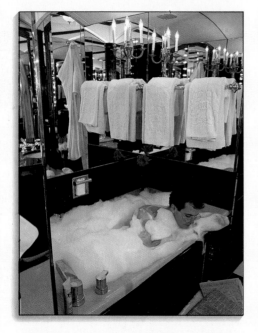

do not sign up for full-page advertising campaigns, so Madison Avenue's advertising and public relations industries were hurt too. Trendy watering spots moved out the decorative ferns and locked their doors. Fine restaurants went belly up.

Housing prices dipped by 25 percent as fewer work opportunities brought fewer people to New York, and couples found that they couldn't move out of Manhattan even if they wanted to, for the simple reason that they couldn't afford to take the losses on the small apartment they had bought for $300,000 but could sell for only $250,000.

Personifications of the 1980s such as Ivan Boesky and Michael Milken went to court, were prosecuted and sometimes ended up in jail, victims of the processes they created and exploited to make awesome fortunes. Even the towers of Donald Trump, for many the ultimate icon of all that is both good and bad about corporate New York, were tarnished. The financial slump showed how his empire had been built on property-based borrowings that could turn precarious when the value that he put on his land and buildings was questioned.

The fact that less money was spent in New York naturally meant lower tax collections, leaving the city with even less money than anticipated to stretch over its sprawling infrastructure. Less money to repair potholes and cracked sidewalks, less money to pay police to arrest drug dealers, less money to collect rubbish, sweep streets or keep Central Park's precious few grassy spots from turning to overtrodden dust.

To emphasize New York's problems, some observers and analysts compared the economic problems of the 1990s to the near-bankruptcy of the mid-1970s, when it took a massive federal government loan to keep the city's finances afloat. To others, however, the way New York recovered in the 1980s was a sign of the never-flagging hopefulness and determination of those people who work in the city.

No matter what happens, corporate America and the people who make up its corporate culture believe New York is the greatest city on earth. It is their playground and their testing ground, a baptism by fire where mere survival says more about the toughness and tenacity of an individual than any sort of faster track in a smaller, easier city. As long as prospering in New York's corporate culture carries the cachet of being able to prosper anywhere, that culture itself will continue to prosper as it attracts America's – and, increasingly, the world's – best and brightest, the young careerists who are not afraid to find out just how good they really are.

<u>Left</u>, reading the *Wall Street Journal* at the Waldorf. <u>Right</u>, the Stock Exchange.

EIGHT HOURS IN A POLICE CAR

Her name is Yolanda. She tells a police officer that she is 25 years old and from Hoboken, New Jersey, and that all she wants is for someone to let her call her babysitter to say she will not be home tonight.

Yolanda is on her way to Central Booking. John Dempster and his partner, Robert Shuell, are her police escorts. Yolanda waits in the security office of Lord & Taylor, the Fifth Avenue department store where she spent an afternoon shopping without paying. She wears a purple coat with padded shoulders, a silky dress and pumps with gold toes.

Dempster asks, "Why did you come across the river to New York, Yolanda?" And Yolanda, in a voice at once weary and ingenuous, replies, "To shoplift."

Dempster shrugs and says, "Time to try on a new pair of bracelets."

It is dusk in New York, or more specifically in that seven-tenths of a square mile tract that falls under the scope of the Midtown Police Precinct. Midtown South has dubbed itself the Busiest Precinct in the World. It extends from 29th Street to 45th Street, from Ninth Avenue to Lexington Avenue. It includes Times Square, the Port Authority Bus Terminal, Grand Central Station, the wholesale fur, flower and costume jewelry districts, Hell's Kitchen (now called Clinton) and Murray Hill, "which," Dempster says, "is where the city's rich people live."

There are nights, Dempster and Shuell say, when they can measure the time between calls on their radio in nanoseconds, when work means drawing their service revolvers, when all the madness, cruelty, senselessness and danger of New York City explodes frantically around them. According to a survey published in *New York* magazine, every 24 hours five people are killed, nine are raped, 256 are robbed, 332 homes and stores are burglarized and 367 cars disappear. A grim record was set on July 9,

Preceding pages: Manhattan's finest. Left and right, policing the streets.

1988, when 20 people were murdered in just 24 hours.

But there are also nights like this night, when the city seems almost tranquil, when the congestion, pollution and cacophony of rush-hour traffic abates, when the theater audiences have taken their seats and the sidewalks, save for 42nd Street, feel empty.

The radio crackles. Dempster asks the dispatcher, "Anything for us?"

"Nothing," says the dispatcher. Dempster

and Shuell drive on, reading the streets.

They drive past a squad of Jesus-Loves-You preachers on Times Square and chess games on Seventh Avenue; past the Please Club boutique, Goldberg's Marine, the Pumping Iron Gym, and Leg Sense pantyhose; past businesswomen in blue suits and sneakers, and a young woman with heavy-lidded eyes dragging herself across 42nd Street, her pregnant belly tightly covered in red velvet.

Tonight will be a night whose languid pace defies prediction, when every call could be a deadly call, but isn't. It will be a night of burglar alarms that sound for no reason, for unexplained shots fired in an empty mortgage office, for dinners of pizza and take-out Chinese food, a night for Dempster and Shuell to keep their heads down in the station house for fear of running into the irate lieutenant trying to find the prisoner who escaped from the precinct holding pen.

But mostly it will be a night for the denizens of Midtown South, for Buster the Wino, Sheldon the Mad Pacer, Enos the Mayor of 31st Street, and, in her one brief and lamentable appearance in the precinct, Yolanda of Hoboken.

Shuell, he lives on Long Island. Like Shuell, he wears a moustache. Shuell is 24 and engaged to be married in a year's time. He has been a policeman for four years. He works with a young man's zeal. Dempster will invoke the privilege of experience, especially when deciding whether it is worth the time, paperwork and hassle of arresting someone for the most minor offense. Shuell, stopped at a red light, will look at vehicle registration stickers on nearby cars, to make sure they are not out of date. Violators will be pulled over.

They have been partners for only a few months, but their rapport is easy, easy

Dempster and Shuell are stopped at a red light in front of Grand Central. A woman approaches. She lowers her head to the window and asks, "Do you guys know what it means to have a monkey on your back?"

Dempster, ever polite, nods, as if to say, "Yeah, so…"

The woman, the light on her side, continues. She says, "Well, if you do would you please explain it to my lawyer, Mr Sizer."

And with that she is gone.

Times Square trade: Dempster is the veteran, with eight years on the force. He is 34 years old, married with two children. Like

enough for them to drive in silence without one or the other feeling the need to fill the void. They share both the policeman's frustration with laws that protect the rights of criminals at the expense – in their view – of fighting crime, as well as a certain nostalgia for the days when heroin was the street drug of choice. Heroin addicts, Dempster says, got high and nodded off. Addicts of crack cocaine explode.

They harbor no such nostalgic views about the central boulevard of their watch, 42nd Street, nicknamed "The Deuce," and its primary intersection, Times Square. "Times

Square," Dempster says, "lives on nothing but a legend, a legend that's 40 years old."

No place in the city has a higher robbery rate. No place has more 25¢ peep shows, shell games, movie houses – most of them pornographic; one, the Selwyn, still inviting families to come see a movie – and, aside from Fifth Avenue in the 50s, stores that swear they must liquidate because they are going out of business.

Times Square is the crossroads of Midtown South, a transient's precinct: people pass through but live elsewhere. Out-of-town visitors come to the precinct to see the Broadway plays, or to have their picture taken with Times Square in the background, or because they think that in Times Square they will find the New York that existed in movies with Ruby Keeler and Dick Powell. The tourists are such easy marks, advertising their out-of-townness by such un-New York behavior as waiting at crosswalks until the light turns green. It is along the stretch of 42nd Street that straddles Times Square that the two halves of New York, victims and perpetrators, come together.

Dempster and Shuell cruise the street slowly. "We try to look for something that might happen," Dempster says. He looks at the droves of tourists. "These," he says, "are the prey." Those who prey upon them lurk in doorways, waiting for Dempster and Shuell to drive past.

A group of 30 Japanese tourists waits for the green light before crossing Seventh Avenue. Dempster waves and a few raise their hands in a tentative response, although the bolder tourists from Japan will ask if they can take their picture. A gaggle of blondes speaking German bounce along Broadway, oblivious to the danger that Dempster and Shuell see all too plainly but are powerless to prevent until a crime occurs. Marking a thief or a crack dealer means nothing if he is standing on the corner, doing nothing more than marking them.

And so they must wait and look, knowing that theirs is often an after-the-fact job. On Broadway, just north of Macy's, a young

man runs up to the patrol car, sticks his face in the window and tells Dempster and Shuell that he has just helped foil a mugging. He wants them to help catch the mugger. They ask where the victim is. The victim, says the young man, is gone. But maybe he can ride with them, searching for the mugger. He is sure he will recognize him.

Dempster and Shuell know this is a fool's errand, because without a victim there will be no arrest. Often they will get a call about a robbery at a clothing store and arrive to see the suspects, a band of teenagers, sprinting away in different directions. They will give chase, but without success, not when they are

running after young men wearing $100 gym shoes. Robberies by the gangs the police call "wolfpacks" generally happen after school is out, when the robbers are on their way home from class.

The radio dispatcher, meanwhile, has work for cars other than theirs. She reports a jack-knifed tractor-trailer clogging the FDR Drive, an off-duty policeman who may be having trouble in a subway station, and a woman assaulting another woman.

For Dempster and Shuell, however, this is a night with little satisfaction. Yesterday there was satisfaction, or rather a moment

Left, a midnight rambler. **Right**, these women are really men in drag.

that seemed to hold the promise of satisfaction. They responded to a call about a 10-year-old boy missing outside a department store. The boy and his mother were from Jamaica. The boy needed to use the toilet and his mother sent him to find it. The boy disappeared. Dempster and Shuell searched for two hours and then found two witnesses who saw him being led through the streets by a crack addict. The two men, sensing something was amiss, stopped the crack addict and discovered that she had taken the boy with her when she saw him at the department store. Dempster and Shuell thought the reunion between mother and son might be joy-

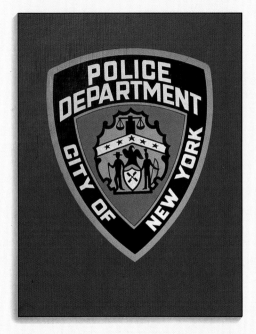

ous. But the mother barely talked to her young son and the son barely acknowledged his mother.

Strange residents: On Eighth Avenue, Dempster and Shuell recognize a woman who used to call 911, the police emergency number, reporting invaders from planets beyond. After too many calls Dempster told her to call the special alert number, 912, and thankfully never heard from her again. They pass the corner on 42nd Street and Dempster recalls the night he was on foot patrol and an 80-year-old woman called out, "Hey, fellas," as she pulled up her blouse. "What do you think of these?" the woman asked, inquiring about her breasts. "I used to be beautiful." Dempster told her, "You're still beautiful. Now get out of here."

A bank alarm sounds and Dempster is all but certain there is no break-in. And though his hunch is proven right, it is a call he and Shuell must make, and which cannot be made casually. Complacency, they say, is their job's greatest danger, because when a policeman is complacent, when he does not have his service revolver drawn, when he too casually strolls over to a car stopped for a routine license-and-registration check, he can discover, only too late, that what seemed so mundane was nothing of the kind.

A prostitute lifts her skirt as they drive north. An old man sits on a shoeshine stand where no one ever comes for a shine. A break-in is reported in the back entrance to a flop house in the 30s. Dempster and Shuell sigh. They know the flop house, know that it is a home for those who share little but a closeness to death – know, too, that it has no back entrance. They scan the windows while climbing the stairs, because the residents do not like police and will throw debris at them. The men at the flop house desk cannot imagine why the police have bothered to come.

The men chat with Dempster and Shuell, which makes for an almost pleasant interlude. Only bums and madmen talk to policemen. Sheldon the Mad Pacer waves to them on 31st Street.

"Did you guys hear about the accident between the cab and the delivery van last night?" Sheldon asks. Sheldon, whose street name is Moses, wears a skull cap, dirty jeans, a long beard and a school ring. He looks like a rabbinical student in need of dry cleaning. Sheldon is Italian. Dempster and Shuell tell him they don't know about the accident.

Sheldon, speaking fast, tells his story about a truck delivering breakfast rolls and how he asked for a roll because he was hungry but how the driver wouldn't give him one which did not seem nice at all and how the driver pulled out onto the street and immediately struck a passing cab. This happened at four in the morning, when Sheldon was still pacing. "Goodnight guys," Sheldon says. "Have a quiet one."

Around the corner they meet Enos the Panhandler. That is the name that Enos uses, even though he calls himself the Mayor of 31st Street. Enos has his mail sent to Miss Kay's 24-hour deli. The mail is addressed to Enos the Panhandler.

Enos once helped Dempster and Shuell solve a rape case. He knows everyone on the block, which is why he also calls himself the mayor. He knew that the rapist lived in a nearby welfare hotel and that is what he told the police. Enos wanted money from the city but the city, he says, "didn't give me jack." Enos, a stocky man dressed in torn shirt and straw hat, could not understand why the

herself and her children. One is 10 years old and the other is nine months. Yolanda responds to inquiries about the whereabouts of the father of the 10-year-old with a shrug. The father of the nine-month-old is still around. He is a drug user and he beats Yolanda when she tries to leave him.

Central Booking is in lower Manhattan, a location that means nothing to Yolanda, who is still feeling her way around the city. "Are we in Brooklyn?" Yolanda asks, knowing only that the ride took a long time. When she hears that Chinatown is nearby, she asks, without success, if she can use the five dollars she brought with her to buy some food.

rapist would need to resort to rape. "Young, healthy dude," Enos tells Dempster and Shuell. "I said, 'What you do that for? The women'll rape you'."

Central Booking: And finally there is Yolanda, who is sitting in the back seat of the patrol car, trying to make herself comfortable with her hands cuffed behind her back. This was Yolanda's plan for her day in the city: she was going to steal things and then sell them and use the money to help support

Left, a shoulder to cry on. **Above**, a Lower East Side mural.

Dempster and Shuell give up Yolanda to the custody of the men and women of Central Booking, who ask her to pause for her mug shots. The jail doors close behind Yolanda, who asks, in a small, tentative voice, if she might be able to call her babysitter. Yolanda says that she does not want her child's life to be like hers. Her child's life, she says, will be "different." Yolanda says "different" in a way that suggests that she can only guess at what it might look like.

Dempster and Shuell depart. They drive north, behind a rising sun. The dispatcher has nothing for them, nothing at all.

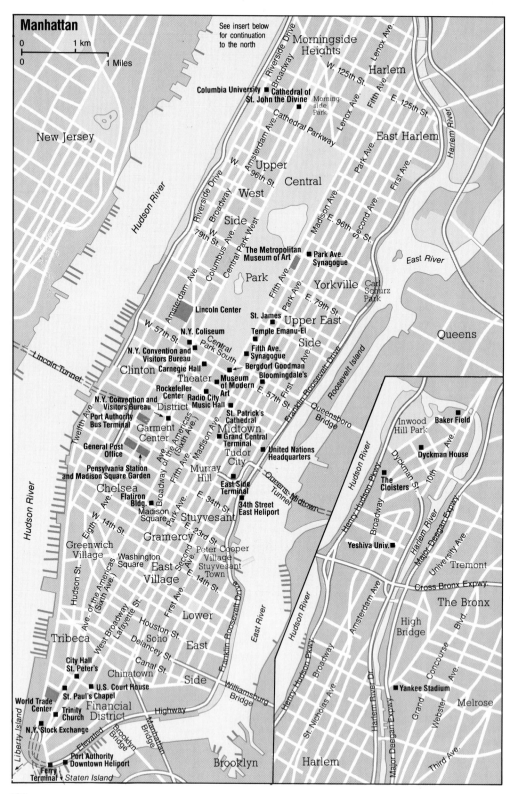

Manhattan

See insert below for continuation to the north

0 1 km
0 1 Miles

New Jersey

Morningside Heights

Harlem

Columbia University

Cathedral of St. John the Divine

Morning-side Park

W. 125th St.

E. 125th St.

Lenox Ave.

Fifth Ave.

East Harlem

Cathedral Parkway

Upper

Central

West

Side

W. 96th St.

E. 96th St.

Park Ave.

Madison Ave.

Second Ave.

First Ave.

Riverside Drive

Broadway

Amsterdam Ave.

W. 79th St.

Columbus Ave.

Central Park West

The Metropolitan Museum of Art

Park Ave. Synagogue

East River

Park

Yorkville

Carl Schurz Park

E. 79th St

Lincoln Center

St. James

Upper East

Temple Emanu-El

Side

Queens

N.Y. Coliseum

Fifth Ave. Synagogue

W. 57th St.

Central Park South

N.Y. Convention and Visitors Bureau

Bergdorf Goodman

Bloomingdale's

Clinton

Carnegie Hall

Theater

Museum of Modern Art

Rockefeller Center

Radio City Music Hall

St. Patrick's Cathedral

Roosevelt Island

N.Y. Convention and Visitors Bureau

District

Midtown

Franklin Roosevelt Drive

Port Authority Bus Terminal

Grand Central Terminal

Queensboro Bridge

Garment Center

United Nations Headquarters

General Post Office

Tudor City

Murray Hill

Inwood Hill Park

Baker Field

Pensylvania Station and Madison Square Garden

East Side Terminal

34th Street East Heliport

Dyckman House

Chelsea

Flatiron Bldg.

E. 34th St.

Queens-Midtown Tunnel

Madison Square

Stuyvesant

The Cloisters

W. 14th St.

E. 23rd St.

Gramercy

Greenwich Village

Washington Square

Peter Cooper Village

Stuyvesant Town

Yeshiva Univ.

Tremont

East Village

E. 14th St.

Hudson River

Lower

The Bronx

Tribeca

East

High Bridge

Soho

Houston St.

Canal St.

Delancey St.

Side

Williamsburg Bridge

Cross Bronx Expwy.

City Hall

St. Peter's

Chinatown

U.S. Court House

Yankee Stadium

Melrose

St. Paul's Chapel

World Trade Center

Trinity Church

Financial District

Highway

N.Y. Stock Exchange

Brooklyn Bridge

Manhattan Bridge

Harlem

Port Authority Downtown Heliport

Ferry Terminal

Staten Island

Brooklyn

Liberty Island

Hudson River

Lincoln Tunnel

Fifth Ave.

Broadway

Ave. of the Americas (Sixth Ave.)

Madison Ave.

Park Ave.

Lexington Ave.

Third Ave.

Second Ave.

First Ave.

Eighth Ave.

Seventh Ave.

Twelfth Ave.

Lafayette St.

West Broadway

Hudson St.

Ave. of the Americas (Sixth Ave.)

First Ave.

Henry Hudson Pkwy.

Broadway

Amsterdam Ave.

Dyckman St.

10th Ave.

Harlem River

Henry Hudson Pkwy.

Major Deegan Expwy.

University Ave.

Grand Concourse

Webster Ave.

Third Ave.

St. Nicholas Ave.

Harlem River Dr.

Major Deegan Expwy.

PLACES

"New York is where I *have* to be," said a character in Jack Olsen's *The Girls in the Office*, "I wish I knew why."

The people who live here, and the ones who visit here, could tell her why. New York's industrial resources are vast. So are its academic facilities. Its cultural life is extensive – witness the fact that the Metropolitan Museum receives almost four and a half million visitors a year. The city's cultural vigor is matched, perhaps, only by its culinary awareness. Take your choice of more than 16,000 eating establishments, from Greek coffee shops to *bijou* bistros, to worthwhile soul food at Sylvia's in Harlem.

There is a mix of freedom and foreignness in New York City which is unsurpassed anywhere in the world. You want to have a drink on a level with the clouds? You want to go dancing, when the moon is high and the mood overtakes you? You want to go roller skating, ice skating or take in that hot new movie? You've come to the right town.

New York City has energy and animosity, clutter and great charm. Not to mention shops. If there are more ways of making it here than anywhere else, there are also more ways of spending it. FAO Schwarz, on Fifth Avenue, sells hundreds of different teddy bears. Maxilla & Mandible, on Columbus between 81st and 82nd Street, is a shop specializing in skeletons (non-endangered species only.) You can buy Art Deco cufflinks; horse tack from an 1875 riding boutique; or any one of a number of edible goodies at Zabar's, the deli located at 2245 Broadway. Zabar's is an Upper West Side institution, each week selling nearly 2,500 pounds of cream cheese, and double that amount of smoked salmon. Then, there's always Tiffany's, Macy's and Bloomingdale's.

But not all of New York comes with a hefty price tag. On sultry summer nights free operas and concerts are held on the Great Lawn in Central Park. Pack a picnic (from Zabar's, of course) and take advantage of Shakespeare in the outdoors, or even the Philharmonic Orchestra. You can visit botanic gardens and historic buildings; Rockefeller Center or the New York Stock Exchange, without disposing of a penny.

The best of almost everything is here for the taking. Cop an attitude and check it out. This is, after all, New York.

Preceding pages: Liberty city; steel and glass; escape from New York.

FIFTH AVENUE

Paris has the Champs Elysées. Rome has the Via Veneto. Los Angeles has Sunset Boulevard. And New York City has Fifth Avenue.

Fifth Avenue plays host to the annual Easter Day Parade, and the annual St Patrick's Day Parade, when New Yorkers take to the streets and Fifth Avenue's center stripe becomes a bright, leprechaun green. At Christmas, Manhattanites, normally taxi and subway users, have been known to rent a car just to to drive at their own pace down this famous avenue, to admire the equally famous holiday displays.

There are few streets that evoke the essence of the city as powerfully as Fifth. It's all here – the audacity of the Empire State Building, the ambition of Rockefeller Center, the glitz of Trump Tower, and the old-world elegance of the Plaza Hotel. Fifth cuts through the heart of midtown Manhattan, dividing the island into East and West. It's a social compass pointing the way to high fashion and the lifestyle of the elite. This is where the rich and powerful make their moves, where New Yorkers come to celebrate, and where the city shows off to the world.

It's also a timeline, chronicling Manhattan's northward and economic growth, then pushing through an area symbolic of the city's decline. Fifth Avenue begins at Washington Square Park, near the crooked streets of Greenwich Village. It continues past the Flatiron Building on 22nd Street, to Madison Square Park, between 23rd and 26th Streets, site of the original Madison Square Garden.

The avenue continues past the Empire State Building, and Rockefeller Center, hugs Central Park for 26 scenic blocks, before plunging into "Museum Mile," which plays host to some of the city's most important collections. Continuing past the mansions and em-

bassies of the Upper East Side, the avenue then runs a course through Harlem, bisecting Marcus Garvey Park and through the heart of this ethnic community, before finally coming to a halt just before the Harlem River. If there's time, you might like to consider traveling many of the 132 blocks which make up Fifth Avenue. South to north, culturally and economically, few streets in the world could offer a better overview.

For the short-term visitor, most of the action is on a 10-block stretch between 49th and 59th Streets, from Rockefeller Center to the Plaza Hotel. There are several spectacular exceptions to this rule, however, so it makes sense to begin with the biggest.

The **Empire State Building** rises like a rocket from the corner of 33rd Street. When it was completed in 1931, this was the tallest building in the world, and in the hearts of many New Yorkers it still is. At 1,4754 feet and 102 stories, it now ranks third behind the Sears

Preceding pages: lunchtime break on Fifth Avenue. <u>Left,</u> Trump Tower. <u>Right,</u> Empire State interior.

Tower in Chicago and the World Trade Center in the financial district. But when it comes to the view, it can't be beat. On a clear day you can see as far as 80 miles. At night, Manhattan spreads out below like a sea of twinkling lights.

You can catch the elevator to the 86th-floor observation deck at the concourse level. From here, a second elevator goes up to the tiny lookout on the 102nd floor, which is just about where Fay Wray had her fateful rendezvous with the "tallest, darkest leading man in Hollywood," a 50-foot ape by the name of King Kong. They're not the only ones who met their fates up here. Of the 16 people who have jumped off the Empire State Building only two were wearing parachutes, and both were arrested as soon as they hit the ground. Fourteen other lives were claimed in 1945, when a B-25 airplane crashed into the 79th floor of the building.

Anyone residing in New York for any length of time will notice that the Empire State Building's upper floors are illuminated at night, often by different color combinations. On St Patrick's Day the summit glows, appropriately, bright green. On Columbus Day, the national holiday for the millions of Italian-Americans who live and work in New York, it turns shades of red, white and green. After six years of intensive lobbying, Manhattan's gay community (thought to be around 700,000) have won the right to have the lights illuminated a symbolic shade of lavender during Gay Pride Week each June.

Back on earth, check out one of New York's most lavish department stores: **Lord & Taylor**. Five blocks north at 39th Street, it is famous for extravagant holiday displays. People have been known to line up on a cold winter day just to peer into the windows.

For the next 10 blocks or so, Fifth gets a bit tedious. The elegant townhouses once owned by the Astors and the Vanderbilts have been replaced by discount shops and the permanent "going-out-of-business" signs they use to bait **Dinner and dancing.**

customers. One major exception is the **New York Public Library**, squatting like a sphinx over two blocks of Fifth Avenue, from 40th to 42nd streets. Built in 1911, this grand Beaux Arts monument now houses one of the finest research facilities in the world, with nearly 20 million books and documents in its collection, including the first book printed in the United States, the Bay Psalm Book from 1640, and the original diaries of Virginia Woolf. An unlikely mix of office workers, layabouts and tourists can usually be found lounging – and smoking – on the stairway under the watchful gaze of Patience and Fortitude, the two marble lions reclining on the top step.

On the other side of 42nd Street, at 500 Fifth Avenue, a shop called **Nat Sherman's** is cigarette-purveyor to the celebrities and other recalcitrant folks who haven't yet given into today's health and fitness mania. At 49th Street, Fifth Avenue begins to live up to its legend, thanks largely to **Rockefeller Center**, one of the world's largest business and entertainment complexes and an absolute triumph of Art Deco architecture. Rockefeller Center has been called a "city within a city," and it's got the numbers to prove it. The Center's daily population is about 240,000 people – greater than all but 60 American cities. There are 100,000 telephones, 48,758 office windows and 388 elevators, traveling a total of 2 million miles per year. That's about 40 times around the planet. Add to this a 2-mile underground concourse, 35 restaurants, four major rail lines and nine foreign consulates, and you've got quite a little metropolis. Scenes from nearly 100 movies have been filmed in the Center since 1943, including *The Sweet Smell of Success* and *Radio Days*.

The **Channel Gardens** – so named because they separate La Maison Française on the left and the British Building on the right, just as these two countries flank the English Channel – draw visitors into the center of the

Newsflash!
St Patrick's
Cathedral.

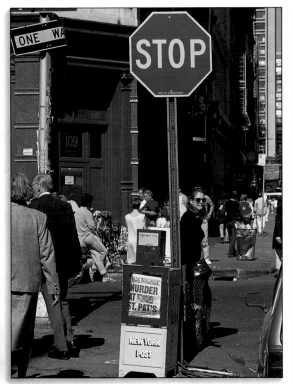

Plaza, dominated by the soaring mass of the **GE Building** (formerly the RCA Building). The GE Building is fronted by a sunken courtyard used as an outdoor restaurant in summer and an ice skating rink in winter. This is also where the famous Christmas tree, lit with countless bulbs, holds throngs of spectators at sway over the holidays. They also pause to read the famous motto on a plaque which reads: "I believe in the supreme work of the individual and in his right to life, liberty and the pursuit of happiness." Inside the GE Building, the main lobby features two murals by Jose Maria Sert. Originally, Diego Rivera was commissioned to do the paintings, but when he refused to change a panel glorifying Vladimir Lenin, the Rockefellers – capitalists to the core – fired Rivera and destroyed the work.

If ever there was a bar in heaven, it would probably be like the one on top of Rockefeller Center. The view on the horizon would no doubt be identical – thousands of twinkling lights stretching as far as the eye can see. **The Rainbow Room**, which reopened in the late-1980s after undergoing a major revamp, is a quintessential Manhattan experience – memorable, a little bit camp, and very, very expensive. To eat in the 1940s-style dining room (jacket and tie required) is beyond the means of most visitors, and even a drink in the bar, which offers the best view, might mean skipping the next few meals in order to save pennies. But dress up in your glad-rags, hold out for a table by the window, devour the complimentary peanuts, and savor the experience, which begins by ascending to the top in an elegant elevator, and even extends to the high-camp ladies' room.

Back on Fifth Avenue, if not real life, **Saks Fifth Avenue**, across the street from Rockefeller Center, is the department store which gave rise to Sak's Fifth Avenue shops from Dallas to St Louis. The **International Building** is on the next corner up, with Lee Lawrie's massive Atlas crouching at its entrance. Although the bronze figure is over 25 feet tall, it is dwarfed by **St Patrick's Cathedral** directly across the way, the largest Catholic church in the country. Opened in 1879, when the city didn't extend beyond 42nd Street, St Patrick's is now one of Midtown's most formidable landmarks, its ornate Gothic facade working an intriguing counterpoint against the angular lines and smooth surfaces of the skyscrapers around it. And yet St Pat's is unmistakably New York: where else would one need tickets to attend midnight Mass? Take some time for a look round the cathedral's magnificent interior, where F. Scott Fitzgerald married his southern belle Zelda. The bronze doors and stained-glass windows are particularly striking.

Beyond St Pat's, Fifth Avenue devotes itself to more worldly concerns. The super-rich (and those who like to pretend) can be seen bouncing between **Cartier, Fortunoff, Bijan** and the twin **Guccis** near 54th Street, just to name a few of the boutiques that give the area

The Rainbow Room.

its characteristic panache. The ornate facade of **St Thomas' Church** overlooks the glamour from 53rd Street, and again, if you have any interest in religious art, see its magnificent sanctuary.

Fifth Avenue's glitz comes to a head at **Trump Tower**, near the corner of 57th Street. The development, which includes four restaurants, about 25 stores and 300 condominiums, is all so self-consciously plush, it's a little hard to stomach. Still, you've got to hand it to realtor Donald Trump. The overall design, with its five-story waterfall and corner terraces, is really quite effective. The shops are pricey, but that's to be expected. The window shopping is good enough. If you get bored at Trump, there's always crystal and jewels next door at **Tiffany & Co.**, the perfect old-money foil to Trump's flashy excesses.

At **Bergdorf Goodman**, shopping has been turned into a fine art. The store is located on the former site of the Cornelius Vanderbilt mansion and retains an air of distinction. Bergdorf is more like a collection of small boutiques than a department store. The atmosphere is refined, the racks are filled with unique designer fashions, and the prices... well, as the saying goes, if you have to ask, you can't afford it.

Grand Army Plaza on 59th Street punctuates Fifth Avenue and marks the boundary between Midtown and the Upper East Side. Usually jammed with bright yellow taxis, limousines and hansom cabs, Grand Army Plaza is surrounded by distinguished hotels including the **Pierre** and the **Plaza**, purchased by – who else? – Donald Trump. If you have a chance, stop in for a drink at the Plaza's Oak Bar, a lavish wood-paneled salon with a gorgeous view of Central Park, not to mention the beautiful clientele. In days past, people like Mark Twain, Frank Lloyd Wright and Eleanor Roosevelt made the Plaza their home away from home. If you hang around long enough, you're likely to see more than one celebrity striding down the stairway to a waiting limousine.

The Channel Gardens at Christmas.

Midtown East is the part of Manhattan the majority of people have in mind whenever they think of New York. This is where the city's corporate heart beats loudest, where power-lunching, power-shopping and even power-walking is a way of life.

Like its counterpart to the west, Midtown East begins in the relatively quiet area above 34th Street, and builds to a bustling climax between 42nd Street and the Queensboro (59th Street) Bridge, beyond which lies the calmer Upper East Side. Stretching east of Fifth Avenue over to the East River, it's a compact, energetic microcosm of the rest of Manhattan, encompassing glass and steel office towers, expensive shops and restaurants, historic landmarks and some very exclusive neighborhoods.

Hills and bays: If you walk east along 35th Street, you'll come to the border of **Murray Hill**, a residential area in the shadow of Midtown office buildings, where cross streets are lined by brownstone relics of a more genteel era. A plaque on the south side of 35th Street and Park Avenue marks the center of an 18th-century farm owned by Robert Murray, "whose wife, Mary Lindley Murray (1726–82) rendered signal service in the Revolutionary War." Close by, at Madison Avenue, the 1864 **Church of the Incarnation** contains some attractive Tiffany stained-glass windows.

The magnificent **Pierpoint Morgan Library** on 36th Street was opened to the public by legendary financier J.P. Morgan in 1924. There are special art exhibits, a glass-enclosed garden café, even a gift shop, but it's the library's collection of rare books that makes this a bibliophile's treasure trove. Permission is needed to visit the second-floor library itself, but visitors are welcome

Preceding pages: autumn in New York. **Right**, Grand Central libation.

in the **East Room**, where ornate vaulted ceilings shelter a display that includes the Gutenberg Bible, an autographed Jane Austen manuscript and a remnant of Milton's *Paradise Lost*, circa 1605.

Continuing north, past **Morgan's**, a chic, streamlined hotel where guests sport ponytails and dark glasses (even the bellhops wear black), you might enjoy a quick coffee break at **Chez Laurence**, on the corner of 38th Street. Though this small café specializes in French pastries, it also serves breakfast and light lunches and has comfortable, quiet tables perfect for enjoying a cup of cappuccino.

From here, walk east on 36th Street, across Park and Lexington Avenues, and you reach one of the city's tiniest and most charming historic districts. **Sniffen Court's** rowhouses were constructed in Romanesque Revival style at the time of the American Civil War, and were originally intended as stables for Murray Hill's grander residences (now they're highly desirable and correspondingly pricey real estate).

East of here is **Kips Bay**, a mainly residential area of high-rise apartment buildings, offices, restaurants and – around 34th Street – a plethora of movie theaters. The area is named for Jacob Kip, a Dutch settler whose farm overlooked a long-since filled-in bay at what is now Second Avenue and 35th Street.

St Vartan's Armenian Church, modeled after a 5th-century house of Eastern Orthodox worship, stands at the corner of 34th and Second, and features a **museum** of Armenian antiquities. Admission is free.

East 42nd Street: Historically, **Madison Avenue** has been a metaphor for the advertising industry, especially the blocks between 42nd and 57th Streets. This is the commercial heart of the city, where attaché-cased men and women buy their clothes at Brooks Brothers on 44th Street and stop off for cocktails at the Yale Club on neighboring Vanderbilt Avenue, before running to catch their trains at **Grand Central Station**.

The hub in a spoke of Metro-North

Detail on the Seagram Building.

THE ADVERTISING INDUSTRY

Madison Avenue was not taken by surprise when the Berlin Wall came tumbling down and the notion of a centrally-directed economy joined the cloud of debris it left behind. America's $165 billion advertising industry was built on the idea that markets always follow media.

Nowhere are markets and the communications arts and sciences which lubricate them more closely watched and translated into the tone, pace and style of the American consumption machine than on Madison Avenue. Apart from the Hollywood film industry, New York holds a near-monopoly on American communications, and nine of the top 10 ad agencies are head-quartered in the city.

Manhattan is a cultural feast, providing both the stimulation and the outlets for creative expression. Among these is a social network based on buyer/seller relationships; everyone is somebody's client and so entitled to lunch, cocktails, or evenings at trendy watering spots. Commercial producers squire agency creative directors and are themselves wined and dined by film editors. Professional communicators, these young careerists are quick to detect shifts in popular culture.

Astronomical rents have driven most companies off Madison Avenue itself (only one of the top 10, Young & Rubicam, still resides there), and it has become a synonym for the advertising business rather than its address. In the 1980s, the huge agency complexes like Saatchi & Saatchi, the Ogilvy Group and J. Walter Thompson found corporate headquarters facilities in signature buildings, moving their subsidiaries and affiliates under one roof. Other, smaller agencies have surfaced in trendy neighborhoods like Chelsea and SoHo, transforming drab, industrial quarters into the glass, brick and gray wall look favored by the photographers and film producers who set the style in advertising circles.

In 1988 the industry suffered a recession which reduced its professional ranks in New York from 24,000 to 20,000, leaving it less confident and prosperous but searching restlessly for the next phase in its history. Marketers had been losing confidence in advertising's selling power and had shifted budgets to promotions and direct selling.

The industry's response testifies to its resourcefulness. A rash of small creative shops has appeared, denying reports of the death of advertising. They find inspiration in the "glory years" style of the 1960s' creative revolution and seek talent outside conventional channels, inclining, for example, toward feature film and foreign directors to shoot their TV commercials.

At the same time, the large agencies have become global supermarkets, purveying "total communications," in which all forms of promotion – advertising, public relations, store merchandising, and design – are coordinated by a single company. During the 1980s the largest agencies swallowed up these ancillary services in a frenzy of acquisition. In turn, some giants – even the mighty J. Walter Thompson – were themselves gobbled up by British agencies.

Consumers became confused as every year 10,000 new items were placed on the shelves of grocery stores. An excess of choice has invaded the world of media, too, as life in fast forward becomes the norm and attention spans shorten. The network TV audience has shriveled from 62 percent of all homes in "prime-time" to 50 percent, under assault from video cassettes, cable, and a rich variety of specialist magazines addressing the interests of highly-segmented lifestyles. All this has produced an opportunistic advertising concept that uses every marketing tool to reach more narrowly-defined audiences.

In the 1990s, these trends are changing the agency business. Up to now agencies have been organized around three groups: the account managers who coordinate and face the clients, the creatives who write, design, and produce the work, and the media and research service groups who plan the buying of time and space. The emerging model calls for a super-communications strategy, with an overall advertising, public relations, design, and merchandising program run by generalists. It will require all the ingenuity the industry can muster, and the role of creative coordination will probably assure that the nerve center will remain concentrated in one place: Madison Avenue. ∎

Darling, I'm tickled pink all over —
I'm head over heels
in New Pink Dove!

Yes, darling, Pink Dove!
New pink color, heavenly new fragrance —
same creamy Dove formula!

Pink Dove, like white Dove, is ¼ cleansing cream. It creams your skin while you wash.

commuter lines reaching deep into the suburbs of Westchester County and neighboring Connecticut, the station is used by almost half a million passengers each day, on over 550 trains. Unlike the old Pennsylvania Station, Grand Central was saved from demolition by the city's Landmarks Preservation Commission, and thus this Beaux Arts reminder of days when travel was a gracious experience remains intact.

Although undergoing a multi-million dollar restoration designed to preserve even more of its former glory, in recent years the station has become an unofficial shelter for the city's homeless, which may lessen your enjoyment of the green-and-gold zodiac fresco on the ceiling of the Main Concourse (one of the world's largest rooms); and the lower-level **Oyster Bar**, a culinary landmark in its own right. Free tours are available once a week; inquire at the information booth for details.

Across 42nd Street, there's a Midtown branch of the **Whitney Museum of American Art** in the lobby of the Philip Morris Building. It's open every weekday, and admission to the gallery and sculpture court is free.

Around the corner on Lexington Avenue, the famed **Chrysler Building** is one of the jewels of the Manhattan skyline. Erected by auto czar Walter Chrysler in 1930, its Art Deco spire rises 1,000 feet into the city air like a stainless-steel rocket ship. Stop in and admire the lobby's marble-and-bronze decor, enhanced by epic murals depicting transportation and human endeavor.

Back on 42nd Street, walk past the glass and glitz of the **Grand Hyatt Hotel** (which adjoins Grand Central, and was built over the old Commodore Hotel), to the former *Daily News* **building**, an Art Deco structure that looks so much like the *Daily Planet* that they used it in the *Superman* movies. Continue past the steps leading up to **Tudor City**, a private compound of Gothic brick high-rises dating from the 1920s

United Nations' symbol of peace.

United Nations & Midtown East

0,25 miles/ 400 m

60 ST.
59 ST.
East
F.A.O. Schwarz
Bonwit Teller
IBM Bldg.
AT & T Bldg.
Bloomingdale's
Citicorp Center
Continental Illinois Center
Helmsley Palace Hotel
Villard Houses
St. Bartholomew's Church
Sak's Fifth Avenue
The Waldorf-Astoria
MIDTOWN
Helmsley Bldg.
Pan Am Bldg.
Grand Central Terminal
Oyster Bar (Underg.)
Chrysler Bldg.
GRAND CENTRAL
Philip Morris Bldg.
42nd Street
Daily News Bldg.
United Nations Headquarters
Franklin D.-Roosevelt Drive (East River Drive)
Sutton Place South

61st St.
60th St.
59th St.
58th St.
57th Street
56th St.
55th St.
54th St.
53rd St.
52nd St.
51st St.
50th St.
49th St.
48th St.
47th St.
46th St.
45th St.
44th St.
43rd St.
41st St.
40th St.
39th St.

Fifth
Madison
Park
Lexington
Third
Second
First

when land along what's now First Avenue was filled with slums and slaughterhouses (this explains why all the windows face west towards the Hudson, not east to the East River), to the **United Nations** building. The UN, built after World War II, is often ignored – not only by cynical New Yorkers – but also by member states who have pledged their allegiance.

A visit to the United Nations building can nevertheless provide a fascinating look at the workings (or non-workings) of international diplomacy. Guided tours take place daily, and free tickets are available for meetings of the **General Assembly**, when it's in session. Don't miss the moon rock display just inside the entrance, or the lower-level gift shop (which features inexpensive handicrafts from all over the world), or the Delegates' Dining Room. Lunch here is surprisingly inexpensive, and the view of the river almost as interesting as the many opportunities for multi-lingual eavesdropping.

Diplomatic impunity.

Back on 42nd Street, the **Ford Foundation**'s glass-enclosed lobby garden of lush trees and flowers is considered one of the city's most beautiful institutional environments, and a small blow for visual harmony in Midtown. Not far away, UNICEF House (East 44th between First and Second) offers multi-media presentations on themes like world peace and global cooperation.

Life of luxury: This part of town is also home to three of the city's classiest addresses, where the rich and famous can be spotted walking their dogs, emptying their garbage and even doing mundane things like grocery-shopping. **Turtle Bay**, for instance, is an historic district between 48th and 49th Streets where 19th-century brownstones share a common garden hidden from the public. Privacy-loving celebs who've lived here include actress Mary Martin and conductor Leopold Stokowsky; current residents include legendary actress Katharine Hepburn.

At **Beekman Tower**, an Art Deco apartment hotel at 50th and First, you can admire the view from the Top of the Tower bar before exploring **Beekman Place** itself, an enclave of elegant townhouses that stretches along the East River.

Named for a wealthy Dutchman who sailed to the New World with Peter Stuyvesant, the area has housed magnates, movie stars, diplomats and members of the exiled Iranian royal family, at one time or another. History was made too, as the plaque on the corner of 51st and First tells you. It was the site of William Beekman's original mansion, which served as British headquarters during the Revolutionary War. American patriot Nathan Hale was imprisoned here, and on the gallows in a nearby orchard supposedly spoke the immortal words, "I regret I have but one life to give for my country."

Sutton Place, an oft-used synonym for luxury in books, movies and TV, starts at 54th Street, its dowager-and-poodle-filled apartment high-rises stretching north for five blocks, with visual relief provided by the occasional quaint cul-de-sac of townhouses, gardens, and promontories offering expensive views of the river.

You can find food for every occasion in this part of town. Sample the neighborhood ambience of **Billy's** on First Avenue and 52nd Street or pricey meat and potatoes at popular steakhouses like the **Palm**, a former speakeasy on Second. **Sparks** on 46th Street is where mobster Paul Castellano met an abrupt end several years ago. If your palate's more delicate (and your pocketbook can afford it), there's **Lutece** just four blocks north, still considered one of the best French restaurants in the world.

Heading uptown from 48th to 54th Streets, Second Avenue is home to the liveliest collection of Irish bars this side of Dublin (**Kennedy's**, **Murphy's**, **Jameson's**, **Ryan McFadden**), culminating with **Eamonn Doran**, where the Guinness is perpetually flowing on tap. Shelter for the homeless.

138

One of the oldest and most colorful is **P.J. Clarke's**, on Third Avenue and East 55th Street. Known simply as Clarke's to generations of drinkers and diners (there's a restaurant in the back), part of *The Lost Weekend*, the movie classic about alcoholism, was filmed here. On another cultural note, on Monday nights you can catch Woody Allen playing the clarinet around the corner at **Michael's Pub**.

You'll find more than enough opportunities to shop around here, starting with the **Citicorp Center**, on 54th Street between Third and Lexington Avenues. The slanted roof of this, one of the world's tallest buildings, makes it a skyline standout, but "The Market" inside makes it a congenial local shopping mecca and hangout. Stores and restaurants are set around the building's central atrium, where you can see and enjoy free concerts and other lunchtime entertainment. (Convenient tables and chairs also makes this a prime spot for people-watching.)

Exit at the Third Avenue entrance, and detour east to Second Avenue; you'll come to the **Manhattan Art and Antique Center** between 55th and 56th Streets, where over 100 small shops sell everything from antique clocks to jewelry and, on the lower level, you'll also find that ever rare NY commodity, public restrooms.

Up at 57th Street, pause to admire Fil Caravan's rare Islamic artefacts. Turn west on 57th and you're on a two-way boulevard lined by boutiques that seem to grow more expensive as you draw nearer to Fifth Avenue. From Third Avenue on, you'll find such fashion fortresses as Hermès, Burberry and Chanel. Upper level – both figuratively and literally – art galleries abound, including Wally Findlay, Tibor De Nagy and **The Pace-Wildenstein Gallery**, all with exhibitions open to members of the public.

Above Grand Central: The once-spacious view down Park Avenue stops abruptly at the towering **Met Life** (for-

Home away from home.

merly the Pan Am) **Building**, which was plonked on top of Grand Central Station in the early 1960s. But this part of the avenue still retains some of its old glamour. The **Waldorf-Astoria Hotel**, between 49th and 50th, is one of Midtown's grandest hotels, and has attracted guests of the royal and presidential variety since it opened here in 1931. The original Waldorf Hotel, on Fifth Avenue, was torn down to make way for the Empire State Building.

Besides Lexington Avenue's row of middle-range hotels (an exception is the elegant **Inter-Continental** at 48th Street, where there's a giant bronze birdcage in the lobby), most of the landmarks in the vicinity are religious ones. **St Bartholomew's Church** opened its doors on Park and 50th Street in 1919 and is a fine example of neo-Byzantine architecture. One block west, the opulent **New York Palace Hotel** incorporates as part of its public rooms two of the **Villard Houses**, 19th-century mansions once used as offices by the Arch-

diocese of New York. Built in 1884 by the architectural firm McKim, Mead & White, these half-dozen houses were originally constructed to look like one large Italian palazzo. The owner was the noted publisher Henry Villard, after whom the houses are named. Almost 100 years later, when two of the mansions were sold to hotelier Harry Helmsley to provide a lavish interior for the Palace, several New York historians took exception to the sale. Now owned by the Sultan of Brunei, the hotel offers afternoon tea under a vaulted ceiling created by architect Stanford White.

At Lexington and 55th Street, the **Central Synagogue** is a national – as well as a city – landmark, its unique onion-shaped dome and Moorish arched windows dating back to 1872. Nearby, the strikingly modern **St Peter's Church**, at the Lexington Avenue entrance to the Citicorp Center, features a chapel designed by artist Louise Nevelson where weekly jazz eucharists are an experience in themselves.

You'll find lines of limos waiting in front of the **Four Seasons** on East 52nd, a restaurant so important it has been declared an historic landmark. The world's largest Picasso can be found inside, as can notable figures from politics and publishing.

In recent years, some of the biggest corporations have created public spaces that vastly improve the quality of Midtown life – including Philip Johnson's mammoth **Sony Building** (originally built for AT&T) on Madison Avenue, where a public arcade is squeezed between shops displaying the latest Sony equipment and gear. Drop into the free **Sony Wonder Technology Lab** to see how it all works.

On the next corner, the **IBM Plaza**, a spacious atrium with glass walls containing clusters of graceful bamboo trees, huge bowls of flowers and dozens of tables and chairs for sitting and snacking, offers a tranquil atmosphere that can make you forget the adrenalin-pumping Midtown madness outside.

Left and right, the Chrysler Building.

140

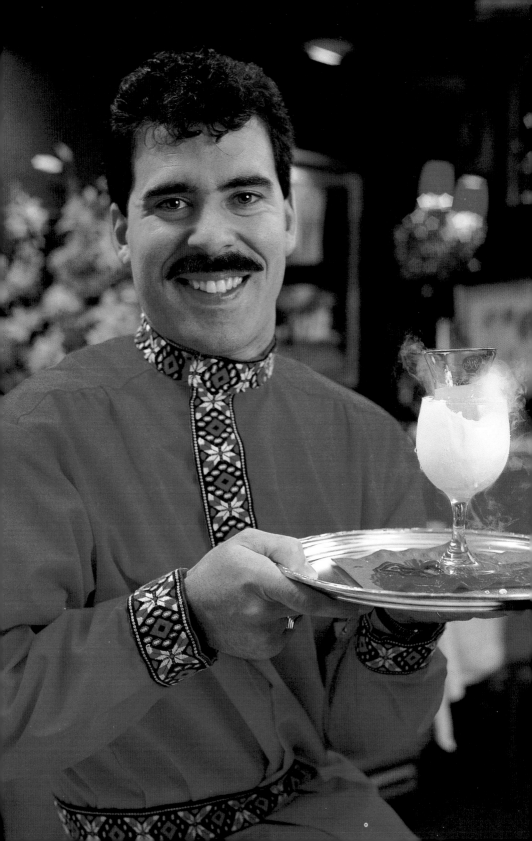

MIDTOWN WEST

The West Side shines less brightly than the east, but never for a lack of sheer neon wattage. What Midtown West lacks in finesse, it makes up for in tenacity. This is hardcore New York, a place where teenage prostitutes do business a few blocks from billion-dollar corporations, where billboards vie with world-class art, and where, as the old saying goes, there's a broken heart for every light on Broadway.

Sweat, grime and greasepaint are the main ingredients here, and they're as potent on the Broadway stage as they are in Hell's Kitchen or the Garment District. At the heart of it all, Times Square wears its neon baubles like an aging beauty queen. The flash and frenzy dazzle the eye, but a profound desperation drives it from below. Even Broadway – the glamorous Great White Way – is more than a little down at the heels. But then, that's the story in Midtown West. It's been bruised and beaten, but it's never gone down for the count. The lights still burn on Broadway, and a bevy of new hotels, plus an ambitious Time Square renovation program, assures that the West Side is still in the fight.

Starting down at 34th Street, the transformation from East to West sides begins at **Herald Square**, where Broadway intersects Sixth Avenue. Given a facelift for the 1992 Democratic Convention, this chaotic intersection is best known for shopping. Immediately south of Herald Square is the **Manhattan Mall**, the city's largest vertical shopping center, with nine floors occupied by at least 70 retailers, including the Sears department store.

The big draw here, however, is **Macy's**, a New York institution for more than 100 years. Like the billboard says, Macy's is the biggest department store in the world, and it's worth seeing for its size alone. Don't count on doing any quick-stop shopping, though. This is definitely not the place to buy that last-minute gift for Aunt Lucille.

In the good old days, Macy's used to be a staple for middle-class shoppers, but lately it's been slapping on the panache – and the designer labels. In fact, these days it's even giving upscale stores like Bloomingdale's a run for their money. In any event, don't expect to find the same bargains your mother came here for. And don't dare leave without visiting the "Cellar," a giant gourmet emporium with every culinary do-dad a creative chef could ask for.

Exiting Macy's on Seventh Avenue puts you right in the middle of the **Garment District**, a jangly, soot-covered workhorse that still turns out the lion's share of American fashion. There's not much to do or see here, although dedicated bargain-hunters have been known to walk away with some first-class deals from the factory floor. Showrooms, too, dot the area, where you can find the latest, if not always the greatest, fash-

ions, although you may have to shop around a bit, both for the bargains and the showrooms themselves.

If you really want to get a feel for the Garment District, your best bet is to have lunch at one of the coffee shops on Seventh Avenue, where you'll find fashion buyers cutting deals and garment workers gobbling down a bite to eat. Check out the diners between 35th and 39th Streets; they're lively, crowded and filled with chatter. One word of warning while you're snooping around, though: keep an eye out for the young men pushing clothing racks through the streets. They've been known to run down a pedestrian or two.

The only landmarks worth noting in this area are on the southern end of the Garment District, which is dominated by the fur industry. At Seventh Avenue and 33rd Street, Madison Square Garden is an enormous barrel-shaped lummox disliked not only for its clumsy design but also for standing on the site of McKim, Mead & White's magnifi-

cent **Pennsylvania Station**. As a result of the demolition, Penn Station was literally forced underground. It now operates approximately 50 feet beneath the sidewalk, belching out a quarter-million commuters daily.

Although long since moved from its original site between Madison and Fifth avenues, ie, Madison Square, **Madison Square Garden** is one of America's biggest entertainment facilities, where rock shows, ice hockey, basketball games and even circuses are held. The center's best-known venues are the **Paramount** and the **Arena**, whose rollicking events attract fans from all over the world.

Those of you with old Glenn Miller records collecting dust in the attic may want to poke your head into the Penta Hotel, across Seventh Avenue at 33rd Street. This used to be the Pennsylvania Hotel, one of the Big Band era's hottest tickets. It was celebrated by Glenn Miller's hit *Pennsylvania 6-5000*, which is still the hotel's phone number.

Angels ♥ Angels.

Otherwise, about the only thing to see in this neck of the woods is the **General Post Office**, located directly behind the Garden on Eighth Avenue. Although it's hardly a tourist attraction, the building really is quite impressive, with a monumental Corinthian design that makes your average Greek temple look like a tiki hut. There's also that terrific slogan inscribed on the frieze: "Neither snow nor rain nor heat nor gloom of night stays these couriers from the swift completion of their appointed rounds." The slogan was actually stolen from Herodotus, who quite obviously never mailed a letter in Manhattan.

Heading back to Herald Square, Broadway slices through the Midtown grid to 42nd Street. This is the downtown end of Times Square, the garish heart of Midtown West, that's as seedy as it is romantic.

Times Square takes its name from the *New York Times*, which used to be headquartered at the Times Tower – still standing at the intersection of 42nd

Street and Seventh Avenue, and now called 1 Times Square (site of the city's first electric moving sign). There's a certain menacing vitality hereabouts. The crowds, the theaters, the traffic, the billboards – they all come together with such a god-awful racket it can't help but get your adrenalin pumping.

Still, Times Square can be dangerous, especially at night. Aside from the muggers, pickpockets and three-card monte players – all of whom make fast work of tourists – there's a sleaze-factor seeping over from the sex shops on Eighth Avenue. Times Square is an essential New York experience, and it really should be seen. But here, more than elsewhere, you need to be careful. Walk with confidence (even if you don't know where you're going), don't wander into any dark alleys, and if possible, travel with a group.

By the end of the 1990s, however, some – if not all – of this will have changed. After years of to-ing and fro-ing, Times Square is now in the initial

stages of a multi-billion dollar renovation scheme to lure tourists and office workers back to the area. Already there are several new high-rise hotels, including the renovated **Paramount** on West 46th Street.

Plans include a massive, much-needed overhaul of the subway station on 42nd Street. And while the station's transformation will cost millions of dollars – and be hugely inconvenient – one trip through this dark, potentially dangerous underground is enough to convince anyone that improvement is urgently needed.

Times Square stretches along Broadway all the way up to 48th Street with the Theater District sprawled out loosely on either side. Back in the 1920s when the Theater District hit its peak, big-name producers like the Shubert Brothers and song-and-dance man George M. Cohan staged as many as 250 shows a year at some of the most lavish theaters in the country. These days, Broadway slips in and out of

slumps with some regularity, and the price of tickets has soared to levels unaffordable by many. But with blockbusters like *Les Misérables* and *The Phantom of the Opera* still packing in the crowds, there seems to be plenty of magic to go around.

If you're in the area for a show, be sure to take a stroll down **Shubert Alley**, a busy walkway that runs behind the Booth and Shubert theaters, between 44th and 45th Streets. **Sardi's**, a restaurant still favored by showbusiness biggies, is right across the street.

Otherwise, nostalgia-buffs can indulge themselves at the **Lyceum Theatre**, one of the oldest on Broadway, and with its elaborate baroque facade and dramatic mansard roof, still one of the most beautiful.

Heading west down 42nd Street brings you face to face with the heart of renewal plans for the Times Square area. Between Broadway and Eighth Avenue, **42nd Street** is lined by a row of seedy derelict theaters that, under

Steamy streets of Times Square.

THE HOMELESS

It's impossible to miss them – people with no place to go and little hope in their eyes. They take refuge in subway stations, churches, or even under trees in Central Park, anywhere which offers shelter from the winter winds and the sticky summer sun. No one knows exactly how many homeless people live in New York City, although estimates put the figure between 75,000 and 125,000.

Every night, more than 20,000 men, women and children are housed in emergency shelters and other temporary housing provided by the city's Department of Homeless Services. But residents claim many of these shelters are poorly maintained, infested with rats and roaches, and even dangerous. One man, living in public accommodation in the Bronx, was stabbed during a robbery there. He now prefers the streets, even the mean streets of Manhattan, to city-funded accommodation.

The options open to such people are few. Some have engaged in a long-running battle with the Metropolitan Transportation Authority for the right to sleep in subway and railway stations, or even on the trains themselves. As many as 5,000 may call the MTA's facilities "home." But occupants say they are constantly harassed. The MTA claims it merely asks people to leave so the facilities can be cleaned

One long-standing "address" was an abandoned railway tunnel on the Upper West Side. The first resident was John Joseph Kovacs, who, in 1975, moved into the 2½-mile tunnel, fixing up his space with chairs, sofas, carpets and kitchen cabinets. In 1991, Kovacs and the other "tenants of the tunnel" were evacuated when the national rail network, Amtrak, decided to run passenger services through their homes.

"The only reason I came here was to find a place that was safer than a park bench," he told the *New York Times* before leaving, "where I could go to sleep without worrying about somebody stealing my shoes."

Unfortunately, a new and even more pressing problem now faces New York's homeless. Whereas before, people tended to be victims of broken homes, job redundancies, and the lack of affordable housing, or the mentally-ill – many of whom were released in the 1960s, in a series of wide-sweeping measures which contained inadequate back-up facilities – the current wave includes an increasing number of Aids carriers, the result of sharing hypodermic needles. There are now an estimated 40,000 HIV-infected homeless people in New York City.

The Aids epidemic has become a priority for the Partnership for the Homeless, a non-profit organization which operates 145 New York shelters as alternatives to city-funded locations. In March, 1990, the Partnership opened the country's first church-based temporary housing residence for homeless people with Aids. Former Mayor David Dinkins earmarked $14 million of the city's money to provide housing, shelter services and early treatment for AIDS victims. Advocates hope this sum will be renewed on an annual basis, and that much of the cost can be shared with the state.

Although the former mayor's involvement was a positive start, the future seems bleak for New York's homeless, even those without Aids. So what do people do?

One couple, Rene Wright and Sean Brooks, set up home in the cash machine vestibule of a Chase Manhattan Bank, conceiving a child one December night under the formica check-writing counter. Bank vestibules are popular spots for the homeless, as they're heated, open all night, and, in the banks that service generous neighborhoods, offer the possibility of a cash hand-out.

Others have become involved with *Street News*, a publication about the housing crisis which calls itself "America's first and only motivational not-for-profit newspaper." Since 1989, more than 3,000 people have sold copies of the paper. Sellers, most of whom are homeless, buy the paper at a discount and pocket the difference. *Street News* claims a good success rate at getting people back on their feet, as the sellers see themselves as self-reliant rather than charity cases.

With *Street News* and other organizations battling the problems that face the homeless, perhaps a few people will end up being better off. ∎

current plans for Times Square's regeneration, will be eventually restored to new versions of their former glory. **The Victory**, for example, was a popular theater in the early 1900s; became a porn movie house in the 1970s; and is now scheduled to reopen as a showcase of wholesome entertainment for young audiences.

At least once a year the facades of closed-down peep shows are enhanced by a series of off-beat, innovative art exhibits. And although thieves, pimps and prostitutes continue to haunt the area, the **Times Square Visitors Center**, in the old Harris Theater on 42nd Street, west of Seventh Avenue, now offers optimistic guided tours. Meanwhile, around the corner on Eighth Avenue, X-rated peep shows and other sleazy "entertainment" still thrive, and the **Port Authority Bus Terminal** attracts an unhappy blend of lowlife and the truly needy. But things start looking up after you cross Eighth Avenue and enter the old **Hell's Kitchen** neighborhood, now known (at least by real estate agents) as **Clinton**. At the turn of the century, Hell's Kitchen was one of the most notorious slums in the country. Immigrants were crammed into unsafe and insanitary tenements, and Irish gangs like the Hudson Dusters and Battle Row Annie's Ladies Social and Athletic Club governed the streets like petty overlords. Even the police were afraid to venture into the neighborhood alone.

In recent years, however, Hell's Kitchen has undergone an impressive transformation. There's still a certain gut-level edginess to the neighborhood, and still plenty of immigrant families, although now they're likely to be West Indian, Puerto Rican, Filipino or Greek, but there's also a new sense of ethnic pride, some trendy restaurants, and an active off-off-Broadway theater scene.

Most of these theaters are located on 42nd Street between Ninth and Tenth Avenues, and present experimental or low-budget works for about the same

A Times Square transaction.

150

price as a movie. A residential high-rise called **Manhattan Plaza** is directly across the street and offers housing to performing artists for a percentage of their income rather than a flat rent. Around the corner on Ninth Avenue, where pushcarts used to gather at the old Paddy's Market, is a strip of ethnic specialty shops that has become a happy hunting ground for local gourmets. During the annual **Ninth Avenue Food Festival** (usually in May), thousands of New Yorkers come to gorge themselves on an endless variety of ethnic delicacies. If you love to eat, it's an event that shouldn't be missed.

West of Ninth Avenue, Midtown doesn't hold much of interest to the majority of tourists. There's the **Jacob Javits Convention Center** – the biggest in the country – and the **Sea-Air-Space Museum** aboard the *USS Intrepid*. Otherwise the riverfront area around here is mostly devoted to dilapidated buildings, although optimists hope that some kind of riverfront devel-

opment may occur here, too – as happened downtown in Battery Park City and, more recently, along the waterfront in Chelsea.

You'll find yourself closer to the mainstream back on Sixth Avenue. The street signs will say **Avenue of the Americas**, but don't be fooled. To New Yorkers, Sixth Avenue is **Sixth Avenue**, no matter how many flags hang from the lampposts.

Kick off the tour at the corner of 42nd Street in front of **Bryant Park**, a restored patch of green directly behind the Public Library that offers summer afternoon concerts. Also during the warmer months, there are usually street vendors doing business on the edge of the park immediately across from the **Grace Building**, whose unconventional facade slopes down to street level like a gigantic sliding-board.

Farther up Sixth, a right turn at 44th Street puts you in the neighborhood of the **Algonquin Hotel**, where Dorothy Parker, Robert Benchley and other dis-

A local drive-in; the Jacob Javits Convention Center.

tinguished *literati* hobnobbed at the famous Round Table. West 44th Street has quite a clubbable atmosphere in fact. No. 27 is the premises of the **Harvard Club**, whose interior can more easily be observed by peering into a back window, rather than shelling out for four years' education; no. 37 houses the distinguished **New York Yacht Club**, whose 1899 facade sports Beaux Arts details with a nautical flair; and at no. 44 is the **Hotel Royalton**.

The Royalton only feels like a club; it is, in fact, a chic and ultra-modern hotel created by Ian Schrager and the late Steve Rubell who also created Studio 54, the jet-set disco once frequented by Warhol, Bianca Jagger and co. Every line and appointment, from the lobby to the lavatories (males and females take turns checking out the men's room) is as boldly, coldly futuristic as the set of a science fiction film. Should you not be sporting minimalist black and a cool attitude, the block-long walk to the restaurant in the back, past row after row of draped sofas draped with beautiful people, will feel much, much longer.

Another quick right at 47th Street takes you into the **Diamond District**, a one-block enclave where close to $500 million in gems is traded every day. Most of the diamond merchants are Hassidic Jews, who wear black suits, wide-brimmed hats, long beards and sidelocks. Book-lovers should also stop at the **Gotham Book Mart**, where the late Frances Stelloff held court over a comfortable clutter of books while lending a helping hand to writers like Eugene O'Neill, Tennessee Williams and James Joyce, at whose censorship trial she defended *Ulysses*.

At 47th Street, Sixth Avenue really starts flexing its corporate muscle. This is actually Rockefeller Center's backyard. The four monumental office-buildings between 47th and 50th Streets make up the **Rockefeller Center Extension**, which kicked off Sixth Avenue's march of corporate monoliths with the Time-Life Building in the

The bright lights of Radio City.

1950s. The buildings feature broad plazas, hidden courtyards and several fine works of art, but they lack the human scale of the original development and are often battered by chilly updrafts.

The one glorious exception to all this buttoned-down modernism is **Radio City Music Hall**, which graces the corner of Sixth and 50th Street. Radio City is the world's largest indoor theater and Rockefeller Center's crowning glory. There isn't much to see from the outside, but the interior is absolutely magnificent and well-worth seeing on one of the guided tours (inquire at the box office). From the 2-ton chandeliers in the Grand Lobby to the plush scallop-shaped auditorium, the Music Hall is the last word in Art Deco extravagance. Even the restrooms are custom designed. In fact, the Stuart Davis mural that once graced the men's smoking lounge has since been installed at the Museum of Modern Art.

The Museum of Television & Radio, at 25 West 52nd Street, is a favorite West Side destination for serious couch potatoes. Founded by CBS magnate William S. Paley, it's also a valuable resource for media buffs, comprising gallery space, two theaters, a screening room showing retrospectives of your favorite directors, and a vast archive of vintage radio and TV programs, which can be hired for an hour at a time. It's the perfect rainy day activity, except for Mondays, when the museum is closed.

One of the city's most celebrated art collections is the **Museum of Modern Art**, known to local culture vultures as MoMA. It has the finest collection of late 19th- and 20th-century art in the whole of the country. Not long ago, a multi-million dollar renovation doubled the museum's exhibition space, and although some critics have bemoaned a loss of intimacy, **MoMA** still makes for one of the most exciting art experiences in the city.

The key to it all, of course, is a superb collection. Picasso, Matisse, Van Gogh, Monet, Pollack – all the biggies are

Hot town, summer in the city.

represented here, often by their most important works. There's also a nifty design collection which includes everything from a full-size helicopter and a flaming red sports car to ordinary items like simple chairs and hair-dryers. One look and you will never regard a common object the same way again.

Although the collection is quite extensive, the new floor plan guides you from room to room so gently you hardly realize how much ground you've covered. Even if you think you're not too fond of modern art and you're absolutely sure you don't like museums, it's worth giving MoMA a try. If you can honestly walk away without being moved, disturbed, enraged, provoked – anything but bored – then it's probably time to see the eye doctor.

In the same block as MoMA, farther down at 40 West 53rd, is the smaller **American Craft Museum**, exhibiting works in clay, glass and even paper. The museum is closed on Mondays. After you soak up all that high-falutin' culture, reward yourself with a down-home New York classic – a thick, fatty pastrami on rye. Fortunately, one of the undisputed champs in Manhattan's deli wars is only a few blocks away. The **Carnegie Deli** on Seventh Avenue near 55th Street is noisy and usually crowded, but then, that's part of life in the Big City. And, oh boy, is the food good! If you don't like pastrami, try the corned beef, the rich French toast, or an old standby, bagels, cream cheese and lox (and don't take off the onion).

From Seventh Avenue and 55th Street, you're two blocks away from the Carnegie Deli's namesake – **Carnegie Hall** – which is located at the corner of 57th Street. As every New Yorker knows, there's only one way to get to Carnegie Hall – practice. The joke is about as old as the hall itself, which was built in 1891 by industrialist Andrew Carnegie. Ever since Tchaikovsky conducted at the opening gala, Carnegie Hall has attracted some of the world's finest performers including Rach-

maninov, Toscanini and Sinatra. It would be nice if the hall's architecture was as inspiring as its history or superb acoustics.

West 57th between Fifth and Sixth Avenues is one of Manhattan's hottest streets. This is definitely "beautiful people" territory, and next to SoHo it boasts the city's densest concentration of expensive art galleries and boutiques. Gallery-hoppers may find that some of the snootier places require an appointment, but you can usually pay a walk-in visit to the **Kennedy** and **Marlborough** galleries or **Frumkin/ Adams**, and **Gallery 84**, about a half-block away at 50 West 57th.

Otherwise, you might want to get a taste of the burgeoning West 57th Street restaurant scene, which in recent years has grown to include a row of popular theme eateries. Between Sixth and Seventh avenues, you'll find glitzy **Planet Hollywood** (fronted by long lines and fake palm trees) and the **Motown Cafe** (equally long lines). Between Broadway and Seventh Avenue, there's the **Brooklyn Diner** (an ersatz "authentic" '50s diner), and – at no. 221 – the **Hard Rock Cafe**, which started it all and still serves up a pretty good burger.

For traditionalists, there's the much more formal **Russian Tea Room**, at 150 West 57th (back between Sixth and Seventh, just past Carnegie Hall). Founded by members of the Russian Corps de Ballet, over the decades the Tea Room has been the setting for more theater deals than any other restaurant in the city – and it still attracts its share of Broadway stars and Hollywood luminaries. The price is high, but there's no better spot in New York to enjoy caviar, blinis, and an icy cold vodka.

Midtown West wraps itself up with a sophisticated flourish just two blocks away on **Central Park South**, famous for its luxurious hotels. It's also a good place to catch one of the **horse-drawn carriages** that clip-clop around the park. It'll be quite pricey for even a half-hour ride, but then you only live once.

The Museum of Modern Art.

CENTRAL PARK

Central Park is New York's year-round back yard, where Manhattan's tired and huddled masses kick off their work shoes and relax – or put on their jogging, tennis or snow shoes to indulge in a few hours of exercise.

At least 15 million people use the park every year, yet there's always a quiet spot to get away from the sounds of the city. Bordered by **Central Park West** (i.e. Eighth Avenue) and Fifth Avenue, this 843-acre urban oasis stretches 2½ miles, from **Central Park South** (59th Street) to **Central Park North** (110th Street).

Besides recreational facilities which include 22 playgrounds, 26 baseball diamonds, 30 tennis courts, almost 5 miles of bridle paths and miles of jogging track, Central Park is also the city's premier place for people-watching and street entertainment.

Most impressive of all is the look of the park itself. Hills, meadows, woods and lakes combine to offer city dwellers the illusion of real country – albeit one surrounded by a multi-story wall of highrises. No small accomplishment, considering this was originally an unsavory expanse of granite quarries and swamp occupied by illegal distilleries, pig farms and wild dogs.

People's park: By the 1850s, New York City was already the biggest metropolis in the United States, with over 700,000 citizens crammed into a growing urban sprawl. Despite street plans that called for a regular series of small parks, there was little (or no) space for relaxation. It was poet-turned-editor William Cullen Bryant who first made an impassioned plea for a city park; he was soon joined by journalists and civic figures. The New York State Legislature eventually approved the purchase of a large tract of land – then open countryside – and appointed Frederick Law Olmsted as superintendent.

<u>Left</u>: **Central Park is 2½ miles long.**

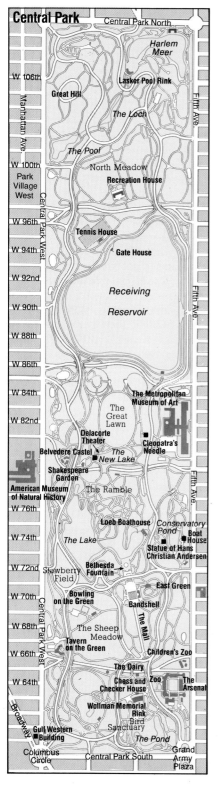

Central Park

Central Park North

Harlem Meer

W 106th

Lasker Pool Rink

Great Hill

The Loch

Manhattan Ave

Fifth Ave

The Pool

W 100th

North Meadow

Park Village West

Recreation House

Central Park West

W 96th

Tennis House

W 94th

Gate House

W 92nd

W 90th

Receiving

Fifth Ave

Reservoir

W 88th

W 86th

W 84th

The Metropolitan Museum of Art

The Great Lawn

W 82nd

Delacorte Theater

Cleopatra's Needle

Belvedere Castel

The New Lake

Shakespeare Garden

American Museum of Natural History

The Ramble

W 76th

Loeb Boathouse

Conservatory Pond

Boat House

W 74th

The Lake

Statue of Hans Christian Andersen

W 72nd

Bethesda Fountain

Strawberry Field

East Green

W 70th

Bowling on the Green

Bandshell

Central Park West

W 68th

The Sheep Meadow

The Mall

Tavern on the Green

W 66th

Children's Zoo

The Dairy

W 64th

Chess and Checker House

Zoo

The Arsenal

Wollman Memorial Rink

Bird Sanctuary

Gulf Western Building

Broadway

The Pond

Columbus Circle

Central Park South

Grand Army Plaza

A Connecticut-born farmer, engineer and journalist, the 35-year-old Olmsted was greatly influenced by the egalitarian People's Park in Birkenhead, England, which he had visited a few years earlier. When the city held a park design contest in 1857, it was his Greensward Plan, created with the help of English architect Calvert Vaux, which won.

While Vaux contributed a formal mall, fountain and ornamental bridges, Olmsted was determined to make the new park as natural as possible, keeping intact the rocky outcrops that once characterized the rest of the island, designing sunken crossroads to keep traffic from intruding and creating meandering pathways to draw pedestrians deeper into his carefully engineered wilderness. The object, he wrote at the time, was not only to give New Yorkers "the most agreeable contrast to the confinement, bustle and monotonous street division of the city" but also to "supply hundreds of thousands of tired workers, who have no opportunity to spend summers in the country, a specimen of God's handiwork."

It took 16 years, more than $14 million, 21,000 barrels of dynamite, the planting of 17,000 trees and shrubs – plus a constant battle with a hostile Tammany Hall – to transform a wilderness into the world's first major public park. And though the "father of American landscape architecture" went on to create more than 100 parks stretching from Maine to California, Central Park is considered his crowning achievement.

Castles and concerts: Roughly divided into a north and south end – with the **Reservoir** (around which the city's fleet of joggers make their rounds) in the middle – the park has entrances at regular intervals around the periphery. The least visited area, at least by out-of-towners, is the northern end above 96th Street. A shame, seeing as this is where the **Conservatory Garden**, the park's only formal horticultural showcase, is located. Benches from the 1939 World's Fair line pathways, and in spring more than 20,000 tulips burst into bloom. (To get here, walk through the elegant **Vanderbilt Gate** at Fifth Avenue and 105th Street.)

Most visitors stick to the park's southern end, entering through the **Maine Monument** at Columbus Circle or at **Grand Army Plaza**, adjacent to the Plaza Hotel at 59th Street.

Pass the statue of General William Tecumseh Sherman astride his horse and follow the path to the **Central Park Wildlife Conservation Center** (formerly known as the Central Park Zoo), where the polar bears have one of the best swimming pools in town. Exhibits include recreations of Temperate, Tropic and Polar Zone environments – and the emphasis is on education, with classes and other programs offered regularly.

Stop to admire the **Delacorte Clock** (with its orchestra of carved animals that dance in a circle every half hour), just past the red-brick **Arsenal**. Once the home of Civil War weaponry and later the Museum of Natural History,

the Arsenal is now the headquarters of the Parks Administration.

Farther into the park **the Dairy** (also reached via the 65th Street Transverse or up the East Drive from Grand Army Plaza) used to be where milkmaids served fresh milk to city kids. Now it serves as Central Park's Visitor Center, and is the best place to go for maps and directions to places like **Strawberry Fields**, Yoko Ono's memorial to the murdered John Lennon.

There are also special exhibits on the park's history as well as information about daily walking tours led by the Urban Park Rangers, and other events.

To the west, **Sheep Meadow** is a 22-acre quiet zone popular with picnickers and sunbathers. The sheep that once grazed here are long gone, replaced by the touristy **Tavern on the Green** restaurant. There's a **carousel** with over 50 handcarved horses and the **Wollman Rink** for ice skating in the winter. (You can rent skates, too.) From here, follow paths north to **the Mall**, Central Park's

Bethesda Fountain.

only formal promenade. This leafy expanse is lined by the country's finest stand of stately elm trees, one planted by the Prince of Wales in 1919. The avenue now comes to a halt at the ornate **Bethesda Fountain**, designed with the surrounding Terrace to be the park's architectural centerpiece. Just beyond the fountain, rowboats can be rented at the **Lake** (there's also a bicycle concession nearby) starting in late March.

Northeast of the lake, the **Ramble** is the wild heart of the park. Its 38 acres of twisting paths and rocky cliffs are a favorite with local birdwatchers in search of the more than 250 migratory species that stop off here; it's also popular with gay couples and the occasional mugger. (Despite its reputation, Central Park actually has one of the city's lowest crime rates, but it is always advisable to explore the more secluded areas with a friend or two.)

A short walk east brings you to the **Conservatory Water**, home of model boat races in warm weather and the occasional free-form ice-skating in winter. (The nearby statue of Hans Christian Anderson is the site of the occasional summer morning storytelling for children, sponsored by the New York Public Library.)

Above the 79th Street Transverse, **Belvedere Castle** sits like a Gothic folly atop **Vista Rock** and serves as a US weather bureau station. Today, it is also a children's environmental education facility and information center – and the best place to go for that quintessential view of the park and surrounding city. The castle is a trick of perspective. It was deliberately built on a small scale because the designers wanted visitors at Bethesda Fountain to think it was farther away that it actually is.

You can wander through the overgrown delights of the **Shakespeare Garden**, planted with trees and flowers mentioned in the playwright's work, or, at dusk peer through the glass at the illuminated Temple of Dendur, inside the Metropolitan Museum of Art. The

Bard's plays are presented free of charge every summer at the **Delacorte Theatre**. Not far away, the **Great Lawn** is where music lovers spread their blankets for free summer evening performances by the Metropolitan Opera and the New York Philharmonic.

On summer weekends, traffic is forbidden, making a stroll, a bike ride or even a carriage ride a particularly pleasant Manhattan experience. But no matter what day of the week, or what time of the year, New Yorkers come to Central Park to find a brief respite from the stress of city living.

Despite an ongoing battle against overuse, litter and erosion, despite the well-meaning but characterless facilities added by subsequent park administrations, despite the occasional sensationalized crime, Central Park endures as Olmsted envisioned: a place where "the mind may be more or less lifted out of the moods and habits into which it is, under the ordinary conditions of life in the city, likely to fall."

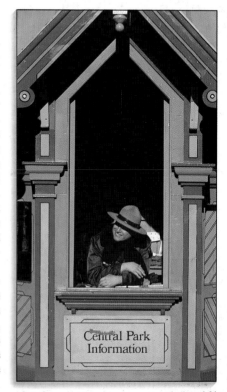

Left, child's play. **Right**, information center.

UPPER EAST SIDE

When New Yorkers think of the Upper East Side, one word comes to mind: money. And lots of it.

The Upper East Side's romance with wealth began in the late 1800s, when the famous Four Hundred – so-called because a contemporary social arbiter had decreed that in all of New York there were only 400 families that mattered – moved into Fifth Avenue to set down roots alongside Central Park. The homes they built were the most luxurious the city had seen – mansions and townhouses decked out like European palaces and filled with priceless art.

Since then, the Carnegies, Fricks and Astors have moved to greener pastures, but the Upper East Side never lost its taste for the good life. Today, Fifth, Madison and Park avenues are still home to the privileged few, people who know the high cost of luxury and make no bones about paying for it. Even the traditional working-class areas east of **Lexington Avenue** are starting to put on airs. Now that gentrification has set in, the old blue-collar neighborhoods once occupied by German, Czech and Hungarian immigrants have become smart and upscale.

As always, the air of wealth is most intoxicating on **Fifth Avenue**, known to old-time New Yorkers as Millionaires' Row. The name doesn't get used much now, but there are still plenty of millionaires – although, unlike the extravagant Four Hundred, they tend to keep a low profile. In fact, most of the newer apartment buildings are understated to the point of boredom. There are still a few eye-poppers left over from the glory days, however, and if you happen to be passing by they are well worth a look.

Standing at the corner of 60th Street, for example, is J.P. Morgan's stately **Metropolitan Club**, founded in 1892 after Morgan and his *nouveaux riches* buddies were denied membership at one of the established downtown clubs. The enormous **Temple Emanu-El** cuts a brooding, Moorish figure at the corner of 65th Street, where 2,500 worshippers can gather under one roof, making this cavernous temple one of the largest reform synagogues in the United States.

Up in the 70s there are several splendid old mansions including the **Harkness House** (1 East 75th Street), the château-style **Duke mansion** (1 East 78th Street), and Payne Whitney's Renaissance *palazzo*, now serving as a branch of the **French Embassy** (972 Fifth Avenue).

International relations are, in fact, the order of the day on the Upper East Side. The former **Stuyvesant mansion** at 79th and Fifth is the **Ukrainian Institute**; the Louis XV-style **R. Livingston Beekman mansion** (854 Fifth Avenue) houses what's left of the United Nations' Yugoslav contingent and the **American-Irish Historical Society** is farther up at No. 991.

Preceding pages: a fur for $60,000. **Left**, a young Upper East Sider. **Right**, a painting from the Metropolitan Museum.

The museum at the corner of Fifth Avenue and 70th Street houses the **Frick Collection**. The building was formerly the home of steel magnate Henry Clay Frick, a man whose passion for art was surpassed only by his ruthlessness in business. The collection, which is made up almost entirely of European works from the 16th to 19th centuries, represents one of the city's most successful combinations of art and ambience – a bit stuffy perhaps, but filled with gracious touches like a tranquil courtyard and soft chairs to sink into when your feet get tired.

The Frick Collection is the first in a series of nine prestigious museums known as Museum Mile, which continues at 82nd Street with the **Metropolitan Museum of Art**.

In a word, the Met is awesome. Opened in 1874, this sprawling Gothic behemoth now contains the largest art collection in the United States, covering everything from an Egyptian temple to modern art. The holdings are so vast that it's not really a single museum at all, but a dozen or more distinct collections housed in a maze of galleries, gardens and period rooms. Half the fun is getting lost, wondering what treasures you'll bump into next. Needless to say, it's not the kind of place you can breeze through in an hour. Be sure to give yourself plenty of time, and whatever you do, don't try to tackle the whole thing in one day. It's much too good to rush through.

Walk four blocks past the Met, and you've hit upon yet another New York classic, the **Guggenheim Museum**. Located at the corner of 88th Street, the white spiral-shaped structure has been a source of debate ever since it opened in 1959. Some people say that Frank Lloyd Wright's design is an architectural masterpiece. Others think it's an abomination, more akin to a parking garage than an art gallery and definitely out of place next to the handsome townhouses that give the area its special charm. Whatever your opinion, it has recently been given landmark status by

Two views of the Guggenheim.

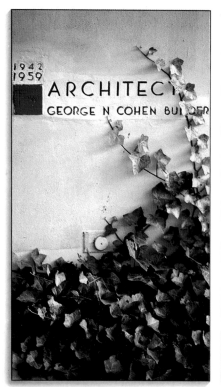

the New York City Landmarks Preservation Commission, the youngest building to be awarded the honor. Take the elevator to the top floor and slowly make your way down the circular ramp. Although exhibitions change frequently, they are likely to include works by Renoir, Van Gogh, Toulouse-Lautrec, Kandinsky, Klee and Picasso. A 10-story tower, opened in 1992, doubled the museum's exhibition space.

After the Guggenheim, Fifth Avenue runs into a barrage of museums between 89th and 104th streets, including the **National Academy of Design**, the **Cooper-Hewitt Museum of Design**, the **Jewish Museum**, the **International Center of Photography**, the **Museum of the City of New York**, and **El Museo del Barrio** – all fine institutions, but of varying interest depending on the exhibits currently in place. The Cooper-Hewitt and International Center of Photography tend to have inventive shows, but it's best to call ahead to avoid unpleasant surprises.

Geographically, Fifth is only one block away from **Madison Avenue**, but in spirit they're worlds apart. You can kiss "prim and proper" goodbye, because Madison is the land of "ritz and glitz" – a slick marketplace tailor-made for the hyperactive consumer.

Madison is a bit mellower at the upper end than it is in the 60s and 70s, but even if you cross over from the top of Museum Mile you'll still find plenty of boutiques and art galleries that are worth exploring. Among them is the Soldier Shop, at 88th Street, which carries miniature battalions of old and new toy soldiers, all rendered with excruciating attention to detail and suitable for adult collectors.

Some of the more interesting galleries in the immediate area include Espiritu (traditional third-world art), and Antiquarium (ancient jewelry, coins and artefacts), as well as several others specializing in modern European and American works. Just below 76th Street, Time Will Tell is a terrific little place filled with vintage timepieces,

Wright's controversial design.

Givenchy represents fashion, and Books & Co. offers the neighborhood's most intelligent selection of titles.

The wheels of capitalism slow down a bit at 75th Street, where the **Whitney Museum of American Art** is located. You can hardly miss it. Marcel Breuer's oddly cantilevered structure is a work of art in its own right, second only to the Guggenheim as one of the area's boldest architectural statements.

The Whitney collection was founded in 1930 by Gertrude Vanderbilt Whitney, whose taste ran to the works of American realists like Edward Hopper and George Bellows. Since then, and especially since the new building opened in 1966, the museum has employed a policy of acquiring pieces that represent the full range of 20th-century American art, including the works of Georgia O'Keefe, Willem de Kooning, Jackson Pollack and Jasper Johns. Every other year, the museum mounts the Whitney Biennial, a survey of the most provocative American art of the previous two years. If you're a fan of contemporary art, it's an absolute must.

Next to the Whitney you'll find a terrific little museum gift shop called The Store Next Door, which features handcrafted jewelry and other *objets*, even furniture, that can also, occasionally, be reasonably priced. Or stop in at the adjacent Madison Avenue Café, a once-funky coffee shop that, despite its recent air of *nouveau* gentility, still manages to maintain a casual popularity with East Side celebrities like Dustin Hoffman and Tony Bennett. For a more down-to-earth New York coffee shop experience, however, try the Three Guys Restaurant a block down and across the street: not only does this tidy establishment have a traditional counter with stools, the food is decent and relatively inexpensive. And it's as good a place as any to savor some java before taking on the rest of Madison Avenue.

From the Whitney Museum to 59th Street, Madison turns into a veritable orgy of conspicuous consumption. The **Penthouse elegance.**

names on the storefronts read like a roster of the fashion elite: Yves Saint Laurent, Giorgio Armani, Gianni Versace, Emmanuel Ungaro and the uptown branch of Barney's. Farther north, Ralph Lauren's Polo is headquartered in the elegant former **Rhinelander mansion** at the corner of 72nd Street. The latest breakthroughs in Japan-wear are available at Kenzo on the corner of 69th Street. Needless to say, unless you're packing a king-size bankroll, most of the stores are more for browsing than serious shopping.

Skipping crosstown to **Park Avenue**, the scene again changes dramatically. Compared to the flashy indulgence of Madison, Park seems rather bland. An exception is the **Colony Club**, located on 62nd Street, which has a stately red-brick facade, appropriately reflecting the stately demeanor of the society women who belong to the Club.

If you happen to be passing by, you might look out for the **Seventh Regiment Armory** at 66th Street, a medi-eval look-alike that occasionally serves as a theater, an exhibition hall and, in one instance, a shelter for the homeless. A few blocks up at 70th Street, the **Asia Society** houses the Rockefellers' fine collection of Asian art. The building also serves as a performance hall, lecture theater and cinema for shows and events dealing with Asian culture.

East of Park Avenue, the Upper East Side falls a few notches in the prestige department, but makes up for it with a healthy dash of self-indulgence. Once dominated by East European immigrants, much of the area is now heavily gentrified, although remnants of the old German, Hungarian and Czechoslovakian quarters remain in **Yorkville**, which runs between 65th and 90th streets. You'll find mouth-watering German pastries at Kleine Konditorei, an inviting little café on East 86th Street between Second and Third Avenues.

A few steps away, the cozy Heidelberg Restaurant specializes in mounds of rib-sticking German food; while far-

Slumbering East Siders.

ther south down Second Avenue, you'll find restaurants with Mediterranean flavor and atmosphere.

In fact, there is a slew of upscale eateries targeted for the under-30 market around here, especially between 60th and 80th. Most tend to be yuppie-esque with a foreign twist, but a few are neighborhood standbys that have outlasted decades of trendier competition.

Two very different classics that must be mentioned are **Elaine's** and Papaya King. Elaine's is the quintessential show-biz restaurant made trendy by all those Woody Allen movies. The crowd tends to be exclusive, so unless you've got a friend who's got a friend who knows Elaine, you might want to think twice about giving it a try. Instead, check out Rathbone's across the way. You get pub-style steaks, burgers and beer for under 20 bucks and a good view of the limos pulling up across the street.

Papaya King falls into an altogether different category. It's not a restaurant so much as a hot dog stand. But this

place certainly doesn't serve just any old wiener. No indeed. Papaya King hot dogs are among the tastiest in the city. And as if that weren't enough, you can wash them down with a luscious assortment of tropical juices like mango, papaya and thick coconut champagne. Keep in mind, however, that this is not the place for a sit-down meal. In true New York fashion, Papaya King supplies about two or three stools. Everybody else has to eat on their feet.

As far as shopping goes, this half of the Upper East Side is scatter-shot with all sorts of specialty stores, antique dealers and galleries. Your best bet is to peruse Lexington Avenue, especially in the mid-60s and 70s. Basically, it's Madison without the froufrou.

Serious shoppers may want to pass on the boutiques and head straight for the retail queen: **Bloomingdale's**, a minor institution that most dyed-in-the-wool New Yorkers could not live without.

Style and quality are keynotes at Bloomies. The shop is almost always crowded – oppressively so during holidays – but if you only go to one department store in New York City, this should probably be it. Corporate raiders have been leveling their sights on Bloomies for some time now, and no one is quite certain whose portfolio its going to wind up in or what they intend to do with it. If you've always dreamed of a Bloomingdale's shopping spree, now is the time to do it, before Bloomies goes the way of the Automat, gone but not forgotten.

Determined sightseers might want to wrap up the tour with a quick look at the neighborhood's eastern fringe. On 61st Street, between York and First Avenues, the **Abigail Adams Smith House** is one of the few early 18th-century buildings still standing in Manhattan. Abigail Adams Smith, daughter of the late president John Quincey Adams, never actually lived here (her husband built it as a stable), but the museum has been meticulously furnished with period antiques, and gives a **Roosevelt Island.**

good indication of what life in the city was like in the early to mid 19th century.

Sotheby's, the high-stakes auction house favored by art collectors, is about 10 blocks away, near the corner of York Avenue and 72nd Street. And still farther up, at about 88th Street, **Gracie Mansion** is the mayor's official residence and another fortunate survivor of the 18th century. It was built by Scots-born Archibald Gracie as a summer home and in 1942 was first used by Mayor Fiorello LaGuardia. It's located in **Carl Schurz Park**, a pleasant patch of green overlooking the treacherous currents of Hell Gate, where the waters of the East River and the Harlem River flow together. If time allows, hitch a ride on the Roosevelt Island Tramway at Second Avenue and 60th Street. The riverfront views are quite spectacular, especially at sunset.

Across the water, **Roosevelt Island** itself is a 147-acre respite from heavy urban living. Lying only 4 minutes by tram from the East Side, this tiny (2-mile), tranquil, cigar-shaped island contains one main street, one church, one supermarket, a few restaurants, and New York City's newest subway extension. This annexation to the Q line makes Roosevelt a suddenly desirable residential area – witness the luxury apartment complex, Manhattan Park, which would not look out of place on the other side of the river. As an added bonus, facilities include an indoor swimming pool, several playgrounds and five small parks – plus an active community center based in the ecumenical Chapel of the Good Shepherd, a landmark Victorian stone-and-brick structure that dates back to 1899.

Walking tours are offered some weekends, providing ample scope to enjoy the panorama of the Upper East Side from specially built walkways, to observe the stone lighthouse (*circa* 1872) at the northern extremity and to savor Roosevelt Island's small-town charm. Madison Avenue seems a long way away.

A doll's life: at home on the Upper East Side.

UPPER WEST SIDE

Geographically, the Upper West Side is laid out like a hot pepper sandwich. It looks tempting on the outside, but it's spicy in the middle.

The spicy bits are Broadway, Columbus and Amsterdam Avenues, a sort of 24-hour circus squeezed between the dignified calm of Riverside Drive and Central Park West. Since the early 1980s, this has been the yuppie capital of New York City – the "Yupper" West Side as local wags put it. The transformation seemed to take hold overnight. Before New Yorkers knew what hit them, there were boutiques popping up all over the place and more sushi bars than in downtown Tokyo.

But it hasn't always been brunch and boutiques. Before the yuppie invasion of the 1980s, the Upper West Side was infested with crime, and even the well-heeled residents of Central Park West were cautious when leaving their apartments at night. Although the area has now been pretty thoroughly gentrified, there are still spots of destitution amid the wealth and more than a little tension between the old residents and the newcomers. But then, conflict is nothing new here. Just as a matter of attitude, life on the Upper West Side has always been hard, and it continues that way today.

The entrance to all this is **Columbus Circle**, a chaotic tangle of cars and pedestrians zipping around a statue of Christopher Columbus, who looks a bit frazzled by all the commotion. Other than the **New York Convention and Visitors Bureau**, located on the southern end of the Circle, there's not much of interest here, although the gateway to Central Park is usually thronged with people eating lunch, passing through or just plain hanging around.

Central Park West branches off Columbus Circle and heads into the area's most affluent residential section. The apartment houses overlooking the park are among the most lavish in the city, and the cross streets, especially 74th, 75th and 76th, are lined with equally splendid brownstones. Among the most spectacular buildings are Art Deco masterpieces like **the Century** at No. 25 and **Majestic Apartments** at No. 115, and the classically inspired **San Remo Apartments**, No. 145–146. At the corner of West 67th Street, the **Hotel des Artistes** has counted Valentino, Isadora Duncan, Noel Coward and Norman Rockwell among its tenants, and is still home to the Café des Artistes, an exquisite hide-away on the ground floor which is perfect for a romantic rendezvous.

The most famous apartment building on this stretch is the **Dakota** (1 West 72nd Street), built in 1884 by Henry Hardenbergh, who also designed the Plaza Hotel. At the time, New Yorkers joked that it was so far outside the city, "it might as well be in the Dakota Territory," which explains the name and the Indian's head above the main entrance.

Preceding pages: an ordinary day at Zabar's. Left, the smooth face of Manhattan. Right, the Dakota.

The rest of the city caught up with it soon enough, of course, but over the years the Dakota has remained the grandest residence on Central Park West, attracting tenants like Boris Karloff, Leonard Bernstein and Lauren Bacall. **Strawberry Fields**, a quiet knoll dedicated to the memory of John Lennon, who lived at the Dakota and was shot outside, is located across the street a few steps into Central Park.

From 72nd Street, it's a short walk uptown past the somber facades of the Universalist Church and the **New-York Historical Society** to the **American Museum of Natural History**, a lumpy, lumbering giant that sprawls over four city blocks. Guarded by an equestrian statue of Theodore Roosevelt, the museum's main entrance is actually one of the many additions built around the original structure. The old facade – a stately Romanesque arcade with two ornate towers – was built in 1892 and is still visible from 77th Street.

If you're traveling with children, vis-iting the museum is an absolute must, though with 34 million artifacts housed in 19 buildings, there's plenty for grown-ups to see, too, not the least of which is a 34-ton meteorite, the largest blue sapphire in the world, a full-scale model of a blue whale and a renowned anthropological collection. The famous dinosaur exhibits, which have been re-installed in six renovated halls, offer an astounding look at life on earth over many millennia. There's even an inter-active computer system for visitors to whom gigantic skeletal remains aren't enough. (The world's tallest dinosaur – the 50-foot-high Barosaurus – can be found in the Theodore Roosevelt Rotunda.)

The museum also features Sky Shows at the **Hayden Planetarium** and other mind-bending programs at the **Naturemax Theater** – which shows films on a screen four stories high and 66 feet wide. As always, it's wise to be selective, especially if you're following a schedule. Don't think about doing the **Columbus of Columbus Circle.**

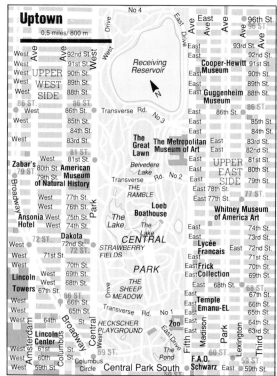

whole place in one shot. It'll only make you crazy – and very tired.

Returning back down to Columbus Circle, Broadway swerves west toward Columbus Avenue and just knicks the corner of the Lincoln Center, flanked on one side by Juilliard and on the other by **Fordham University**.

Even to be accepted at the **Juilliard School of Music** is an honor, as the school's highly selective enrollment practice and small classrooms draw some of the most talented students in America. They no doubt draw inspiration from neighboring Lincoln Center, which is worth a visit even if you're not attending a performance. Guided tours of the complex are given every hour on the hour between 10 a.m. and 5 p.m., but unless you are especially interested, it's just as well to save time and money by exploring on your own.

Construction of the **Lincoln Center for the Performing Arts** started in 1959 as part of a massive redevelopment plan intended to clean up the slum that used to occupy the site. More than 180 buildings were demolished and 1,600 families relocated in order to make room for the complex, inflaming social critics who saw it as nothing more than a playground for the elite. Architectural critics gave it a beating too, citing a general lack of gravity and an overdose of ornamentation. Despite all the fist-pounding, Lincoln Center has become one of the city's most vital outlets for the performing arts. And with yearly attendance now running at about 5 million people, it is obviously meeting a popular need.

Standing at the black marble fountain in the middle of the plaza, you are surrounded by the glass and white marble facades of Lincoln Center's three main structures. The **Metropolitan Opera** is directly in front with two large murals by Marc Chagall hanging behind the glass wall – *Le Triomphe de la Musique* to the left, *Les Sources de la Musique* to the right. The Met is home to the Metropolitan Opera Company from Septem-

Strawberry Fields is opposite the Dakota.

ber to April and the American Ballet Theater, formerly directed by Mikhail Baryshnikov, from May to July. Although marvelous, its lavish productions and big-name performers carry a hefty price tag.

To the left of the central fountain, the **New York State Theater** is shared by the **New York City Opera** and **the New York City Ballet** – both more adventurous than the Met and less expensive. If the doors are open, look at the Jasper Johns painting on the ground floor and the two controversial marble statues by Elie Nadelman in the upstairs foyer.

The third side of the main plaza is occupied by **Avery Fisher Hall**, home of the New York Philharmonic and the Mostly Mozart series held in the summer. For years the hall was plagued with bad acoustics, and after several renovations failed to correct the problem the auditorium was gutted and rebuilt. Peek in for a look at Richard Lippold's *Orpheus and Apollo*, a hanging metal sculpture that dominates the foyer.

Two secondary courtyards flank the Met on either side. To the right, the **Vivian Beaumont Theater** is fronted by a shady plaza and reflecting pool where brown-baggers gather for lunch. The oxidized bronze sculpture in the center of the pool is by Henry Moore. A spindly steel sculpture by Alexander Calder is located near the library entrance. **Damrosch Park** is located to the left of the Met. The **Guggenheim Bandshell** at the far end is used for free concerts during the summer, usually around lunchtime although occasionally in the early evening as well.

When you've finally finished gazing around Lincoln Center, head uptown on Columbus Avenue for some high-grade browsing. Like Madison Avenue on the opposite side of Central Park, Columbus is committed to the art of mass consumption, although fortunately most of the shops and restaurants don't take themselves as seriously as their east side counterparts. As usual, there are far too many places to list by name, **American graffiti.**

178

but those that deserve a special mention are all located north of 69th Street.

For the hippest collection of jewelry this side of SoHo, try Jerry Grant, marked by equal smatterings of glitz and folky charm at expensive prices. Picking up the trail again at 77th Street, you'll find a vintage clothing store called Alice Underground, located in the basement of a stately old mansion; there are other vintage wares for sale at the P.S. 44 market, held every Sunday between 76th and 77th streets. A few doors farther up puts you at the entrance to Penny Whistle Toys, which offers an intriguing assortment of old-fashioned games, stuffed animals and other items designed to delight all those childish hearts. And, at 450 Columbus Avenue, Endicott Booksellers is one of the city's best bookstores.

Skipping west to Amsterdam Avenue, the scene is slightly different, with a few boutiques and twenty-something bars scattered amidst Latino-flavored groceries and other traditional

neighborhood shops. Amsterdam hasn't felt the full brunt of gentrification yet; nevertheless, you'll also find some good restaurants, which generally tend to be less crowded, as well as slightly more casual in price and atmosphere, than the eateries on Columbus Avenue.

If you're into home cooking, for instance, check out **Good Enough to Eat**, a cozy little nook on Amsterdam between 83rd and 84th streets that serves basic American "country-style" food – and has country-style decor to match (the Sunday brunch is particularly good). Just next door, a more typical urban scene can be found at the sprawling **Hi-Life Bar and Grill**, where the eclectic cuisine plays second fiddle to the lively and attractive young crowd that hangs out here after work. If neither one suits your fancy, there are plenty others to choose from in the area.

A few blocks up, on 89th Street, you'll find **Claremont Riding Academy**, which celebrated its centenary in

1989. At the time the Claremont was built, this part of town contained many stables; now this is the only one left on the island. But if you want the experience of riding through Central Park, with your horse's nostrils flaring and mane flying, this is the place to come.

It's not until you hit Broadway that the Upper West Side really gets down and dirty. Up in this part of town, Broadway is a round-the-clock stage, the one place where all the incongruities of the Upper West Side flow clamorously together. Boutique-hoppers, stockbrokers and carriage-pushing mothers mingle with street vendors, artists, panhandlers and con men.

In general, the shopping isn't as rich here as it is on Columbus Avenue, but Broadway boasts a few places that are practically institutions. **Zabar's**, for example, is the gourmet shop against which all gourmet shops are measured. The people at Balducci's downtown in the Village may not agree, but take a look around and judge for yourself.

Even if you're not in the mood for buying, it's a kick elbowing your way up to the counter for a free taste of all the cholesterol-soaked goodies. It's worth visiting for the glorious smells alone.

A stone's throw from Zabar's, Shakespeare and Co. is the neighborhood's best bookstore and a sociable place for late-night browsing. Should you find yourself in dire need of a bagel smothered in cream cheese, H&H Bagel – located just down the street – makes over 60,000 every day.

Farther down Broadway, the **Ansonia Hotel** occupies the entire block between 73rd and 74th streets. Although a bit worn around the edges and in need of a good bath, this is the *grand dame* of west side apartment buildings, with a resident guest list that included the likes of Enrico Caruso, Igor Stravinsky, Arturo Toscanini and Theodore Dreiser. Although retailers now dominate the ground floor, the Ansonia's mansard roof, corner towers and terracotta detailing still add up to a Beaux Arts fantasy that captures the gaze and refuses to let go.

Past the Ansonia, Broadway crosses Amsterdam, near the bench-lined concrete strip known as **Needle Park**, the subject of a national magazine article that became the basis for the movie *Panic in Needle Park*, a depressing *tour de force* about heroin addicts.

From here you can wrap up the tour by going west on 72nd Street to **West End Avenue** and **Riverside Drive**. North of 72nd Street, West End is affluent and strictly residential. It's a great street to live on, but not terribly exciting. All the drama seems to have been stolen by Riverside Drive, which winds along the edge of Frederick Law Olmsted's **Riverside Park**. This is one of the most picturesque corners of Manhattan, blessed with exceptional architecture and sweeping views of the Hudson River. Be sure to get a look at the houseboats at the **79th Street Boat Basin**, where a few salty Manhattanites brave the elements all year round.

Left, Riverside Park. Right, Riverside Church.

180

HARLEM

Nearly everyone has heard of Harlem. It has the highest name recognition factor of any neighborhood in the state of New York; most likely more than any neighborhood in America. In fact, very few of the world's cities have areas that are as famous. People may not know a true thing about the place, but they are familiar with the name.

An African-American, Alabama-born professor remembers being in Europe at the age of 18 in the late 1950s. He was asked repeatedly about Harlem, a place that he had never been close to in his life. His inquisitors didn't want to hear it. The man was black; he lived in the United States; therefore he had to be from Harlem. What they didn't know was that the only thing he "knew," based on the same stereotypes shared by the Europeans, was that Harlem was a destination full of naughty nightlife which featured devilish dancing, mind-blowing music, dangerous dudes and wicked women. Harlem, of course, was and still is much more than that.

In common with other urban neighborhoods, it is not a readily hospitable place for the adventurous and overly romantic loner. It is best to visit Harlem in groups and to use common sense. When making plans, note that there is an **East Harlem** (Madison Avenue to the East River Drive), where most Latino residents live and sometimes called **Spanish Harlem**; a **Central Harlem**, (Fifth Avenue to Amsterdam Avenue), whose citizens are overwhelmingly African American; and a **West Harlem**, which extends to Riverside Drive. West Harlem has many more white residents than the other two and includes the neighborhoods of **Morningside Heights** and **Hamilton Heights**. **Washington Heights** is a separate neighborhood far to the north, almost at the tip of Manhattan, and is an ethnically-mixed area with a couple of cultural treasures.

Going Dutch: Before the influx of black residents in 1910, Harlem passed through various hands. Originally the home of Native Americans, it was seized by the Dutch in 1658 and named Nieuw Haarlem, after a city in the Netherlands. Then, in 1664, it fell to the British, who tried to change its name to Lancaster.

Serious protest prevented this happening, but Haarlem was anglicized by dropping one "a," making it Harlem. Which raises the question, would Harlem be the same if it had been called Lancaster? It's hard to imagine watching the Boys Choir of Lancaster rather than the Boys Choir of Harlem, or attending Lancaster's famous Apollo Theater. Maybe a name does make a difference.

Harlem was basically farmland and was considered to be New York City's first suburb, where prominent folks like Alexander Hamilton, the country's first Secretary of the Treasury, maintained a home. This exclusivity changed in 1837 with the opening of the Harlem River Railroad; in 1873 with its annexation to

Left, artwork on iron barrier. **Right,** a soulful smoke.

New York City; in 1880 by the extension of the elevated rapid transit lines; and in 1904 by the building of the IRT Lenox Avenue subway. All of this made Harlem more accessible to the rest of the city, which in turn led to an influx of European immigrants.

One of the biggest changes occurred in 1910 when African Americans, to the dismay of white residents, moved into homes on 134th Street, east of Lenox Avenue. From that time on Harlem became a place where people of African descent from throughout the world have made their presence felt. People as diverse as Marcus Garvey, Adam Clayton Powell Jr, Malcolm X, Langston Hughes, Duke Ellington, Louis Armstrong, Sidney Poitier, Ella Fitzgerald and Lionel Hampton launched their careers in Harlem.

It was Harlem that housed legendary places such as the Cotton Club and the Savoy Ballroom, and it was Harlem that in the 1920s, 1930s, 1940s and 1950s gained an international reputation as an exotic playground for thrill-seekers from around the globe. According to the late Charles Buchanan, who was general manager of the Savoy Ballroom from its opening in 1936 to its closing in 1958, eager Europeans would check into their hotels, and then make mad dashes to the Savoy to savor its dazzling dancers and never-ending music.

Much later, Harlem, or to be more precise, a restaurant called Sherman's Barbeque on 151st Street and Amsterdam Avenue, was where the female singing group the Ronettes brought the Beatles in 1964. It was the Fab Four's first American tour and their hotel, the Plaza, was surrounded by hysterical fans. It was only by sneaking out a side door and escaping to Sherman's that the Beatles were able to breathe easily, play the well-stocked juke box, and relax with like-minded musicians. To a large extent, it is this Harlem which is conjured up in the minds of visitors.

That Harlem no longer exists, nor does the Harlem portrayed so often in **Street scene** *circa* **1930s.**

the American press – a place where every other resident is either a drug pusher or an addict, and where a white person with a concern for life or pocketbook dare not tread.

What does exist is a neighborhood with a diverse population. Like many neighborhoods, it is a place where good and welcoming people live alongside other people who may be no good. It's also a place where a visitor who wants to see, hear and learn more about African Americans and Latino-Americans can have a memorable time.

Harlem is where you can listen to most kinds of modern music, from jazz to blues to gospel to rap to reggae to salsa; where you can consume a wide variety of foods favored by people of African descent from around the world; where you can see and purchase arts and crafts created by talented black artists; where you can experience a rodeo with black cowboys or see future basketball greats "do their thing" on community playgrounds; and where you can see

theater, dance and music artists work their magic.

Central Harlem: The place to begin is **125th Street**, Harlem's famous main drag. It's Fifth Avenue and Times Square compressed into one river-to-river street, a street where every north–south Manhattan subway stops, and several north–south buses cross over. A main shopping area, it's vibrantly alive with throngs of people and music blasting from nearly two dozen record stores.

Several of Central Harlem's most important attractions are located on 125th Street, most notably the **Apollo Theater**, the launching site of many great singing careers. The Apollo's amateur nights provide the experience of seeing and hearing rising young talent, while at the same time being a part of the highly responsive, often appreciative and sometimes harshly critical Apollo audience. Apollo crowds are noted for their knowledge of what great black music is all about, and are notorious for panning performers who don't live up

Doing the jitterbug.

to their expectations. For a visitor, an evening at the Apollo Theater can be the highlight of a trip.

The presence of legendary artists such as Billie Holliday, Duke Ellington, Louis Armstrong, Mahalia Jackson, Dinah Washington, Bob Marley and of super-artists such as Aretha Franklin, Ella Fitzgerald, Nina Simone, Al Green, Gladys Knight and Carmen McRae can still be felt, even in the newly renovated Apollo. The theater's finances have been rocky, though, and threats of closure are unfortunately commonplace.

The **Studio Museum of Harlem** is also on 125th Street, with a permanent collection and archives consisting of over 10,000 objects. The largest holdings are in the area of contemporary black art. It has been called "the premier museum in the world devoted solely to the art and artifacts of Black America and the African Diaspora." Besides exhibitions, the Studio Museum also features lectures, films and workshops.

Equally interesting is the **Black Fash-ion Museum** nearby on 126th Street. It is a one-of-a-kind museum that exhibits the most comprehensive collection of black fashion memorabilia in existence. The collection consists of items used in Broadway shows, films and television as well as outfits worn by more private style-setters. The history behind each item is provided.

If you're interested in what is sometimes called "street art," make an attempt to be on 125th Street before the shops open in the morning to see the works of **Franco the Artist** on the iron storefronts installed by merchants to thwart burglaries. The paintings are colorful and imaginative, striking examples of how an artist can take a negative situation and make it into a positive one. It's worth getting up an hour early to see.

The office of the **Audience Development Committee** (AUDELCO) is also located on 125th Street. Its staff will provide you with most anything you want to know, historical or current, about

Time out at Sylvia's.

black theater in Harlem or elsewhere in the city. If you're in town on the third Monday in November, check out the annual AUDELCO Awards ceremony, which is the black equivalent of Hollywood's Oscar presentation. A host of theater artists are usually in attendance. AUDELCO can also provide information on other local cultural events.

All around 125th Street you will find clubs and restaurants, the best of which include **La Famille**, **Showman's Café**, **Bombay Restaurant** and **The Cotton Club**. All are popular with local residents and provide the chance to meet Harlemites in their favorite and most convivial hang-outs.

Name change: From 125th Street in Central Harlem, walk up one of the neighborhood's north-south streets, like **Malcolm X Boulevard (Lenox Avenue)** or **Adam Clayton Powell Jr Boulevard (Seventh Avenue)**. Malcolm X Boulevard is probably Central Harlem's best known street after 125th Street.

Several Harlem landmarks are located here, including **Sylvia's Restaurant**, a family-owned eatery whose southern-inspired food is worth traveling for; the **Liberation Bookstore**, for those interested in books about the experiences of people of African descent; and the **Schomburg Center for Research in Black Culture**, one of the top institutions of its kind. The library is a goldmine of books, magazines, records, films and photos about black Americans in general and Harlem in particular. The Schomburg is where writer Alex Haley did much of his research for the book *Roots*, which later became the basis for a record-shattering television series.

Malcolm X Boulevard was once better known as the location of the original, gangster-owned Cotton Club, which barred blacks from entering, and the legendary Savoy Ballroom, also known as the "Home of Happy Feet" in honor of its innovative dancers. The avenue is not a pretty sight these days, but its institutions are well worth a visit for anyone who wants a true feel of Harlem.

Harlem's townhouses.

If you walk up Malcolm X Boulevard, it's best to come back down Adam Clayton Powell Jr Boulevard, the location of lots of nightclubs which jump all night long.

The area around Adam Clayton Powell Jr Boulevard and 137th to 139th Streets is known as **Striver's Row**, and contains four rows of handsome townhouses completed in 1891. It was called Striver's Row because of the professionals, striving to succeed, who moved into the elegant houses.

On the corner of Adam Clayton Powell Jr Boulevard and 125th Street stands the old Theresa Hotel, which during its heyday in the 1930s, 1940s and 1950s, was *the* place for VIPs to stay, since most downtown hotels barred black visitors. The Theresa's most famous guest was Fidel Castro, who in 1960 moved in after a dispute with a downtown hotel. World leaders like Nikita Kruschev came to visit Castro in his room at the Theresa Hotel. Every evening before dusk the Cuban dictator would step out onto a small balcony and wave to the enthusiastic throngs gathered below. It was perhaps Harlem's grandest moment in the international arena. The Theresa's last major claim to fame was as the site of the office of the Organization of Afro-American Unity, which was founded by the African-American leader Malcolm X in 1964, a year before he was assassinated.

If you happen to be in Central Harlem on a Sunday morning, make an effort to attend services at a Baptist church. Some visitors may have heard a touring gospel choir or gospel singer but to really get the feel of this type of music, you must hear it in an African-American Baptist or Pentecostal church. The fervor of the singing and the response of the congregations is stirring; a spiritual experience that is hard to get back home. Many visitors are already aware of this, as evidenced by the number of people who show up at places like **Canaan Baptist Church** on Sunday mornings. Visitors from Japan, Germany, France, Sweden, Brazil, Switzerland, Italy, Nor-

The Abyssinian Baptist Church.

way are often in attendance and are introduced to the congregations along with local visitors – a custom in most black Baptist churches.

Central Harlem churches play a significant role in the political, economic and cultural life of the community. Besides the aforementioned Canaan Baptist Church, institutions such as the **Abyssinian Baptist Church, St Phillip's Episcopal Church** and **Mother A.M.E. Zion Church** have played a crucial role since the early 1800s. The singing style favored in these three churches is more traditional, and may be more familiar to visitors.

East Harlem: The languages most often heard in East Harlem are English and Spanish, its residents by and large having close ties with Puerto Rico.

The most colorful place to start a visit is **La Marqueta**, located under the elevated train lines on Park Avenue from 111th to 116th Street. La Marqueta, or the Market, calls itself "the world's largest supermarket," with the look and the smells of the type of markets often found in Latino and African countries. Now mainly active in the block between 114th and 115th streets, you can still find mangos, papayas, cassavas, tamarinds, exotic herbs and other imported tropical staples here, along with fresh-grown regional produce. Fridays and Saturdays are the best time to come and shop – or just stroll around and experience it.

Another East Harlem attraction is **El Museo de Barrio**, the only museum in the city devoted to Puerto Rican and other Latin-American art. Located in the same building is the **Heckscher Theater** which for several years was the home of Reach Productions, the producers of *Mama I Want To Sing*, the longest-running black musical in history.

The music pounding out from East Harlem record shops and played in local nightclubs has more of a Latin beat than the music in Central Harlem, but it is just as African-influenced and deserves to be heard in authentic settings.

West Harlem: Finally there is West

Harlem, which extends from around Amsterdam Avenue to Riverside Drive, taking in the Convent Avenue area. Most of Harlem's white residents live in this district, which includes **Barnard College** and **Columbia University**.

Around each institution are the types of clubs and restaurants usually associated with large, urban universities. On any given night you can attend music concerts, dance concerts, art exhibitions, lectures, poetry readings, plays and athletic events. The universities' public relations offices or Offices of Student Affairs can provide information.

Some residents of West Harlem vehemently deny that they live in Harlem at all, preferring to say that they live in **Morningside Heights**, or **Hamilton Heights**, most pleasant-sounding names. What they can't get around is that if there is an East Harlem and a Central Harlem, then there's bound to be a West Harlem. And Columbia University is in West Harlem.

West Harlem is also the home of

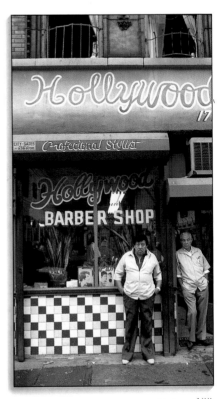

East (Spanish) Harlem.

important historical sites such as **Hamilton Grange**, built in 1801–02, which was the home of Alexander Hamilton, the country's first Secretary of the Treasury. The **Morris-Jumel Mansion**, at 160th Street and Edgecombe Avenue, is surrounded by a garden which once boasted a clear view of the Hudson River. It was a headquarters for George Washington during the American Revolution. Adjacent to the mansion is **Jumel Terrace**, a series of 20 beautifully presented row houses built around the turn of the century.

The impressive **Cathedral of St John the Divine** is the world's largest Gothic cathedral, while the **Ulysses S. Grant National Memorial**, tomb of the former president and Civil War general, is said to be inspired by the Invalides, Napoleon's final resting place in Paris.

Audubon Terrace, on Broadway between West 155th and 156th Streets, is lined by stately neoclassical buildings built between 1905 and 1923 as a planned cultural complex. Among them is the **American Numismatic Society**, which has exhibits of old money; and the Hispanic Society of America. (**The National Museum of the American Indian**, which opened here in 1922, is moving the bulk of its collection to the Washington DC area; the remainder can be viewed in downtown Manhattan's historic Custom House.)

WASHINGTON HEIGHTS: This far northern area was once an Irish neighborhood. Now it's ethnically mixed, with Dominicans, Puerto Ricans, blacks and others claiming it for their own. **Fort Tryon Park**, on West 192nd Street, is a 62-acre public park designed by Frederick Law Olmsted. Inside the park is **The Cloisters**, a branch of the Metropolitan Museum of Art and home to most of its medieval collections.

French and Spanish monastic cloisters, a 12th-century chapter house, the Fuentaduena Chapel and a Gothic and a Romanesque chapel were imported and reassembled stone by stone. The result is a beautiful and inspiring spot. The

The Morris-Jumel Mansion.

190

prize of the medieval collection is the Unicorn Tapestries, six handwoven tapestries from the 15th century. Even farther to the north, at 204th Street and Broadway, lies the **Dyckman House**, a two-story Dutch colonial farmhouse that was built in 1784.

Back down in Harlem Central, around 125th Street, the neighborhood also provides an opportunity to experience annual events that highlight Harlem's cultural diversity. They include the **Black World Championship Rodeo**, held every spring, whose goal is to bring the African-American role in the history of the American West to wider public attention; the **Dancemobile and Jazzmobile concerts**, presented outdoors throughout the summer months; the **African-American Day Parade**, held in early September; the lighting of Harlem's **Christmas Tree**; and the previously mentioned **AUDELCO Awards celebration**, which takes place most years on the third Monday of November.

For serious fans of basketball, there's the **Doc Turner East Coast Holiday Classic**, which features top high school teams, during the week between Christmas and New Year. In the summer months, there's the **Golden Hoops Tournament**, which features major college basketball players.

The largest annual event is **Harlem Week**. It began as a one-day celebration in 1975 and now runs for three weeks every August. With a multitude of activities and conferences throughout the neighborhood, Harlem Week has become one of the city's best summer attractions.

Highlights include Uptown Saturday Night, and Harlem Day, on the final weekend. The former is a huge music concert and fashion show, while the latter features a bit of everything, from foods to fashions to arts and crafts to concerts. Parts of 125th and 135th Streets become a giant market and outdoor concert hall that attracts thousands of participants and visitors. This is the best time to check out Harlem.

Courtyard of the Cloisters.

NEW YORK TALES

New York is full of contradictions, a place of hits and misses, genuine "firsts" and monstrous myths. Tales of the unexpected are as commonplace as the misconceptions about the city itself. Here are a few of each.

Crime in New York makes headlines around the world. The truth is somewhat less sensational: the city recently ranked only ninth for murders in the US, and a lowly 13th for overall crime rates. In fact, New York can sometimes seem surprisingly spiritual, with almost as many churches, synagogues, temples and mosques as there are good restaurants, and it has had, over the years, more than its fair share of saints.

The first canonized American citizen was Mother Cabrini, who came to New York from Italy (her shrine lies in **Washington Heights**) and the first American-born saint was Elizabeth Ann Seton, who hailed from lower Manhattan, and later converted to Catholicism in Little Italy's **Old Saint Patrick's Cathedral**.

To complete the trinity, Pierre Touissant, an 18th-century Haitian slave who is buried in the same church, may soon become the country's first black saint. Even a vision of the Virgin Mary has been seen in New York, at the site of the 1964 World's Fair Vatican Exhibit in **Flushing Meadows**. The faithful still turn up occasionally there and at a tree on **East 71st Street**, where a statue of Our Lady was embedded and is said to have left a permanent shadow.

(Further proof of New York's saintliness is an old but still-active law which states "no license can be issued for sale of hard liquor for a premises that is on the same street and/or avenue and within 200 feet of a building used as a house of worship...")

New York's water may no longer be the purest in the country, but it's still very clean – all 1½ billion gallons which arrive daily from upstate reservoirs. And while the streets aren't exactly paved with gold, they are paved with glassphalt, a mix of glass and asphalt that makes them sparkle at night like an opera diva's spangled gown.

The sidewalks have a certain cachet all their own, too. There's a Cartier clock set under glass at the corner of **Broadway and Maiden Lane**, put there as an advertisement for a neighboring clockmaker. If you step on a certain grate in **Times Square** (south of 46th between Seventh Avenue and Broadway), you'll hear a strange, musical groaning. This is not an injured pedestrian, but an aural installation created a few years ago by site composer Max Neuhaus.

Eccentrics have always thrived in New York. In the 1950s, the Collyer brothers' **Harlem** mansion was discovered crammed with 120 tons of junk, including 14 grand pianos and a Model-T Ford. In the 1960s and 70s, Moondog, a poet renowned for his Viking helmet and wild-eyed recitations was a staple on city streets. Fifteen years later Adam Purple left purple footprints in the sidewalks, and high-wire daredevil Philippe Petit was artist-in-residence at the **Cathedral of St John the Divine**. Should you care to join a club of like-minded enthusiasts, you might consider the Count Dracula Fan Club or the Royal Charter of Catfish Lovers.

New Yorkers, of course, like to think things happen here first. And they do. The city can claim America's first 24-hour bank, first algebra book, first car accident and first speeding ticket. Even the first flea circus ("an extraordinary exhibition of industrious fleas") held its opening night at **187 Broadway** in January, 1835. The first elephant to step ashore in the New World landed here on April 13, 1796.

Nowadays, exotic wildlife includes the elephants that march through the **Queens Midtown Tunnel** when the Ringling Brothers Circus comes to town; the alligators which persistent forklorists claim roam the city's sewers (so far only rats and waterbugs have been discovered lurking); and a mysterious colony of ants that were spotted on top of the **Empire State Building**. No one knows how they got there, or why. Closer to earth, animal lovers can find rabbits and racoons in Central Park (along with snapping turtles and the occasional woodchuck), or sip cocktails underneath a 92-foot (28-meter) blue whale at the **American Museum of Natural History**.

Shopping opportunities are equally eclectic.

When financier Diamond Jim Brady wanted to impress actress Lillian Russell in the 1890s, he bought her a diamond-encrusted bicycle to ride in **Central Park**. Nowadays you can purchase the skeleton of your choice at Maxilla and Mandible, an **Upper West Side** shop specializing in bones; miles of hair at the Lugo Hair Center in **Brooklyn**, where they import in 55-kilo boxes; and buttons of every conceivable shape, size and material at Tender Buttons, on **East 62nd Street**. (Even non-humans have a wide selection of outlets to choose from: for instance, at Karen's For People and Pets, on the Upper East Side, you can invest in matching outfits for you and your poodle, while the Dog Lover's Bookshop on West 31st Street stocks the latest in canine videos.)

Bike riding is as popular as it was in Diamond

inches – at the intersection of **Christopher Street and Seventh Avenue**. During the summer, Central Park's **Wollman Rink** turns into a miniature golf course where each hole features a model of a local landmark – so you can really knock the city down to size.

There's always something new to discover. Like the fact that 20,000 Native Americans live in New York (and an annual Thunderbird American Midsummer Pow-wow takes place at the **Queens County Farm Museum** in **Floral Park**). Or the five antique carousels that make the rounds in city parks, or even what may be the only concrete piano in existence. Built during World War II, when wood was scarce, it sits in the **Museum of the American Piano** on **West 58th Street**.

There are almost 8 million stories in the naked

Jim Brady's day, although modern New Yorkers are a hyper-active bunch, seldom satisfied with conventional means of exercise. They may join aerobics classes and work out at gyms, but they also ice skate any time of the day or night at **Sky Rink** (16 floors above street level). Or they'll join in the New York Roadrunners Club's annual Backwards Mile Race. Or they'll gasp and pant up 1,575 steps in the Empire State Building's annually exhausting Run-up (the record: 10 minutes, 47 seconds from lobby to 86th floor).

New York can be intimidating, especially for first-time visitors. You can, however, put it all in perspective at the **Queens Museum of Art**, where there's a model miniature metropolis, complete in every detail. Or stand on the world's smallest piece of real estate – a triangular plaque measuring 24 by 26

city, and you'll find some of them at the **New York Society Library**. Chartered by King George III in 1772, it's the oldest institution of its kind in New York.

A close second is the **New York Historical Society**, a museum cum library founded in 1804 (making it the oldest in New York State). It includes some of the country's rarest manuscripts. Or stop by New York Bound, just inside the Associated Press Building at **Rockefeller Center**. A bookshop devoted exclusively to works about the Big Apple (everything from an 1885 *Ladies Guide and Directory* to *Secrets of the Metropolitan Police*), it's also browser-friendly, contradicting the myth that New Yorkers are invariably rude. "We have people who've sat here for hours and we don't even glare," says one of the owners. ∎

COSMOPOLITAN
COSMOPOLITAN
FALL COLLECTION
BIT
PRODUCED BY KRAZE
A Bitch Named JOHANNA
AVAILABLE IN

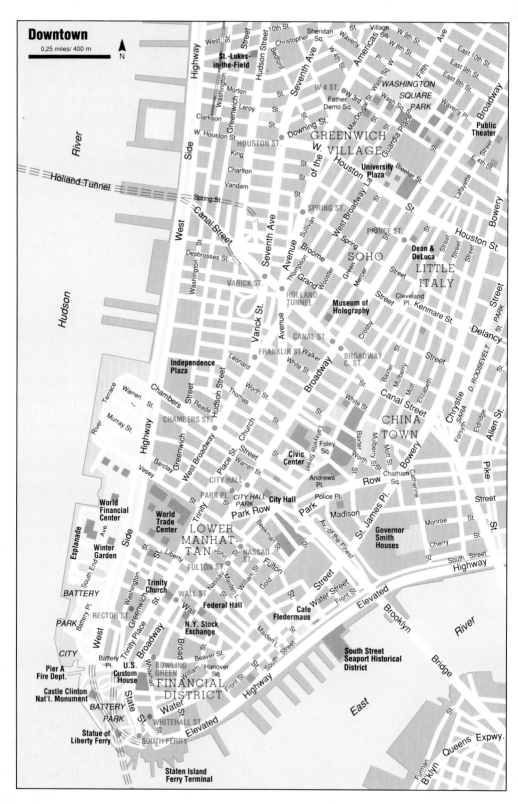

Downtown

0,25 miles/ 400 m

N

St.-Lukes-in-the-Field

WASHINGTON SQUARE PARK

Public Theater

GREENWICH W. VILLAGE

HOUSTON ST.

University Plaza

SPRING ST.

PRINCE ST.

SOHO

Dean & DeLuca

LITTLE ITALY

HOLLAND TUNNEL

Museum of Holography

CANAL ST.

Kenmare St.

Delancy

FRANKLIN ST

BROADWAY C. ST.

Canal Street

Independence Plaza

CHINA TOWN

CHAMBERS ST.

Civic Center

Foley Sq.

CITY HALL

PARK PL.

CITY HALL PARK

City Hall

Police Pl.

Andrews Pl.

Chatham Sq.

World Financial Center

World Trade Center

LOWER MANHAT-TAN

Park Row

Governor Smith Houses

Winter Garden

Esplanade

NASSAU ST.

Madison

FULTON ST.

Trinity Church

WALL ST.

Federal Hall

Cafe Fledermaus

BATTERY

RECTOR ST.

Wall

Water Street

N.Y. Stock Exchange

South Street Seaport Historical District

Brooklyn Bridge

Pier A Fire Dept.

U.S. Custom House

BOWLING GREEN

FINANCIAL DISTRICT

Hanover Sq.

Castle Clinton Nat'l. Monument

BATTERY PARK

WHITEHALL ST.

Statue of Liberty Ferry

SOUTH FERRY

East River

Staten Island Ferry Terminal

Queens Expwy.

Hudson River

Holland Tunnel

DOWNTOWN

Downtown and uptown New York are two very different places. Uptown, where life can scream with a neon fury and adrenalin is high, passions run hot and furious. Downtown's attitude is cool. Uptown is for museums and Broadway and shopping, downtown is for strolling around and having another cup of cappuccino.

Some of the oldest sites in the city are located downtown, like Trinity Church in lower Manhattan, where in the cemetery notables like Alexander Hamilton, America's first Secretary of the Treasury, and inventor Robert Fulton are buried. Downtown also contains most of New York's newest sites. These may be historic, like the Ellis Island museum, which chronicles the story of American immigration, but they're more likely to be glitzy affairs. Downtown is where nightclubs spring up with energizing regularity, and close again quicker than you can change your dancing shoes. Restaurants, too, are fashionable and then scorned, at a pace which only *cognoscenti* with a keen sense of direction can follow.

Downtown is Alphabet City. There's Avenues A, B, C and D, plus SoHo and TriBeCa; NoHo and SoFi. A large-scale map of downtown looks like a kidnapper's ransom note.

The latter two are among New York City's newer neighborhoods. An amorphous section North of Houston Street, known locally as NoHo, appeared in that guise in 1990 in a variety of publications. So the name NoHo is official. SoFi (South of Flatiron) is not. Watch this space.

The southern portion of downtown is corporate New York, where Wall Street banks keep tabs on everybody's money and South Street Seaport takes it away again with a series of shops, watering holes and seafood restaurants. The World Trade Center stole a great deal of the Empire State Building's thunder when the first of its twin towers opened in 1970. Insult was added to injury when, six years later, it stole King Kong as well, in a remake of the movie classic. (The film flopped.)

The outer boroughs of NYC – Brooklyn, Queens, Staten Island and the Bronx – are included in this section of the book purely for convenience. They are a mystery to those who don't know them; to those who do, the outer boroughs are places to find world-famous hot dogs, a movie museum, Edgar Allan Poe and even a little bit of New England.

"The Bronx? No thonx," said poet Ogden Nash. You may be surprised.

GRAMERCY, UNION SQUARE AND CHELSEA

Gramercy Park, Union Square and Chelsea fall into the border area between midtown and downtown Manhattan, and share qualities of both. The major avenues slice through the neighborhoods, but they aren't nearly as formidable as they are farther uptown.

These are some of the less-traveled areas of the city, stable, mostly residential sections that tend to their own business and attract little attention from outsiders. There are no major commuter lines or tourist attractions, and as a result, few people have reason to pass through. Union Square has recently attracted its share of the hip young publishing crowd, Chelsea is teetering on the verge of gentrification, and Gramercy Park maintains its usual well-heeled reserve, but for the most part these areas seem to enjoy life outside the mainstream.

GRAMERCY PARK: Starting on the east side **Gramercy Park** is a tidy little square surrounded by trim townhouses, some with fancy iron balconies that give it a charming European look. The park, neatly landscaped and well-maintained, was established in the 1830s by a wealthy lawyer named Samuel Ruggles along the lines of a London square. It is Manhattan's only private park, for, like many of its European counterparts, only residents of the houses which ring it are allowed in. Ruggles named the area south of the park **Irving Place**, for his friend, the writer Washington Irving.

This elegant atmosphere lingers for a few blocks surrounding Gramercy Park (19th Street between Second and Third Avenues is especially charming) before the city's normal clang and clatter reasserts itself. One block farther up, on 20th Street, is the **Police Academy and Museum**, which gives a history of New York's boys in blue. Entrance is free. The little café called Friend of A Farmer (Irving Place between 18th and 19th

Streets) features homebaked goods and a great Sunday brunch. For something more urban, check out **Pete's Tavern** across the street. A dark, historic bar where the atmosphere reeks of old speakeasies and spilled beer, it's also where short story scribe O. Henry is said to have written many a tale.

Drifting northward, in the triangle created by Broadway crossing Fifth Avenue, is one of Manhattan's favorite architectural whimsies, the triangular **Flatiron Building**. Created by David H. Burnham, this ocean-liner of a building, 285 feet high, raised eyebrows and hopes for a bright future when it was erected in 1902. It soon became known as the Flatiron Building (original name: Fuller Building) because of its distinctive shape. Reflecting the area's growing reputation in media circles, the neighborhood is colloquially known as SoFi, which stands, of course, for **S**outh of **Fl**atiron. An attractive little café, inside the building itself, gives the appelation even more cachet.

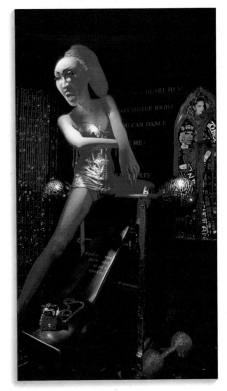

Left, the Con Ed Building. **Right**, Madonna in window of Barney's.

UNION SQUARE: Drifting southward, Broadway loops around Union Square. Years ago it looked like Union Square was yet another lost cause, one of those threatening public spaces you made a point of avoiding. Since then, the city has cleaned up the square and recent developments have breathed new life into it. One of the first was the bustling, weekend **Greenmarket** (also open some weekdays), which brings farmers and their produce into the heart of Manhattan; other plans include an outdoor cafe and two new playgrounds.

During the last decades of the 19th century, fashionable retailing centered on the "Ladies Mile," a glittering main drag that ranged from the old John Wanamaker store on 9th Street, up Broadway and Sixth Avenue, to 23rd Street. While the stores themselves have long since closed or moved on, these ornate monsters remain. Among the notable emporiums were Siegel-Cooper Dry Goods, on the east side of Sixth Avenue between 18th and 19th Streets,

which opened in 1898 to a crowd reported at 150,000; and Arnold Constable at Broadway and 19th, purveyor of expensive fabrics. Over a period of years, the Constable store expanded, until it filled the entire block from Broadway to Fifth Avenue. Lord & Taylor, which began as a small shop downtown on Catherine Street, opened its ornate headquarters on the southwest corner of Broadway and 20th Street in 1872 – not moving uptown (where its fashionable doors are still open) until 1914.

Union Square, named for the convergence of Broadway and Fourth Avenue, was a stylish prospect in the mid-1850s. In the second half of the 19th century, deserted by genteel residents, it became a theater center. When even theater had moved to Midtown, the square became best known for the political meetings it hosted. In the years preceding World War I, anarchists and socialists addressed sympathizers here. In 1927, a large crowd gathered to protest and mourn the execution of Sacco

A sign of the times.

and Vanzetti, anarchists widely believed to have been wrongly accused of murder. Through the 1930s, rallies in the square continued to draw crowds, but finally even radicalism dwindled, and the area went into decline until its recent resurgence.

The **Consolidated Edison Building**, with its gently lit-up clocktower, used to be the dominant presence, but the **Zeckendorf Towers** has now stolen its thunder and obscured the view. The **Con Edison Energy Museum** provides a bright spot in more ways than one. Nearby are several trendy restaurants, so expect to see lots of Italian suits and tortoise-shell eyeglasses about. For those who prefer to spend money on food for the soul rather than for the stomach, the **Union Square Theatre**, at 100 East 17th Street, stages contemporary plays, and tickets can be reasonable priced.

CHELSEA: West of Fifth Avenue, **Chelsea** occupies the area from 14th to about 30th Streets. Adrenalin trickles down from the Garment District in Midtown into that part of Chelsea which has been genrified. The fuzzy border between the two areas is marked by the **Flower Market**, which runs along Sixth Avenue between 28th and 30th Streets. It's actually an indoor/outdoor warehouse where wholesalers store plants before they're transferred to various parts of the city. In the spring and summer, the avenue is crowded with leafy vegetation and bathed in a sweet loamy odor. After all those miles of concrete and asphalt, it's a little bizarre to find yourself in the middle of a small jungle.

The **Chelsea Hotel** is only a short walk away on 23rd Street between Seventh and Eighth Avenues. Along with the Algonquin and Ansonia, the Chelsea stands as one of the city's most famous residential hotels because of the long list of artists who lived, worked and died here. Thomas Wolfe, Arthur Miller, Jack Kerouac and William Burroughs produced some of their best work while living at the Chelsea; Andy Warhol filmed a bizarre tribute called

Fire and water.

Chelsea Girls; it's where Dylan Thomas spent some of his last boozy days, and punk-rocker Sid Vicious murdered his girlfriend in their room, only to die of a drug overdose several weeks later. If you can appreciate the weirdness, it's a reasonable place to stay. By all means, have a look at the unusual artwork in the lobby and check out some of the characters; then have a drink in the bar of the adjacent restaurant.

Chelsea has as its core a large piece of land acquired in 1750 by Captain Thomas Moore. His grandson, Clement Clark Moore, a Greek and Hebrew scholar best remembered for his poem *A Visit from Saint Nicholas*, inherited the land. Faced with the onslaught of the northward-creeping city, Moore divided his legacy into lots and sold them off with certain restrictions: "undesirable" uses, like stables, were prohibited, and all houses had to be set back from the street. Moore also contributed an entire block to the **General Theological Seminary**, with which he was affiliated. The

Seminary's most interesting building is the **Chapel of the Good Shepherd**, which boasts massive bronze doors and a 161-foot bell tower.

The tree-lined quadrangle acts as a spiritual and visual oasis in heavily urban Chelsea. Passersby may visit on weekday afternoons by entering at the Seminary's modern, main building on Ninth Avenue.

South of the Chelsea Hotel, the neighborhood starts melding into the West Village. This is the more gentrified end of Chelsea, although the tidy townhouses below 23rd Street are still punctuated with a scattering of fix-it shops and Puerto Rican stores that hint at the area's working-class foundations.

The population in Chelsea was and is mixed. But the dominant change is the influx of the young and prosperous, hard-working professionals who are able to pay the rents blue-collar workers are not. Aside from **Barney's**, which is a premier address for men's and women's fashion, big attractions for many New

Yorkers are the trendy restaurants constantly popping up on Eighth, Ninth and Tenth Avenues.

Retro-chic is all the rage at the Empire Diner on the corner of Tenth Avenue and 22nd Street. It looks like an old-time aluminium-sided diner on the outside, but inside it's an Art Deco fantasy. The clientele is predictably hip and the prices are inflated accordingly, but this is where you'll find the diehards after a long night of partying. A few other entries on the top ten list include Mary Ann's which stands on Eighth Avenue near the corner of 16th Street, and specializes in hearty American cuisine with a Tex-Mex-Cajun twist. A nearby doubleheader – Trattoria Tiziano and Man Ray – stand side-by-side on Eighth Avenue at 19th Street, the former Italian, the latter French.

These restaurants cater to the discerning crowd that attends performances at the **Joyce Theater**. Once a decaying movie house, the premises have been extensively remodeled to present some of the most innovative performances in the dance world. Anyone even remotely connected to dance stands by the Joyce, which is not well-known outside rather arty circles. (Performers range from Spanish Gypsy flamenco artists to Native American dance troupes.)

Performances of an experimental nature have always been on the bill at **The Kitchen** (19th Street between Tenth and Eleventh Avenues). This latter-day institution used to be in SoHo before moving "uptown" to Chelsea. Video, dance, and performance art are staple fare, with many a budding artist on hand, sometimes onstage, sometimes in the audience. Catch them here before these young innovators move to venues where you have to dress up.

Another venue which caters to the "see it here first" crowd is the **WPA Theatre**, 519 West 23rd Street, where hits like *Little Shop of Horrors* and *Steel Magnolias* made it – not to Broadway but all the way to Hollywood and the rest of the world via the cinema.

Left, the Chelsea Hotel. **Right**, the Flatiron Building.

GREENWICH VILLAGE

"The greater part of New York is as soulless as a department store; but Greenwich Village has recollections like ears filled with muted music and hopes like sightless eyes straining to catch a glimpse of the beatific vision."
— Djuna Barnes, *Greenwich Village As It Is* (1916)

Greenwich Village was the country's first true bohemian neighborhood, a place where, at the turn of the century, writers and poets, radicals and runaway socialites, artists and others seeking freedom from conventional lifestyles flocked to live in romantic surroundings. Mark Twain, Walt Whitman and Edgar Allan Poe lived here, as did later seekers like Dylan Thomas and Eugene O'Neill.

Since bypassed by the hipper (and at first cheaper) pastures of SoHo, TriBeCa and the East Village, some New Yorkers consider Greenwich Village – or "The Village" – one big tourist attraction. Untrue. Though a commercial element exists, some parts are as quietly residential as they were in the late 18th and early 19th centuries, when the village of Greenwich was first settled by New Yorkers fleeing a series of epidemics at the tip of the island.

As in other Manhattan neighborhoods, spiraling real estate prices have forced out all but the most successfully hip (and lucky holders of rent-controlled leases), but the Village is still where many people would prefer to live – and barring that possibility, where they go to walk and shop and enjoy the variety of street life. Here you can find cobblestone streets, graceful architecture, Italian bakeries, outdoor markets, galleries, and the largest gay community in New York. In addition, there's a remarkable array of restaurants, bars, theaters and jazz clubs.

Bordered by 14th Street to the north,

the Hudson River to the west and Broadway to the east (where the East Village begins), it's where the off-beat is the norm, and where the annual Halloween Parade has to be one of the world's best spectacles.

Manhattanites who dwell downtown are fond of saying they never go above **14th Street**, a bustling ethnic bazaar lined by discount stores and street vendors that stretches from Avenue D west to the meat packing district near the Hudson River. Encompassing everything from appliance stores to porno shops, 14th Street also forms the southern border of historic Union Square – once fashionable, later radical, still later derelict, and now surrounded by major publishing houses, chic restaurants and hot nightspots.

Walk down Fifth Avenue, past **East West Books** – stocked with the latest in new age tapes, incense and crystals – and Reminiscence, a low-price clothing store that specializes in recycled fashions, and you'll see the famous **Wash-**

ington Square Arch rising in the distance. Built in 1892 and designed by Stanford White, the Arch marks the entrance to **Washington Square**, the geographical and spiritual heart of Greenwich Village.

A quick detour: Before continuing, walk east to Broadway and you come to the **Strand bookstore**, one of the last survivors of what was once known as "Booksellers' Row." Located at the corner of 12th Street, the Strand offers "eight miles" of used books, and the stalwart searcher may just discover that rare first edition he or she has been trying to find. Just down the street, **Grace Church** is one of the city's loveliest ecclesiastical structures. Built in 1846, its exterior white marble, now a muted gray, was mined by convicts at infamous Sing Sing prison in upstate New York.

Turn right on 10th, walk west towards Fifth Avenue, and you cross **University Place**, which runs parallel to Fifth from 14th to Eighth Street. You can grab an inexpensive burger at the Cedar Tavern where artists Jackson Pollack and Willem de Kooning used to hang out; listen to some of the finest jazz in town at **Bradley's**; or do both at the slightly more upscale **Knickerbocker**, on Waverly Place, where there's great jazz *and* great food.

On West 12th Street, the **New School for Social Research** offers city dwellers classes in everything from Arabic to screen-writing. At *Forbes* magazine's Fifth Avenue headquarters around the corner, a gallery holds the late Malcolm Forbes's collection of tin soldiers and Fabergé eggs. Nearby is the **Salmagundi Club**, the country's oldest artists' club, founded in 1870.

Take a stroll west along 9th and 10th Streets, two of the most picturesque in the city. Lined by stately brick and brownstone houses, these desirable residential streets have been home to numerous artists and writers (Mark Twain lived at 14 West 10th). You might catch Jack Nicholson having din- **A crumbling corner.**

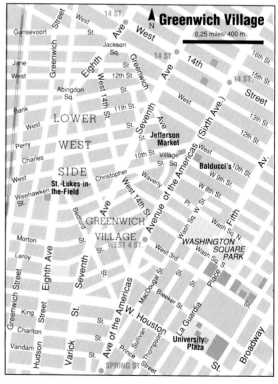

ner at **Marylou's**, a discreet lower-level restaurant that attracts a wide spectrum of celebrities. The **Church of the Ascension**, on the corner of Fifth and 10th Street, was designed by architect Richard Upjohn in 1840, and features a marble altar relief by sculptor Augustus Saint-Gaudens.

Positively 8th Street: If 14th Street forms downtown Manhattan's northern border, then **8th Street** is the bridge between the east and the west. East of Fifth, you'll find one of the city's most outrageous clothing stores, **Patricia Field**, where vinyl *bustiers*, heavy metal jewelry and formidable hats and wigs are displayed with tongue-in-chic irony. West 8th, on the other hand, is a commercial strip consisting of bargain shoe stores, rock 'n' roll regalia, and even a psychedelic rock nostalgia store.

Tucked away just above Washington Square Arch are two tiny dead-end streets that look like stage sets. **Washington Mews** lies just south of **One Fifth Avenue** (a stately building that houses an ever-changing bar and restaurant), situated between Fifth and Washington Square North, an extension of Waverly Place. Originally built as stables for the townhouses along Washington Square North (where the artist Edward Hopper lived), the mews row houses here and along nearby **Macdougal Alley** are now highly sought-after residences.

All of this could distract you from **Washington Square Park** itself. Originally a potter's field, where the poor and unknown were buried, it later became a parade ground, and still later a residential park. Although it's lost the cachet it knew in the days of Henry James – who lived by the park and was inspired to write his well-known novel by the same name – on any afternoon you'll find guitars, mime artists, jugglers and even the occasional fire-eater performing to appreciative crowds of New York University students, mothers with babies in strollers, Japanese camera crews, passers-by and pot dealers.

A quiet moment in Washington Square Park.

With its two blocks of Greek Revival townhouses, **Washington Square North** retains a 19th-century elegance at odds with the monolithic **New York University** buildings which adjoin the park. The large gray building on **Washington Square East** claims to be the Washington Square College of Arts and Sciences, but is actually NYU's main building. Inside you'll find the **Grey Art Gallery**, which showcases some of the savviest contemporary and historical art exhibits in town.

Continue on Washington Place to NYU's **Brown Building**, built on the foundations of the 1900 Asch Building, a garment factory that in 1911 was the site of the Triangle Factory Fire, where 146 young women workers lost their lives in a tragedy that was to instigate wide-reaching labor reform laws. Past NYU's Loeb Student Center, Library and Catholic Center (all on Washington Square South), you come to **Judson Memorial Church**. Designed in 1890 by the ubiquitous Stanford White in Romanesque Revival-style, for decades the church has been a cultural as well as a religious center, featuring avant-garde art exhibitions and music, dance and theater presentations.

Tourist Central: Turn left off Washington Square South onto **MacDougal Street**, and you're in the heart of what was once beatnik heaven, where world-weary poets sipped coffee and discussed the meaning of life late into the night. These days, it's a tawdry mecca for out-of-towners, drawn by the bevy of ersatz crafts shops and "authentic" ethnic restaurants. A stroll around here offers the added pleasure of a pilgrimage to past grooviness; some nights you could swear you see the ghost of the young Bob Dylan hovering over the intersection of Bleecker and Mac-Dougal Streets.

Many of Eugene O'Neill's plays were first produced at the **Provincetown Playhouse** on MacDougal. Stop in at the **Minetta Tavern** where Ernest Hemingway hoisted a beer or two, or **Caffé Reggio**, one of the old-time coffee houses made famous in the 1940s and 50s. Another is **Le Figaro** on Bleecker, which along with **Café Borgia** across the street offers maximum sidewalk people-watching opportunities, along with first-rate espresso and cappuccino.

Nearby entertainment includes live performances by the world's jazz greats at the **Blue Note** (on West Third Street between MacDougal Street and Sixth Avenue), and excellent contemporary theater at **Circle in the Square Downtown** and the **Minetta Lane Theater**.

Except for a profusion of juice bars, shoe stores, leather and souvenir shops, every other door seems to lead to a restaurant, and the smell of Indian, Spanish, Japanese and Italian cuisines spills out onto the sidewalk in a miasma of olfactory overkill. One of the best places is Mamoun's, next to Caffé Reggio. The *falafal* is very inexpensive (take out or eat in), and they serve the best mint tea this side of Marrakesh.

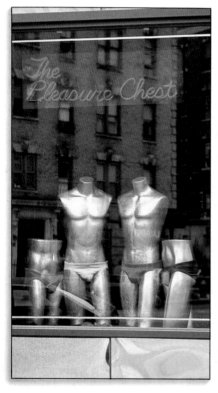

The Village caters for all tastes...

Not far away, you can feast on splendid Italian specialities at **The Grand Ticino** on Thompson, founded in 1919, and where, years later Cher spent time in the movie *Moonstruck*. If you're in the mood for old-world atmosphere and service, walk down to Bleecker Street and back over to MacDougal: a few doors down on the right, at No. 69, **Villa Mosconi** is another Village classic: a friendly, family-run eatery where the portions are huge and the atmosphere unabashedly Southern Italian.

The West Village: The area west of Sixth Avenue is referred to as the **West Village**, and runs all the way west to the Hudson River and north to 14th Street. This is the Village that hosts the annual Halloween Parade, saw gay-rights riots at the Stonewall Inn in the late 1960s, and has pretty streets that wind confusingly between the major avenues.

A good place to start exploring is the striking Gothic building at 10th Street and Sixth Avenue, just up the road from the famous **Balducci's** indoor market, a mecca for food enthusiasts. Originally part of a complex which included the old Women's House of Detention (where black activist Angela Davis was once imprisoned), this red brick structure was built over an even older market. Now it's the **Jefferson Market** branch of the New York Public **Library**, and borders a pretty community garden which is occasionally open to the public.

Walk west on 10th Street, past **Patchin Place** – a mews where Eugene O'Neill, the journalist John Reed and the poet e. e. Cummings lived – to Greenwich Avenue, and you reach **The Peacock Caffé,** yet another traditional Greenwich Village coffeeshop. With its ivory-toned interior and operatic portraits, this is a wonderful place to sit sipping coffee on a rainy day, and read the paper (or study a detailed map – you'll need it around here).

Next door, the playground of Public School 41 transforms into an **outdoor bazaar** and **flea market** on Saturdays. In the other direction, Greenwich

...including theatergoers'.

Avenue leads to **Christopher Street**, symbolic center of the gay community and a main cross-street that slants across the heart of the West Village. The farther west you walk, the more explicit the displays in menswear shops become, starting with respectable T-shirts, continuing with stylish manacles (and other essential items), and ending up at West Street, which runs past the Hudson River's abandoned piers.

Just past **Gay Street** (so named long before current implications), with its row of small Federal houses, is the **Northern Dispensary**. A non-profit health clinic from 1827 until recently, it's one of the oldest public buildings in the city. Nearby, Abracadabra sells everything from holograms to juggling equipment and even has a magician on the premises. A few doors down and close to three decades ago, the modern gay rights movement got its spontaneous start one night at the Stonewall Inn – a gay bar whose habitués were tired of being rousted by police.

Into the night: The **Lion's Head** on Christopher Street is that rarity, a famous literary bar where literary types still hang out. Actress Jessica Lange was a waitress here, and besides the journalists, novelists and playwrights hanging out in the front bar, there's good food in the restaurant at the back.

Tiny, fenced-in **Christopher Park**, at the junction of Waverly Place and Christopher Street, features a statue of the Civil War general Philip Sheridan. In the traditional Village spirit of confusion, **Sheridan Square** itself is actually a few steps away, where Grove, Christopher and West 4th Streets all meet Seventh Avenue South in a nightmare of city un-planning.

Playwright Lanford Wilson's work is often showcased at the **Circle Repertory Company** theater on Seventh Avenue South, and more good off-Broadway productions take place at the **Lucille Lortel Theater** on Christopher. Across the street from the Circle Rep, you can enjoy the great music of

If pigs could fly...

the late Gil Evans on Monday nights at **Sweet Basil**, one of the great Village jazz venues.

Another is the **Village Vanguard**, an historic basement club several blocks north. Just around the corner, you can join the *cognoscenti* who've discovered Chez Brigitte, one of the world's smallest restaurants (it seats only 11 people). Here, dinners are cooked right before your eyes, and your wallet will enjoy a treat, too. Farther along, **Greenwich Avenue** runs into the heart of Manhattan's meat district, where a small stainless-steel restaurant called Florent, on Gansevoort Street, has the best onion soup in town.

Hudson Street runs south from 14th Street, and includes Myers of Keswick, a British specialty shop, where Keith Richards, Elton John and Princess Margaret find delicacies like Peter Myer's homemade pork pies, as well as imported teas and biscuits. The **White Horse Tavern** has been serving drinks since 1880, and is where Dylan Thomas had one too many before expiring at nearby St Vincent's Hospital.

Across from the White Horse, **Abingdon Square** (named after a local girl who married the Earl of Abingdon) leads to the start of Bleecker Street.

Bookstores, birdstores, restaurants and antiques abound on this end of **Bleecker Street**, bisected by some of the Village's prettiest thoroughfares. For example, **121 Greenwich Street**, west of Bleecker on the corner of Charles Street, is one of those urban anomalies, a white wooden house surrounded by a white fence and a yard, that looks like it belongs in a country village, rather than leaning up against a city tenement.

Bank Street is particularly scenic, with its cobblestones and pastel houses, and lies in the center of the Greenwich Village Historic District's finest 19th-century architecture. Not that it's all historic houses around here. Automatic Slim's, on the corner of Bank and Washington, was named the best bar in

the West Village a few years back, and there always seems to be a party going on at nearby Tortilla Flats, a lively Tex-Mex restaurant where patrons have been known to sing along to raunchy rock 'n' roll.

Across the street, **Westbeth** is a sprawling, government-funded artists' enclave that looks out over the Hudson River. A combination of subsidized apartments and theater complex, it was once home to Bell Laboratories, and the development of sound production as well as early television took place on the premises. Today it contains four performance spaces, as well as rehearsal spaces often used for Broadway and off-Broadway productions. At the corner of Greenwich and Christopher streets is **White Columns**, a non-profit art exhibition space located on the ground floor of a large high-rise.

St-Lukes-in-the-Field is the city's third oldest church, and was built in 1821, when this area was still pretty much open countryside. Easily reached

Dylan Thomas' last watering hole.

by walking west on **Grove Street** from Seventh Avenue South, the route takes you through a rabbit-warren of lanes and byways, which cross themselves or change names without warning.

Number **17 Grove Street**, built in 1822, is another wooden relic of days gone by, as is **Grove Court**, an alleyway with a cluster of white-brick houses hidden inside. Grove Street intersects **Bedford Street**, one of the oldest Village byways.

If you turn right here, you'll discover the original "Twin Peaks" (102 Bedford Street), which was built as an artists' residence in 1830 – long before director David Lynch's infamous television production. As its name suggests, the gabled roof comes to two peaks, not just one peak.

Tiny poet Edna St Vincent Millay once lived at **75 Bedford Street**, Manhattan's skinniest house at just over 9 feet wide. Not far away, the atmosphere is appropriately secretive at **Chumley's**, a hidden former speakeasy turned bar and restaurant where novelist John Steinbeck was a regular.

Named for a local artist Thomas Barrow, **Barrow Street** is one of the quietest, quaintest streets around, and intersects Bedford at **Commerce Street**, which is an equally secluded lane. The **Cherry Lane Theater** on Commerce, where a pre-stardom Barbra Streisand worked as an usher, was originally a farm silo, later a box factory, and was converted to a theater in 1922.

The old **Blue Mill Tavern**, a local hangout since Prohibition Days, has been transformed into a 30s-style eatery called The Grange Hall.

From here, a walk south on Hudson Street takes you to **St Luke's Place**, a slow curve of a street lined by gracious Italianate houses. One of New York's favorite mayors, Jimmy Walker, lived at No. 6, and two lamps – a sign of mayoral honor – can still be seen at the foot of the steps. Nearby **James J. Walker Park** is named after this famous son of New York.

Left, a hot club for cool jazz. **Right**, Marilyn pauses on Lexington Avenue.

NEW YORK IN THE MOVIES

When Marilyn Monroe, dressed in high heels and a flimsy white dress, cooled off over a subway grating located at 52nd Street and Lexington Avenue, an image of New York on film was confirmed. *The Seven Year Itch* was sweaty and high-spirited, brimming over with good dialogue and good-humored sexuality, hallmarks of a movie filmed or located in New York City.

Scores of landmarks have featured in films shown around the world, from the Plaza Hotel (*Crocodile Dundee, The Great Gatsby, Funny Girl*) to Grand Central Station (Hitchcock's *North by Northwest*) to just about every street corner and café in town (Woody Allen's *Manhattan*).

The city has played a prominent role in the history of the movies. *The Lights of New York*, released in 1927, is commonly held to be the first all-spoken movie, as distinct from *The Jazz Singer*, premiered the same year, which featured singing and just a few lines of dialogue. King Kong hit the screens in 1933, only two years after the Empire State Building was completed. Kong atop the Empire State, fending off disasters and airplanes and the defenders of Fay Wray, is an enduring cinema image to movie fans everywhere.

Contemporary films about the city can be divided roughly into three categories: hard-hitting stories like Martin Scorsese's *Mean Streets, Taxi Driver*, Francis Ford Coppola's Godfather films and cop flicks like the *Die Hard* series, where the action is fast and the talk is tough; Woody Allen films, in which New Yorkers are stylish purveyors of an elegant, if neurotic, culture; and period dramas.

This last category poses special problems for film makers. When *Ragtime*, the film based on E.L. Doctorow's novel, was first proposed, location managers scoured the streets to find a neighborhood which could convincingly pass for the Lower East Side, *circa* 1900. The final choice was East 11th Street, which, with its rooflines and tenement buildings, exactly fitted the bill – if the local community could be persuaded to put up with the day and night disruption.

Production designer Patrizia Von Brandenstein was quoted as saying, "I think 11th Street was a classic model of a good way to do a street location. We had a production office there. We canvassed the entire neighborhood. We explained in detail, in English and Spanish, what we were going to do and why. We asked them to be a part of this historic thing. We told them we would give them a summer camp for their kids, which we did. We utilized their businesses. And we offered to park their cars."

Neighborhood politics resolved, the next step was to hide any modern references. Clotheslines and flags, banners and bunting were erected to flutter across the street, in order to obscure electrical wires and television antennas. Van Brandenstein explains: "One of the first things I did on 11th Street was bring the buildings out onto the sidewalk to cut down (the width of the street). All the facades were built out. It made it a much narrower street and more accurate. And as we got down to the end of the street, we closed it in even more, creating a false perspective point of view."

The *Ragtime* tenements on 11th Street are only one of many locations which film buffs can spot while crossing the city. There's the *Ghostbusters'* building at 55 Central Park West (it moved uptown after residents of the original Greenwich Village location, One Fifth Avenue, objected) and the dazzling, revolving globe in the lobby of the *Daily News* building on East 42nd Street, which doubled as the *Daily Planet* in the *Superman* films. The classy apartment rented by those sassy dames Monroe, Grable and Bacall in *How to Marry a Millionaire* is located at 36 Sutton Place South in Midtown East.

Lauren Bacall was actually a downtown girl, having earned the title Miss Greenwich Village in 1942, while living in the area with her mother. Quite a few other well-known Village locations have made it to the big screen over the years: these include the Bleecker Street Cinema, which featured in rock star Madonna's first movie, *Desperately Seeking Susan*; Washington Square, where a pre-aerobics Jane Fonda frolicked innocently with Robert Redford in *Barefoot in the Park*, and the swimming pool by St Luke's Place, where Robert De Niro met Cathy Moriarty in Martin Scorsese's 1980 boxing drama *Raging Bull*. ∎

THE EAST VILLAGE TO CHINATOWN

THE EAST VILLAGE: Younger in spirit than the West Village, the East Village has more adventurous nightlife, with fewer cabaret and more rock clubs, more performance art and less "straight" theater. Roughly bounded by 14th Street to the north, East Houston to the south, Broadway to the west and Avenue B to the east, this is a place that stays up late, where clothes and politics have historically been more radical than anywhere else in the city.

Beneath its avant-garde surface, the East Village is also a neighborhood of immigrants, with Ukrainian social clubs next to galleries and offbeat boutiques, and Puerto Rican health clinics beside pricey, restored brownstones. Like other downtown neighborhoods, old and new are juxtaposed in a mind-boggling mosaic.

St Mark's-in-the-Bowery, at Second Avenue and 10th Street, is the second-oldest church in Manhattan – and a good place to start exploring. Built in 1799 on a *bouwerie* (farm) belonging to Dutch governor Peter Stuyvesant, St Mark's has a long history of liberal religious thought, a reflection of the neighborhood that manifests itself in such long-standing programs as the Poetry Project, where renowned East Village poets like Allen Ginsberg and ex-Fug Tuli Kupferberg give readings.

The red-brick Anglo-Italianate houses across from the church on East 10th Street and on Stuyvesant Street, which veers off at an angle from Second Avenue, form the heart of the **St Mark's Historic District.** Number 21 is the **Stuyvesant Fish House**, a national historic landmark built by Peter Stuyvesant's great grandson in 1804.

In the beginning: Keep walking on Stuyvesant Street and cross Third Avenue to **Astor Place**, once one of the city's most fashionable addresses. It is named after John Jacob Astor, who arrived in New York in 1784 as a penniless immigrant and was the richest man in town by the time he died 36 years later. Today its most notable landmark is the giant rotating black cube by Tony Rosenthal called **The Alamo**. One of the first abstract sculptures installed on city property, it has stood at the intersection of Astor Place and St Mark's Place and Lafayette Street since 1967.

Nearby, the brown Italianate **Cooper Union Foundation Building** opened in 1859 as one of the country's earliest centers of free education. Famous as an art school, it's also where Abraham Lincoln gave the speech said to have launched his presidential campaign. A statue of founder-philanthropist Peter Cooper by Augustus Saint-Gaudens, who studied here, stands behind Cooper Union at **Cooper Square**.

Colonnade Row on Lafayette Street is a once-elegant group of columned homes built in 1833. Four of the houses still stand. Across the street, **Joseph Papp Public Theater** was originally

the Astor Library, John Jacob's only public legacy, which he envisioned as a center of learning for the common man. The fact that it was only open during working hours didn't strike Astor as a problem. Built between 1849 and 1881, it later became the headquarters for the Hebrew Immigrant Aid Society, and since 1967 has been home to some of the city's best theater and film productions.

NoHo: At the turn of the century, the stretch of Broadway from around 9th Street to 23rd Street was the "Ladies Mile" of fashionable retailing. More recently, it was just a dingy pause before reaching SoHo, but all that changed when Tower Records, the now defunct Unique Clothing Warehouse and other young consumer centers moved in. Now it's part of **NoHo** (an abbreviation for **No**rth of **Ho**uston), a gritty, lively district which runs from Broadway on the west to Astor Place on the north down to Houston on the south. The eastern boundary, in keeping with the area's general character, is somewhat vague.

On the corner of Astor Place and Broadway, the huge **Astor Place Hair Designers** is a downtown institution. The latest in hair-dos is yours for the asking – cutting time: 10 minutes. Just across Houston Street in SoHo, the exhibits at the New Museum of Contemporary Art are always worth a visit; or you can drop in and see the city as it was at the **Old Merchant's House** on East 4th Street, a small Greek Revival-style brick townhouse built in 1832 and open as a museum on Sunday afternoons.

St Mark's Place, a continuation of 8th Street between Third Avenue and Avenue A, is the East Village version of main street, and in the 1960s was the East Coast's counter-culture center. These days, head shops and psychedelic clothing stores have been replaced by book and video shops. The Dom (a former Polish social club where Andy Warhol presented Velvet Underground "happenings" and later barefoot freaks tripped out at the Electric Circus) is now a **community crafts center**.

Waving to the Public.

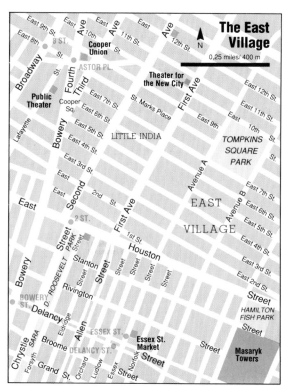

The East Village

However, this is still one of the city's liveliest thoroughfares. The sidewalk cafés and restaurants are always heaving with customers, and the bazaar-like atmosphere is enhanced day and night by street vendors selling socks, T-shirts, and jewelry. Stop in at Trash and Vaudeville for the latest in retro-punk gear; around the corner on Third Avenue, **St Mark's Bookstore** is one of the best places in town for new fiction and poetry.

Also around the corner, **McSorley's Old Ale House** on East 7th Street – across from the Ukrainian Catholic church – has been around since the 1850s. A true drinking man's pub where women didn't break the sex barrier until 1970, it was one of Irish playwright Brendan Behan's favorite hangouts.

Theater 80 on St Mark's Place recently converted from a cinema for vintage flicks to a theater – appropriate, as the East Village has been a center for live performances since Second Avenue was lined by Yiddish theaters at the turn of the century. Today there's **La Mama E.T.C.** just west of Second Avenue, a pioneer of avant-garde theater. You can see more of the best downtown performance artists in action at **P.S. 122** (on First Avenue at 9th Street), where an annual benefit offers a microcosm of what's happening on the cutting edge of music, dance and poetry.

As befits a neighborhood that's a typical melting pot, you can find just about any cuisine here, from trendy to traditional. If cheap and exotic is your preference, you can't do much better than "**Little India**," on 6th Street between First and Second Avenues. Interspersed with boutiques selling Japanese kimonos and Guatemalan dresses are restaurants with names like Mitali, Taj and Prince of India. All are incredibly inexpensive, most stay open pretty late, and some even feature live Indian music on weekend evenings.

Walk north up Second Avenue, past the **Middle Collegiate Church** (a Reformed Protestant Dutch church built in

McSorley's dates from the 1850s.

MAKING A BUCK

Once upon a time in New York, if you wanted to spurn the corporate route but had no capital to start on your own, you could fall back on door-to-door sales. The classics were the Fuller brush men, their demo cases abristle with boar's hair, and encyclopaedia peddlers. Today, few people stay at home in the daytime, and those who do don't open their doors to strangers. So that option is no more.

The answer in the 1990s: start your own business and be creative about it, because you've got to capture the imagination of the world's most persnickety consumers. A rifle through the *Yellow Pages* shows what's been done. You can find firms renting hairpieces, meditation coaches and dominatrixes by the hour. Twenty-four-hour dart stores, haircutters, and luxury laundromats have all made their splash, plus mobile home financiers, animal carcass removers, and even while-you-wait gun repairers.

Costa Mantis is a feature film director, screenplay writer and a father. Late one night in his Times Square apartment, a friend – ultimately his backer – told Mantis his cookies were good enough to sell. "Yeah, right," he replied, "and I'll sell them in the streets off bicycles

that look like rockets!" But as the tang of sarcasm died from his tongue, Mantis's mind was already racing ahead. A year later, the "Mothership" landed, and Alphamen bakery products invaded the streets.

Alpha Chips merged many things in Costa's life, he says. A native of Reading, Pennsylvania, Costa had two Greek-born grandfathers, one a restaurateur, the other a philosopher. So, as a child, he learned to bake and to ask questions.

Costa's cookies asked questions, too. Alphamen comics were included inside each bag. In the balloons issuing from Alphaman's mouth were philosophical conundrums like: "What has man made?" The *Wall Street Journal* and *Forbes* lauded not only the entrepreneurial spirit involved but also the metaphysics of the venture.

The company had a great street presence and, briefly, a Japanese branch. But Alpha Chips didn't make it in the end, for the classic reason: costs outstripped profits. Recouping the costs on the bicycles alone was daunting – they'd cost $5,000 each. The business folded.

"It was devastating," said Mantis, but the business acumen he picked up hasn't gone to waste. He now contracts as a consultant to a marketing company, while still writing screenplays and seeking film directing work.

Helen and Kerry Prep ("yes, it's really our name") started Preppygram as a stop-gap measure to supplement other careers, but it took off like a racehorse. Helen thought Preppygram was a dead loss of a name for a singing telegram company, but Kerry prevailed. The name decided, they searched for a gimmick and chose wisely: personalized singing telegrams. The Preps wanted to keep the act classy, so all the telegram deliverers wear top hats and tuxes – "no chickens, no strippers." And no orders for mad, bad, or sad occasions like divorces. "I value everyone's face, I don't want anyone getting punched," says Kerry.

The Preps borrowed $500 to start Preppygram. It was paid back in six months. Within three years, the average week's take was approaching $2,000. Problems? Only that business was taking Kerry away from acting and Helen away from creating children's stories and comic strips. They hired help. The company roars on.

So there is failure and success; but there is a non-profit business culture, too. Terry Adell, busily self-employed as a bellydancer and sometime actress, makeup artist and film producer, volunteers at New Leash on Life. New Leash finds stray animals foster homes.

Terry volunteers because she loves animals, yet admits she probably couldn't do it if she had remained in modern or classical dance. "I would have had to waitress on the side," she says. But her dusky looks and attraction to ethnic dance led neatly to the freelance world of bellydancing. "It's really well paid and I'm never out of work." She also dances with Ibrahim Farrah's Near East dance troupe, and it was from the contacts she made while on a Mid-East tour that she was able to get backing for the film she's now producing, "a sort of a classy horror film." Clearly, the key to survival in New York is diversification. ∎

1891), and you'll find the Kiev. Great Eastern European-style meals can be enjoyed cheaply here, and it stays open late. Kosher meals are the staple at the Second Avenue Kosher Delicatessen and Restaurant on the corner of 10th Street. And if you're hungry for something sweet, there's Veniero's on 11th Street, near First Avenue, where the Veniero family have been baking delicious Italian pastries since 1894.

East 10th Street is where you'll find everything from art galleries to drug dealers – even an old-world health club. The **Russian & Turkish Baths** has been offering steam baths and *platzas* (rub-downs with brooms made of oak leaves) since 1892. Newfangled additions include an exercise room and health bar, but they still have bunk beds where you can collapse after a particularly debilitating steam, as well as special ladies and men-only days.

The **Theater for the New City** on First Avenue was founded in 1971 as another venue for experimental Broad-

East 3rd Street.

way productions. Not far away, the lovely **St Nicholas** Carpatho-Russian Orthodox Greek Catholic Church is another reminder of this ethnic and religious melting pot. Originally built for a predominantly Anglican parish as St Mark's Chapel, its interior tiled walls and beamed ceiling date from 1894.

At 10th Street and Avenue A, you come to the top of **Tompkins Square Park**, a patch of reclaimed swamp used as a drill ground and recruiting camp during the Civil War. It was later the center of the *Kleine Deutschland* (Little Germany) community that thrived here more than a hundred years ago. Recently, Tompkins Square Park has been the focal point for an ongoing conflict between homeless activists and local police, the former creating instant communities of cardboard boxes, and the latter trying to clear them out.

Many of the homes in this area have been renovated by young professionals (the 19th-century row houses on 10th Street at the park's northern border are

a good example). This has also created tension between the haves and the have-nots, a group that includes African Americans, Latinos, aging hippies and neo-punk/anarchists.

Farther east on 10th, the neighborhood goes downhill – this is Alphabet City (Avenues A through D), home of housing projects, burned out cars, drug dealers and graffiti-covered walls. Strolling around, especially late at night, is not recommended, unless you're feeling adventurous. However, even the most bombed-out looking block occasionally reveals a new art gallery or performance-art bar; and sometimes a trendy new restaurant or two is tucked unexpectedly behind the drabbest of storefronts.

Walk through **Tompkins Square Park**, past the children's playground, and you're back on Avenue A – and right near the Odessa restaurant, another Eastern European neighborhood favorite where specialities include homecooked *pirogi*, *blintzes* and *borscht*. Next door at

Alphabets, you can buy T-shirts with logos like "New York – It Ain't Kansas." Nearby, the Pyramid Club is a dark bar famed for wild music and an eclectic clientele.

Nightlife in the East Village includes **CBGB-OMFUG**, on the Bowery, the club where the city's punk and new wave scene exploded in the 1970s; still a popular rock venue, it attracts a mixed crowd of uptown adventurers and hardcore downtown attitudes. (More upscale attitude is evident at newer hangouts like the nearby **Bowery Bar**.)

Though **the Bowery** is traditionally synonymous with Skid Row, this continuation of Fourth Avenue was lower Manhattan's "Great White Way" in the 1800s, when the street was lined by a dozen or more theaters. Today, the **Bouwerie Lane Theatre** in a handsome 1874 cast-iron building and the tiny, family-run **Amato Opera Theater** at Second Street, carry on the tradition.

THE LOWER EAST SIDE: This area technically starts east of Tompkins Square Park, where Avenue C becomes Losaida Avenue, but the traditional **Lower East Side**, with its Jewish roots firmly in place, is south of East Houston Street, bordered by the Bowery and the East River.

This is where bargain hunters flock for wholesale deals in everything from bridal gowns to bathroom fixtures, and where the narrow streets are lined by tenements that haven't changed much in the past 150 years.

Starting in the mid-19th century, successive waves of immigrants arrived here in pursuit of a new life: first free Africans, followed by Irish and Germans, and later by Eastern European Jews, mainly from Russia and Poland. These days you see stores with Jewish names and Chinese or Hispanic owners, a reminder that this neighborhood still attracts new arrivals to New York.

Walk along East Houston Street to the top of **Orchard Street** and you've reached New York's favorite **Sunday shopping bazaar** (stores close Friday

Lower East Side pickles are famous.

afternoons and all day Saturday for the Jewish sabbath). Once crowded with peddlers selling everything from old clothes to cracked eggs, today you can find designer clothes, jewelry and shoes at prices often half as much as uptown. Ron's Leather Center, for example, is where to go for snazzy bags and shoes.

The next street down is **Delancey**, named for the old New York De Lancey family, who lost their vast land holdings during the Revolution because of their Loyalist leanings. Between Delancey and Broome Streets is the old **Essex Street Market**, a red-brick building opened in 1938 as a way to keep peddlers off the streets.

For the best onion rolls in town stop in at Ratner's, or sit down to a memorable feast at **Sammy's Famous Roumanian Restaurant** at 175 Chrystie Street, just north of Delancey, where a traditional pitcher of chicken fat comes with every meal. Not far away, at **Katz's Delicatessen** on East Houston, the menu has hardly changed since it opened in 1898

Katz's Delicatessen.

– they make a pastrami sandwich that's considered a culinary landmark.

The corner of Hester and Essex Streets, on the other hand, offers the city's best pickle experience – namely **Essex Street Pickles** (formerly Hollander Pickle Products) where you'll find barrels filled with home-made, authentic pickles – the same kind featured a few years ago in the movie *Crossing Delancey*. After munching on one of these, stride up the block for a coffee at **Gertel's**, 53 Hester, a small bakeshop specializing in kosher pastries.

Walk west on Grand Street back to the Bowery and you'll come to the **Bowery Savings Bank**, an 1894 landmark designed by McKim, Mead and White in classic Roman-temple style.

The two-block stretch of the Bowery south of Delancey might be considered the lighting capital of the world, and possibly the best place in town to pick up a cheap chandelier. Nearby, the jewelry stores by the entrance to the **Manhattan Bridge** are all that remains

of a once-thriving downtown diamond district, which has since been transplanted to 47th Street. **Allen Street**, which runs parallel to Orchard, was well-known as a center for brass and copper antiques, and still has a couple of such shops.

History lives on: Grand Street's **Seward Park High School** counts actors Tony Curtis and Walter Matthau among its graduates. Sam Jaffe, another actor, was born in the tenement on Orchard Street that's been the **Lower East Side Tenement Museum** since 1988. In addition to a small gallery on the first floor, the museum offers neighborhood walking tours and historic dramatizations. You can also explore the bleak 1863 building's tiny upstairs apartments. The area's substandard working and living conditions (ably chronicled by journalist-reformer Jacob Riis) were instrumental in spawning various anarchist and socialist movements. Emma Goldman preached her gentle anarchism here, radical newspapers, such as the *Jewish Daily For-*

ward, flourished, and settlement houses offering immigrants health and education assistance were formed.

Some of them are still in operation, including the **University Settlement House** on Eldridge Street, and the **Henry Street Settlement**, founded in 1893 by Lillian Wald as the country's first volunteer nursing and social service center.

Religion also played an important role in the lives of immigrants and, though many of the old synagogues in the area are boarded up, the **Eldridge Street Synagogue**, a Moorish-style landmark close to Division Street, has been restored.

CHINATOWN: The largest Chinese-American settlement in the United States, as well as one of Manhattan's most vibrant and exciting neighborhoods to visit, **Chinatown** got its start in the 1870s, when Chinese railroad workers drifted east from California in the wake of rising anti-Asian sentiment. Reforms in US immigration laws have **Altered** caused a population boom, with the **eating.**

result that Chinatown – once squeezed into a three-block area bordered by Mott, Pell and the Bowery – now encompasses almost 40 blocks.

Chatham Square was named after William Pitt, the Earl of Chatham, and is where Worth Street, East Broadway and the Bowery meet. The **Kim Lau Memorial Arch** here was built in honor of a Chinese-American pilot who died a hero in World War II. Nearby, **Confucius Plaza** is a high-rise complex that includes apartments, shops, an elementary school, and an interior tree-shaded park. A bronze statue of the philosopher Confucius stands in front, facing Chatham Square.

Tucked away among the Chinese banks lining the Bowery is a remnant of Old New York: **No. 18 Bowery**, a Federal-style house built in 1785 and now the oldest surviving row house in Manhattan. Its original owner, Edward Mooney, was a wholesale meat merchant who dabbled in racehorses; ironically, in later years there was even an off-track betting parlor on the premises. Another interesting building on the Bowery worth noting is the pagoda-style **Manhattan Savings Bank**.

Walk west to **Columbus Park** and you're at the beginning of **Mulberry Street**, which, along with **Mott Street**, forms Chinatown's two main thoroughfares. In the early 19th century this area was part of the notorious Five Points slum region, where street gangs ran rampant and squatters' huts formed an equally notorious shanty town, later torn down to make way for the park.

The turn-of-the-century school building situated on the corner of Mulberry and Bayard Streets houses the **Chinatown History Museum**, the best place to learn more about the neighborhood. Founded in 1970, when the area's population began to explode, the Project sponsors walking tours by appointment and also runs a fascinating little museum and bookstore.

From here, walk past sidewalks thick with stands selling fruit, vegetables,

Death in Chinatown.

fish and leaf-wrapped packets of sticky rice, and turn right on **Canal Street**. Crowded with vendors hawking Taiwanese tapes, old men in conical hats reading fortunes, and shops stocked to the brim with imported goods, it's a scene that seems far from the rest of Manhattan. Turn right down Mott Street, and you'll notice shiny Singapore-style restaurants with marble facades and plastic signs, part of the "new" Chinatown built by recent, wealthier immigrants from Hong Kong and Taiwan.

Signs of the "old Chinatown" can also be found, including the **Chinese Community Center** run by the Chinese Consolidated Benevolent Association, which first opened on Mott Street in 1883. Next door, there's a multi-armed statue of the Goddess Kuan-Yui inside the **Eastern States Buddhist Temple**, where the air is thick with the scent of sickly sweet incense.

Nearby, **Quong Yuen Shing** opened as a general store in the 1890s. The oldest emporium in Chinatown, it's an interesting place to browse. Farther along, the **Church of the Transfiguration** was constructed for an English Lutheran congregation in 1801, became the Zion Protestant Episcopal Church in 1810, and was sold to the Roman Catholic Church in 1853. Today, it offers services in Cantonese and also runs a school for local children.

Heart of Old Chinatown: Turn right down **Pell Street** and you'll see the **Sun Wui District Association** across from the **First Chinese Baptist Church**. This type of organization afforded Chinese immigrants another means of coping with the new world they found themselves in. Unlike some of the other associations, this group constructed a more traditional-looking edifice, perhaps in an effort to combat homesickness. The pagoda roof is topped by two "good luck" ceramic fish.

Nearby is the headquarters of the Hip Sing Association, one of Chinatown's many *tongs*, or fraternal organizations. **Mott Street.**

From the 1870s until well into the 1930s, these groups were involved in often-violent disputes that were sensationalized as "*tong* wars", mainly by the non-Chinese press.

The narrow lane off to the right is the most crooked street in Manhattan; in the 1600s it was a cart path leading to Hendrik Doyer's brewery. Later, **Doyers Street** became an important communications center, where men gathered to get the latest news from China, and drop off letters and money for home with the small shopkeepers who served as combination banks and post offices.

In keeping with this tradition, the current Chinatown post office was built on the site of the old brewery. Just before it is the **Nom Wah Tea House**, the oldest restaurant in the neighborhood. Unlike many places in the area, this one generally closes early (around 8 p.m.), but it has some of the best *dim sum* in Chinatown. The interior is much the same as when it opened in 1921, with sagging red leather banquettes, linoleum floor, and ceiling fans. The prices are just as old-fashioned.

Food is one of the main attractions of Chinatown, and with hundreds of restaurants to choose from, the hardest part is making a decision about where to eat. Choices range from the tiny five-table Malaysia Restaurant in the **Chinatown Arcade** to the Silver Palace which seats 1,000. There's also the Golden Unicorn on East Broadway, where house specialities are served in a rather luxurious atmosphere, and the Peking Duck House on Mott Street, a favorite of former mayor Ed Koch.

For a taste of Chinese culture, drop in at one of the movie theaters that show films from Taiwan, Hong Kong and China, or visit the **Asian Arts Institute**, across from the Confucius Plaza complex, which features ongoing exhibits. Upstairs, the **Asian-American Dance Theater** presents both traditional and contemporary dance productions.

Chinese New Year combines feasts,

Chinese take-away.

dance and musical presentations. Traditionally, it begins with parades and fireworks in a noisy, crowded celebration held between the end of January and the beginning of February.

LITTLE ITALY: Crowds – along with a bevy of tantalizing food stalls and raucous games of chance – are an integral part of two annual festivals in this neighborhood: the Feast of St Anthony in early June, and the Feast of San Gennaro, in September. Otherwise, Little Italy is generally quieter than its Chinese neighbor, and its landmark status gives it some protection from developers. However, a major change occurred when a hotel, the Holiday Inn Downtown, opened in a renovated building on nearby Lafayette Street, a block north of Canal.

Wedged between Chinatown and SoHo, this area has been an Italian enclave since the late 1800s, when large numbers of immigrants arrived in New York from Italy, and many of the local restaurants and bakeries date from that

time. The most pleasant bit is along **Mulberry Street**, north of Canal, where the atmosphere changes suddenly from boisterous to almost mellow, and the sidewalks are lined by cafés and social clubs rather than clamorous street vendors.

As in Chinatown, most outsiders come here for food or festivals, but there are some historic surprises along the way. **Luna's**, on Mulberry, is a longtime favorite, a reasonably priced restaurant that's been run by the same family since 1878.

On the corner of Hester Street, **Umberto's Clam House** stays open until 6am but its biggest claim to fame is as the place where gangster Joey Gallo met an abrupt and bloody end in 1972 while having dinner with his family. **Puglia** on Hester Street is another neighborhood standby which has been around since 1919.

Keep walking north on Mulberry, past the headquarters of the Society of San Gennaro (a statue of the saint sits in

the window), and you come to one of the oldest houses in Little Italy. Now **Paolucci's Restaurant**, where strolling violinists entertain during dinner, the small white Federal-style house was built for Stephen Van Renssellaer, a well-to-do New Yorker, in 1816. Originally located at 153 Mulberry Street, the entire house was moved to its present site in 1841.

At the corner of Mulberry and Grand, you can browse through the gifts, novelties and religious relics sold at E. Rossi & Co., before sampling some of the famous products of **Ferrara**, a pastry shop since 1892.

Di Palo's on Grand is a great place for take-out cheese and salami. Alleva, at Mulberry and Grand, is even better. Nearby, the **Police Building** on Centre Street, an elaborate Beaux-Arts structure that dates from 1909, was police headquarters until 1973, and was recently divided up into expensive apartments. A reminder of the building's former use can be found just to the north on Broome Street where a small shop sells police equipment and advertises a "gunsmith on the premises."

Old **St Patrick's Cathedral**, on the corner of Mott and Prince Streets, was the seat of the New York archdiocese until 1879 (when the "new" St Patrick's Cathedral on Fifth Avenue was completed). Construction on the Cathedral began in 1809, was interrupted by the War of 1812, and was eventually finished in 1815. It was rebuilt in 1868 after being destroyed by fire – and remains, if less impressive than the original, a unique landmark on Little Italy's northern fringes.

Across Mott Street from the cathedral's graveyard, there's a small plaque on the wall of a Victorian building. Now apartments, this was the **School of the Children's Aid Society**, for the care and education of neighborhood immigrant children. A handsome, red-brick building, it was designed by Calvert Vaux in 1888, the architect who also helped to create Central Park.

Left, Italian activities. **Right**, flower of the Orient.

SOHO AND TRIBECA

Thirty years after the first artists moved into industrial lofts, SoHo is still one of Manhattan's most stimulating neighborhoods. Cast-iron warehouses house high-tech galleries and cobblestone streets are lined by glossy boutiques and restaurants.

When Abraham Lincoln made his first campaign speech at nearby Cooper Union, this was the center of the city's fashionable shopping and hotel district, but by the end of the 19th century most of the old houses were torn down in order to make way for factories whose imaginative facades hid sweatshop conditions so appalling that the city fire department later dubbed the area "Hell's Hundred Acres."

The area was almost razed to make way for an expressway, but in the early 1960s conservationists got the city to protect these elaborate "temples of industry" by establishing the SoHo Cast Iron Historic District. Around the same time local artists discovered it was an ideal place to live and work.

Now too expensive for all but the very successful, SoHo, an acronym for **So**uth of **Ho**uston, is bordered by **Canal Street** to the south, **Lafayette Street** to the east, and the **Avenue of the Americas** to the west. The area is still a uniquely New York combination of industrial grit and flair, where brawny men unload trucks next to futuristic video displays.

West Broadway: The kind of street where you might see a living statue posed in one window, or a talkative red parrot staked outside another, **West Broadway** is lined by stores that offer everything from Japanese suits to Ecuadoran sandals – and on Saturdays (in particular) is packed with crowds of uptown and out-of-town tourists. Just below West Houston Street, you'll find a clutch of boutiques hawking French fashion and Italian footwear, as well as a bracing dose of imported attitude. Farther along, there's a wide selection of color-coordinated household goods at **Ad Hoc** – and an even larger choice of enormous toothbrushes, pencils, and other overscaled ordinary objects at **Think Big**. Drop in and browse the book selection at the narrow-fronted **Rizzoli** – or walk around the corner to Spring Street Books, one of the city's best independent literary outlets.

More than anything, you can find art galleries. At last count, there were more than 140 in the immediate vicinity, making SoHo gallery hopping an endurance as well as a cultural marathon. Most are pretty crowded on Saturdays, so weekdays may be the least hectic time to explore them. A good place to start is **420 West Broadway**, home to some of SoHo's most important galleries, including Leo Castelli, one of the first dealers to move downtown (and the first to represent Roy Lichtenstein, Willem de Kooning and Andy Warhol). Nearby, the **Mary Boone Gallery**, in a

Preceding **pages**: would you buy a used car from this man? **Left**, Vesuvio Bakery. **Right**, key to the city.

small yellow brick storefront, is another prestigious space with exhibits by the art world's *crème de la crème* – not far from the Dia Center for the Arts gallery, where Walter De Maria's *The Broken Kilometer* (rows of polished brass rods) has been on exhibit for several years.

Some of SoHo's **best galleries** are located on the side streets that branch off West Broadway, including **Prince Street**. Louver New York, for instance, can be found in a renovated former bakery at **No. 130**. A more permanent art installation can be viewed on the Greene Street side of 114 Prince Street, a turn-of-the-last-century building whose cast-iron facade has been reproduced there in a *trompe l'oeil* mural by artist Richard Haas.

Stop and shop for French ready-to-wear at Agnes B.'s downtown store, or take a coffee break across the way at the Dean & DeLuca café, located in an 1895 warehouse between Greene and Wooster Streets. The original site of Dean & DeLuca's famed gourmet gro-cery store (since moved to lower Broadway), it's now an airy, palm-filled atrium with counter-service breakfast and lunch.

Two other good places on this street for meals include the diner-style Jerry's, a local, not too expensive favorite; and **Fanelli's**, a landmark neighborhood bar and restaurant that's been standing on the corner of Mercer Street since the 1890s.

Greene Street: Named after a Revolutionary War general, **Greene Street** runs parallel to West Broadway. In the late 19th century it was the center of New York's most notorious red-light district, where brothels with names like Flora's and Miss Lizzie's flourished behind shuttered windows. An 1824 red-brick Federal-style survivor of the wicked old days still stands at **139 Greene Street**, just across from the **Pace Gallery**'s SoHo branch.

As befits one of the SoHo Cast Iron Historic District's prime thoroughfares, Greene Street also offers a rich concen-

Duck under glass.

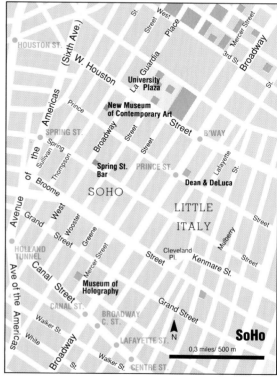

tration of this uniquely American architecture at its best, including (at the Canal Street end) the city's longest continuous row of cast-iron buildings. At the corner of **Broome Street**, the **1872 Gunther Building** houses **SoHo 20**, a women's cooperative art gallery where past exhibits have concentrated on issues like the civil rights movement and South African apartheid.

Further along Greene, you'll find a mind-boggling array of classic Wurlitzer jukeboxes at Back Pages Antiques. Before continuing onwards, stop and admire the cream-coloured "king" (architecturally-speaking) of cast-iron splendor at **72-76 Greene Street** just opposite. It's an impressively ornate structure designed by Isaac Duckworth and built in 1873.

It looks like another antique store, but 5 & 10 No Exaggeration is really a quirky, cluttered restaurant where everything's for sale – the only place in the city, according to the owner, with both a liquor and an antique dealer's license.

In the mid-1800s, the fashionable American House Hotel stood at the corner of Spring Street and West Broadway, across from where the just as fashionable **Spring Street Bar and Restaurant** stands today. And, though the ghost of a young girl found murdered near the spring that once flowed here has been known to haunt neighboring waterbeds, this central SoHo wayfare is particularly lively.

Across from the informal **flea market** on the corner of Spring and Wooster is a white clapboard and brick house built in 1818, now Tennessee Mountain, a popular rib joint. The entrance is round the corner on Wooster Street and there's a nice view of Soho's weekend action from the second-floor windows.

Turn onto stone-cobbled **Wooster Street** for another group of galleries, including Tony Shafrazi, which like many SoHo art spaces seems to hop from street to street in search of the perfect long-term lease. A few have managed to anchor themselves at the

Art entrepreneur Leo Castelli.

same spot for years, however, including **Printed Matter**, a wholesale and retail specialist in books by artists, and the **Paula Cooper Gallery**, farther up Wooster toward West Houston. The same block is home to *New York Earth Room*, another Walter de Maria installation, at the **Dia Center for the Arts** Wooster Street gallery.

On the block of Wooster that stretches between Prince and Spring Streets, you'll find minimalist display areas as an art form (along with clothes as art on display) at the stylish **Comme des Garçons**. And near the corner of Grand Street, the **Performing Garage** is home to its own theatrical company and has presented experimental theater, dance and performance art since 1967.

Broadway and beyond: Continue east on Spring Street to **lower Broadway**, once home to the city's most elegant shops, and more recently inhabited by textile outlets, discount stores and Spanish delis. As SoHo expanded, this stretch of stately cast-iron structures has

reacquired cachet, as more new stores, galleries and restaurants move in.

The **New Museum of Contemporary Art** may have paved the way when it relocated from lower Fifth Avenue to Broadway between Houston and Prince Streets in 1983. Since then, it's become the best place in Manhattan to find out what's new on the art horizon. Exhibits focus on everything from recent social and political issues to television's influence on society. The **Alternative Museum** at 594 Broadway is another cutting-edge exhibition space worth visiting, as is the **Museum for African Art**, across the street at No. 593.

Opposite the **Little Singer Building**, a 1904 cast-iron confection designed by Ernest Flagg, the $3 million **Dean & Deluca** store at the corner of Prince Street is filled with a cornucopia of fruits, vegetables and imported gourmet grocery specialities; there's also a stand-up coffee bar stocked with mouthwatering pastries. Upstairs, each floor has several important galleries.

An even more important venue is the **Guggenheim Museum's SoHo branch**, which opened at 575 Broadway in 1992. The building was constructed in 1881 and 1882 for John Jacob Astor III, on the site of the Astor family's original estate office. It was designed by the architect Thomas Stent, who worked extensively with the Astor family at the time. Now transformed into two floors of minimalist exhibition space, even the entranceway feels auspicious: from Broadway, you pass through the museum store and walk across a blackened raw-steel bridge hung by stainless steel cable railings.

Walk east on Prince Street to **Lafayette Street**, and you're at the northern fringe of Little Italy, where misplaced New York can, literally, be purchased at Lost City Arts, a store that sells discarded gargoyles, street signs and other romantic remnants. To the north, across from the Pop Shop, where late artist Keith Haring's vibrant work is displayed on reasonably-priced T- **The Puck Building.**

shirts, hats and condom holders, the **Puck Building** was home to *Spy* magazine – an appropriate locale considering it was built in 1886 as headquarters for the equally satirical *Puck*. Golden imps hang mischievously over the entrances.

To experience art with a child's eye, head back toward Broadway along Spring Street, where (at No. 72) the **Children's Museum of the Arts** offers creative play space, interactive exhibits and a great little gift shop. Across the street, you can take classes in everything from Middle Eastern drumming to dream interpretation at the **New York Open Center**, a non-profit holistic learning center that sponsors full-moon meditations and Saturday night "open dances." Drop in for a catalogue.

Not far from the rare "bishop's-crook" lamppost unceremoniously draped with No-Standing signs in front of 515 Broadway, the Palazzo-style **Haughwout Building** is one of SoHo's oldest – and most striking – cast-iron edifices. Designed by John Gaynor, it

was constructed in 1857 as one of the country's first retail stores, complete with the country's first elevator. Today, the second floor SoHo Mill Outlet is the best place around for inexpensive sheets, blankets and other bedding.

Cast-iron stomachs: John Broome was a successful merchant who imported tea and silk from China at the end of the Revolutionary War, but the stretch of Broome Street from Broadway to West Broadway is one of SoHo's least jazzed-up thoroughfares, with dental repair services and textile businesses housed behind decaying cast-iron facades alongside galleries, antique shops, and a combination pet store/human deli called Little Arf 'n Annie. Among the more interesting buildings here is the ornate Calvert Vaux-designed edifice at No. 448, built in 1872.

Turn onto Mercer Street to reach The Enchanted Forest, a whimsically decorated fantasy of toys and children's games. (Lately this nondescript, narrow thoroughfare, named for a Scottish sur-

SoHo espresso.

THE SOHO ART SCENE

BandMental is a rocking, danceable band that "kicks Captain Beefheart's ass a little." Their lyrics are hard-hitting political statements and their shows benefit most from grandiose performance spaces like the Anchorage at the Brooklyn Bridge, on the Brooklyn side.

For band members Liliana Luboya and Dave Hatchett, BandMental is a significant obsession, but not a full-time one. When not fronting BandMental gigs, Lil is a science fiction comic strip writer and underground clothes designer; but mainly, she is a painter. When you ask how she first got noticed as a painter, she is sublimely nebulous. "I don't know," she says. "I come from an artistic family. I've never done the artist's hustle, I've just been an artist all my life." Lil is from Hawaii.

Dave, BandMental's chief lyricist, puts most of his time into sculpting. But he was first recognized for his painting by collector Seymour Knox, who invited Dave to exhibit at the museum he founded, called the Albright-Knox.

Dave moved permanently to SoHo in 1971. He met Lil at a local group show. They live in a loft which is both home and showspace, a set-up that is an utter rarity now. When they moved in, SoHo was a wasteland of abandoned warehouses. When artists showed interest in them, landlords were glad to have their derelict properties occupied, despite the fact that they were zoned for commercial use only.

Dating from 1805, Dave and Lil's apartment building on Canal Street features in a landmark court case highlighting why artists aren't getting into SoHo any more. In 1980 their building was designated for certified resident artists only.

But many non-artists, once they saw SoHo was habitable, moved into protected buildings under false pretences (the easiest way was to present a bunch of sham slides of "their" work). Prices rose precipitously. After the late 1970s, according to Dave, genuine artists couldn't afford loft space.

Landlords now want to root out long-term residents and sell lofts at current market values, but the artist-resident clause bars their way – hence the court case. (Peak loft spaces now hover around $400,000. In the 1960s and early '70s, an entire building could be bought – as artist Jeffrey Lew found with the 112 Greene Street artists' space – for $25,000.)

In SoHo today, both real estate and art seem to have suffered the same syndrome. If investors don't care for what they buy but are simply following a trend, values will bloat, then collapse.

SoHo real estate investors may never recoup their losses. But in the art world, after the end of a decade of greedy buying by dilettante investors, the window has been left open for the reclaiming of values, which, according to Dave, is the spirit of the 1990s. Near the beginning of this decade, signs were contradictory. Overall, the art market was quiet, although sales of work by artists like Van Gogh were still breaking records. Bold leads were also taken by museums like the Guggenheim, which sold three masterpieces – by Chagall, Kadinsky, and Modigliani – to raise capital for a new collection of American Minimalists.

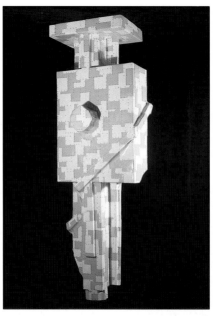

What the trickle-down effect will be on the downtown art scene and how values will be reclaimed at street level is a question mark, which will probably remain until the end of the century. One reason is that, with radical revamping of values, newer movements will remain in embryonic form for some time; another is that it's now much more difficult to get a reading on the New York art world because it's so dispersed. Once SoHo prices became prohibitive, artists scattered to more affordable surrounding areas – Brooklyn, New Jersey, and Long Island City.

The exodus was stopped for a while with the movement to contiguous areas like the East Village (home to an enclave of Norwegians living on arts stipends from their own government), and TriBeCa. But, wherever artists moved in and fixed up derelict space, the rest of New York soon followed. As in SoHo, the creative people were rapidly priced out of the very neighborhoods they'd brought back to life.

If Dave and Lil's building and others like it can be reclaimed for creative purposes, SoHo may once again become a place to find artists – not just art galleries. ∎

geon who became a general in the Revolutionary War, has experienced a mini-Renaissance that includes the construction of SoHo's first loft-style hotel.)

If you're starved for lunch, stay on Broome Street until you reach the corner of West Broadway, and the Broome Street Bar. Located in an 18th-century house, this relaxed hangout is also open for brunch and dinner (no credit cards accepted). Next door, the friendly Cupping Room Café specializes in breakfast, but offers lunch and dinner too.

The **Manhattan Brewing Co.**, across West Broadway at the corner of Thompson Street, opened several years ago in this abandoned Con Edison plant and serves home-brewed beers and ales, along with meals, in the noisy second-floor tap room.

Turn right on Thompson Street – which runs parallel to West Broadway – and you're on the fringe of the "South Village," where in between chic little shoe salons and boutiques you find, on Prince Street, places like the tiny

Vesuvio Bakery, run by the same family since the 1920s, and **Milady's**, a recently shined-up neighborhood bar and restaurant that's been around for 40 years, has a pool table in back, and "serves the best home fries in town" (they say). For some of the best *escargots* in town, pay a visit to **Raoul's**, a cool-and-pricey bistro favored by a hip, international crowd.

If your taste runs to something hotter and you've got the stamina, turn onto Spring at the Thompson Street playground and walk several blocks west to the **New York City Fire Museum** between Varick and Hudson Streets. It's worth the hike to the former Engine Company No. 30 headquarters to see the 15 antique hand- and horse-pulled wagons, colonial firemen's hats and cumbersome old extinguishers.

Canal Street has been called New York's attic and can be a bewildering experience for the uninitiated – especially the blocks west of Broadway, where stores sell plastic odds and ends,

Paper, bags
sugar, wax...

rubber tubing, neon signs, household appliances, and barrels of nondescript industrial leftovers. It's all mixed together in a bedlam of hot dog carts and street vendors displaying old books, new cassettes and, on occasion, genuine treasures.

For creative types, Canal Street is an endless source of "found art," bits and pieces that can be used for sculpture, collage or decorating a loft. For others, it's the place to go for car radios (installed at the curbside) and the kind of hardware necessities difficult to find in uptown stores.

TRIBECA: By the late 1970s, adventurous artists seeking cheaper rents moved south from SoHo to **TriBeCa**, a section of the Lower West Side known as Washington Market when the city's major produce business was conducted here. The market has since moved to Hunts Point in the Bronx.

TriBeCa, the **Tri**angle **Be**low **Ca**nal which lies south of Canal Street to Chambers Street, and west from Broad-

way to the Hudson, is quieter than SoHo and is also one of Manhattan's fastest-growing neighborhoods. It's an eclectic combination of renovated warehouses and new condominiums. What TriBeCa lacks in the shopping department it makes up for in innovative art galleries and hip new clubs and restaurants.

To find out what's new on the New York art scene, walk south on West Broadway to **White Street**, where the brick house on the north corner has survived since 1809.

Although the **Alternative Museum** – the country's first museum founded by artists – moved "uptown" from White Street to lower Broadway (where it continues to present exhibits with a provocative social and political slant), **Artist Space** at 223 West Broadway still offers a unique TriBeCa focus on contemporary visual art. Laurie Anderson, Cindy Sherman and David Salle, among others, got their start here, and there's a regular series of video screenings as well as special evening events.

Half a block after the ersatz Statue of Liberty crown that peeks dramatically from the top of El Teddy's restaurant, turn left on Franklin Street, where **Franklin Furnace** is a combination museum-and-archive for "book works" created by artists. This is also one of the most important – and controversial – downtown venues for avant-garde performances and installations, many of which utilize the printed word as an artistic medium.

From West Broadway, walk east on **Leonard Street** to Broadway, past some of TriBeCa's finest cast-iron architecture, and you'll see the former New York Life Insurance Building looming ahead, topped by an ornate clock tower. Remodeled by Stanford White in 1898, the building has belonged to the city since the late 1960s and now houses various municipal offices as well as the **Clocktower Gallery**. Enter at 108 Leonard Street, then take the elevator up to the 12th floor – the gallery is up a flight of stairs, at the

The glowing words of the Constitution.

240

end of a hallway lined by artists' studios, and offers some of the best views of downtown New York to be had anywhere in the city.

Produce to pâté: On the corner of Thomas Street and West Broadway, a red neon sign spells out "Cafeteria," but this 1930s mock-stone building has been one of downtown's hippest restaurants since 1980, when the eaterie, actually called The Odeon, first opened. Unlike other trendy spots, however, this one shows no signs of fading away and is still a favorite with the *cognoscenti*, especially late at night.

Across the street, you may want to browse through the city's largest collection of charts, maps and sailing accessories at the **New York Nautical Instruments and Service Corps**, a store that's been serving the sea-going public since 1910, before turning right on Duane Street.

Named after New York's first post-Revolution mayor, **Duane Street** meets Hudson Street at tiny triangular **Duane**

Park – all that's left of a farm the city bought for $5 in 1795. Alongside the **New York Egg Auction** building, a remnant of the area's once-thriving egg and butter market, you'll find million-dollar lofts in converted warehouses and **Bouley**, one of New York's best and most romantic restaurants.

Staple Street, a narrow strip of cobblestone where "staple" produce was once unloaded, connects the park with the ornate red-brick **Mercantile Exchange Building**, on the corner of Harrison and Hudson Streets. Built in 1884 as the trading center for the egg and butter business (but now offices), the ground floor is home to the decidedly upscale **Chanterelle**, another TriBeCa temple of Gallic cuisine.

The neighboring **Western Union Building** on Hudson soars 24 stories above the rest of the neighborhood like a layered missile and is made of 19 different shades of brick. Its interior lobby, where even the letterboxes are marvels of Art Deco artistry, is equally

Match me, Sidney.

breathtaking. This route makes for a diverting short cut if you're heading back to West Broadway.

Nearby, Puffy's Tavern on Hudson is a former speakeasy that serves down-to-earth steak and kidney pie and has an unpretentious atmosphere that attracts artists, truck drivers and downtown *literati* until 4am each morning. Even more down-to-earth is McGovern's on Reade Street, another late-night bar favored by local artists and working folk, and one of the few places which still has sawdust strewn on the floor.

If you walk west on Franklin from either West Broadway or Hudson you'll pass Riverrun, a pleasant, reasonably priced restaurant that's been around since 1979. You'll also reach the corner of Greenwich Street, where actor Robert De Niro recently transformed the ramshackle Martinson Coffee Factory into the **TriBeCa Film Center**. Whether the ground-floor **TriBeCa Grill**, co-owned by De Niro and a group of fellow actors, will outlast its initial

success remains to be seen – but you may want to stop for lunch and find out.

Old and new: Greenwich Street is where much of TriBeCa's new condominium and office developments are centered, but you can still find some authentic early remnants – like the row of late 18th and early 19th-century brick houses on **Harrison Street**, standing like a stage set in the shadow of Independence Plaza's three gargantuan 1970s towers.

A block farther down, on the other side of the street, is the Old World ambience of **Bazzini's**, a fruit and nut wholesaler since 1886, whose retail outlet sells tempting 5-lb bags of pistachios and other delicacies.

Across from a block-long stretch of upscale condo dwellings, **Washington Market Park** was (until recently) TriBeCa's only real recreation area, where there's a thick grassy meadow to stretch out on, a fountain to splash in, and even a fanciful gazebo to daydream in. Turn right on **Chambers Street** and right again to the entrance of the Borough of Manhattan Community College, in a sprawling southern extension of Independence Plaza.

The **Triplex Theater** opened here in 1984 as downtown Manhattan's largest performance space. It has three separate venues for multi-cultural productions, which are scheduled each year from September to June.

The imaginative Public School 234, its ironwrought fence embossed with Spanish galleons in full sail, is one indication of TriBeCa's transformation into a family neighborhood. The Stuyvesant High School is another. Even newer is the 8-acre **Hudson River Park** – part of Battery Park City's northernmost development – that stretches along the water's edge. A pedestrian bridge connects TriBeCa's southern boundaries with this development. Or keep walking south on West Street to reach lower Manhattan's World Trade Center, and the World Financial Center's soaring atrium, the Winter Garden.

Left, climb every mountain. **Right**, I ♥ NY.

242

LOWER MANHATTAN

"Manhattan crowds, with their turbulent musical chorus! Manhattan faces and eyes forever for me."
    – Walt Whitman, from *Song of Myself*

Below Chambers Street to the west and the Brooklyn Bridge to the east is the original New York, where the Dutch and later the English first settled, the country's first hotel was built, the first president was sworn in, and the city's first theatrical opening night took place.

Clipper ships bound for the California gold rush sailed from lower Manhattan's East River piers in the 1850s; by 1895, the first skyscraper stood 20 stories above lower Broadway. Today, the city's financial and city government areas provide a staid contrast to lively developments like South Street Seaport and the Winter Garden in the World Financial Center – and Manhattan's oldest neighborhood is quickly becoming the city's newest weekend hangout.

Earliest New York: At the island's tip, **Battery Park** is where New York's history (and geography) began. Named for the battery of protective cannons that once stood here, it's a green oasis at the harbor's edge, with spectacular views of the **Statue of Liberty**.

Walk from the top of the park down to **Castle Clinton**, a reddish stone building that was once a fort. Originally it stood 200 feet offshore as a defense against the British in the War of 1812. Renamed Castle Garden in 1824, it became the city's premier place of amusement, where Samuel Morse gave his first public telegraph demonstration and Swedish singer Jenny Lind made her American debut in a tumultuously acclaimed concert in 1850 (to which some wealthy New Yorkers paid a then unheard-of $30 a ticket).

Not long after, it was joined to the mainland by landfill and served as the New York State Immigration Station, where more than eight million immigrants were processed between 1855 and 1890. For two years, potential settlers were processed on a barge moored in the Hudson River, but when the new headquarters opened on Ellis Island in 1892, the tide of immigration shifted. Site of the New York Aquarium until 1941, Castle Clinton was declared a national monument in 1950 – and opened to the public in 1975. Today it's run by the National Park Service, and houses an exhibition area, an information kiosk, and the ticket booth for the Statue of Liberty/Ellis Island ferries.

Exit through the back and you're on the **Admiral Dewey Promenade**, which runs along the water from the endearingly ramshackle Marine Company No. 1 building (a fireboat station built in 1886) on Pier A at the end of West Street to the Coast Guard Station at the park's eastern corner.

Walking along the promenade, you pass several monuments, including one to Giovanni da Verrazano, who sailed

past here in 1524 (85 years before the arrival of Henry Hudson and the Dutch West India Company), and the **East Coast War Memorial**, eight tombstone-shaped slabs of concrete engraved with the names of men who died in World War II Atlantic Ocean battles. Not far away, there's a wall plaque, hidden in a corner of the park's beer garden and snack bar; it honors John Wolfe Ambrose, planner of the Ambrose sea channel "whose vision... and courage ended in making New York the greatest seaport of the world."

Early immigrants: East of Battery Park, **Peter Minuit Plaza** is named for the first governor (director general) of New Amsterdam – but in a tiny park nearby, another plaque commemorates some of the city's lesser-known arrivals: 23 Sephardic Jews dropped off by a French ship in 1654, who founded New Amsterdam's (and the country's) first Jewish congregation. Their graveyard is located south of Chinatown, at the corner of Oliver Street and St James Place.

Turn left on State Street, once lined by wealthy merchants' houses, and you come to the last 18th-century mansion still standing – the **Rectory of the Shrine of the Blessed Elizabeth Ann Seton**, the first American-born saint. The chapel located next door contains a statue of this very woman who, in 1809, founded the Sisters of Charity, and was canonized in 1975.

New York novelist Herman Melville was born in a house near 17 State Street, where a shiny modern high-rise now stands. Across from the equally-shiny Bowling Green subway station is the former **US Custom House**, designed by Cass Gilbert and opened in 1907 on the spot where Fort Amsterdam stood from 1626 to 1787. A magnificent example of Beaux-Arts architecture, with a facade embellished by ornate limestone sculpture representing the four continents and "eight" races of mankind, it has striking Reginald Marsh murals inside on the rotunda ceiling.

In a somewhat ironic development – **City Hall Park.**

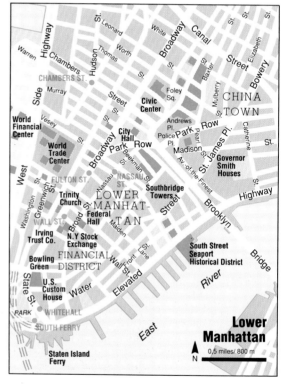

Lower Manhattan

0,5 miles/ 800 m

considering that Bowling Green Park, right across from the entrance, is where Peter Minuit "purchased" Manhattan from local Native Americans for $24 – the Custom House houses the George Gustav Heye Center of the **National Museum of the American Indian**.

Back on State Street, turn north on Pearl Street, one of the city's oldest byways. Not far away, **Hanover Square** (the city's smartest shopping center in the mid-to-late 18th century) burned to ashes in the Great Fire of 1835, one of many fires that virtually destroyed all remnants of Dutch New Amsterdam. According to an eyewitness in Brooklyn, "the sparks from that fire came over the river so thick that the neighbors... were obliged to keep their roofs wet all night."

Happily, the square made a complete recovery, to become a thriving commercial center again. You have to be a member to dine at **India House**, an 1850s Italianate brownstone that's been home to a private club for maritime movers and shakers since 1914, but anyone can drop in for a bit of refreshment at Harry's on Hanover Square, right underneath.

Another popular eating place is **Fraunces Tavern**, at the corner of Pearl and Broad Streets. It's actually a 1907 reconstruction of the old Queens Head Tavern run by Samuel Fraunces in the late 1700s, where the New York Chamber of Commerce got its start over a few mugs of ale and where George Washington gave an emotional farewell address to his troops in 1783. The tavern and four adjacent 19th-century buildings house a **museum** that offers the curious a look at a lock of Washington's hair, a fragment of one of his teeth, and a shoe that belonged to his wife Martha – along with a regular schedule of films, lectures and changing exhibits. The museum is often closed on weekends, so check before visiting.

NY's financial heart: Nowhere else in the city can you find the same concentration of power and money as in lower

Legal eagle.

Manhattan. Though some firms have moved their headquarters uptown, this is still the traditional center of city commerce, where narrow stone canyons are lined by towering banks, brokerage houses and law offices.

Until recently, captains of industry could dine at **Delmonico's** on Beaver Street just as they had since the mid-1800s, when two Swiss brothers established the city's first formal French restaurant here. The end of an era came when this, the city's earliest example of power dining, finally closed – but you can still admire the impressive marble portico, supposedly brought over from Pompeii.

Walk north on William Street to **Wall Street**, where in the 1600s there really was a wall – or, more accurately, a wooden stockade built by the Dutch as protection against the threat of Indian and British attacks. The privateer Captain William Kidd and his wife lived in a house at **56 Wall Street**, and the country's first stock exchange began

just in front of **60 Wall Street** in 1792, when 24 brokers gathered beneath a buttonwood tree.

The present **New York Stock Exchange** building was constructed at the corner of Wall and Broad Streets in 1903. Although fronted by an impressive facade of Corinthian columns, the building seems smaller than its status would imply. There's a **Visitors' Gallery** that's open on weekdays, and admission is free. The **American Stock Exchange**, a few blocks away, has a more secretive members-only policy.

Across the street, the Greek temple-style **Federal Hall National Memorial** is also open to the public on weekdays, though the visitors' entrance is around the corner on Pine Street. Built on the site of the original Federal Hall where George Washington was sworn in as the first President of the United States, it later became a branch of the US Treasury. Today, the suit George wore to his inauguration can be seen inside, along with other historical memorabilia. Occasional concerts are also staged here.

Renowned as the legendary site of high-diving bankers in the crash of 1929 (and of more recent insider trading scandals), Wall Street can also claim to be one of the first publicly-lit streets in the country. The marble-sided **Morgan Guaranty Trust** at Wall Street stands on the site of the former Drexel-Morgan building, where Thomas Edison turned on the lights, supplied by a commercial generating station, in 1882. Nearby is the city's first **Bank of New York**, established in 1784 by Alexander Hamilton, the country's first Secretary of the Treasury, who lived in a house at **33 Wall Street** and who was later killed in an ill-fated duel with his arch-rival Aaron Burr.

If you keep walking north on **William Street** (its twists and turns redolent of the days when it was known as Horse and Cart Street), you'll reach **Nevelson Plaza**, a narrow urban breathing space inhabited by a cluster of seven tall abstract sculptures by the late **Easy street.**

Louise Nevelson, a long-time New York resident. Nearby, **more sculpture** (including works by Isamu Nogachi and Jean Dubuffet) graces the pedestrian plaza in front of the Chase Manhattan Bank, an 800-ft tower between Pine and Liberty Streets.

Money may not be art, but there sure is a lot of it at the **Federal Reserve Bank** on Liberty Street, just west of Nevelson Plaza. Constructed in 1924, this appropriately imposing edifice houses an equally imposing amount of the world's gold, as well as virtual wheelbarrows full of old and counterfeit cash. Tours are available, but you have to book a week ahead. Nearby, the elegant Beaux-Arts building at Liberty Street housed the **Chamber of Commerce** of the State of New York until 1980; it was built in 1901.

A spiritual oasis: At the very top of Wall Street, where it meets Broadway, the neo-Gothic **Trinity Church** is a serene survivor of early New York. First established in 1698 (when its char-

ter included the rights to all unclaimed shipwrecks and beached whales found in the vicinity), the present 1846 church is the third one built on the same site. The three bronze doors at the entrance were donated by William Waldorf Astor (John Jacob Astor's great-grandson). The church's graveyard contains the city's oldest graves, including Alexander Hamilton's. Public recitals and concerts are held at Trinity on a regular basis, and the adjoining museum offers a look at the original charter, among other artifacts.

Behind the church, the **Trinity Bookstore** is a good place to find books on theology and religion.

Five blocks north on Broadway, George Washington's personal church pew is still preserved at **St Paul's Chapel**, part of the Trinity Church Parish and Manhattan's oldest public building in continuous use. Built in 1766, this Georgian-style national landmark is the only church left from the colonial era, when luminaries like

Money talks.

Prince William (later William IV) and Lord Cornwallis worshipped here. The interior, where 14 Waterford chandeliers hang from a pastel-green ceiling, is also a popular venue for recitals.

Though not exactly spiritual, the gargoyle-topped **Woolworth Building** on Broadway was known, in its heyday, as the "cathedral of commerce." From 1913 until 1930, when the Chrysler Building was completed, it was also the tallest building in the world. Designed by Cass Gilbert, the Gothic Revival edifice cost five-and-dime baron Frank Woolworth $13 million, and was officially opened by President Woodrow Wilson, who pushed a button in Washington that successfully lit up all 51 floors. Take a walk around the marble-encrusted lobby and admire the sculptural detail of Woolworth counting nickels, or take the elevator to the 24th floor, where access to a 27th-floor office, now a tiny shrine to his rags-to-riches success story, is sometimes granted on weekdays.

Turn left onto Barclay Street and walk to the corner of Church Street to see the granite-and-colonnaded **Old St Peter's Church**, New York's oldest Catholic parish. Farther south on Church Street, you'll spot a small white building stranded in the middle of a parking lot between Cedar and Liberty Streets. Built as a tavern in 1832, it's been the **Hellenic Orthodox Church of St Nicholas** since 1920, when this area was an enclave of Middle Eastern immigrants.

Best view in town: The Twin Towers of the **World Trade Center** rise 110 stories into the city sky like parallel lines of stainless-steel. The towers are the most photographed part of this 16-acre, seven-building complex that took 17 years, 200,000 tons of steel and 425,000 cubic yards of cement to build – enough for a sidewalk all the way to Washington DC. They also attract more than a million visitors each year.

In early 1993, a terrorist bomb exploded in the car park, killing several office workers. Security has improved now, and the crowds keep on coming. Most come to ride the ear-popping express elevators to the **107th-floor Observation Deck** or to admire the even more spectacular view from the rooftop promenade. Both are open seven days a week, but there's usually a line of thrill-seekers winding right around the lobby, so try to get there early in the day.

You can dine in lofty splendor at **Windows on the World** (One World Trade Center), browse through an exhibit on what not to bring into the country at the **US Customs Service** (Six World Trade Center), or even get lost while shopping in the underground concourse beneath it all. Then wander around the Trade Center's central **Austin J. Tobin Plaza**, which in warm months is packed with office workers having lunch or enjoying free noontime concerts and performances. Stop and admire the huge sculptures (including Fritz Koenig's 25-ft high *Globe*, and James Rosati's *Ideogram*), which – along

Reflections on lower Manhattan.

with their spectators – are dwarfed by the surrounding heights.

If you walk through the Plaza to Three World Trade Center, or around to West Street, you'll come to the **New York Vista Hotel**. When this handsome 22-story structure opened in 1981, it was the first hotel to be built here since 1836, when the rich and powerful booked rooms at the Astor House or the Great Eastern (both long gone). Nowadays, neighbors include the sleek, 55-story Millenium Hilton, with amenities like in-room fax machines and computer hook-ups, and the New York Marriott Financial Center Hotel – both of which opened in the early 1990s.

Along the river: Stretching along the **Hudson River**, between Chambers Street and Battery Park, **Battery Park City** is the most expensive real estate venture in the city's history. It's a 92-acre mini-city with apartments, condominiums, restaurants and parks offering the best views of the river since the island's uncluttered colonial days.

Although some parts are still under construction, this multi-billion dollar development, built on river-reclaimed land that includes 24 acres of earth left over from the construction of the World Trade Center, will have at least 25,000 residents when it's finished. That's more than were counted in all of lower Manhattan in the 1980 census.

Battery Park City includes the **World Financial Center**, four domed office towers that are home to American Express and Dow Jones, as well as the glittering **Winter Garden**. Opened in 1989, this modern-day Crystal Palace – which gives new meaning to the term "public space" – is accessible by two enclosed pedestrian bridges from the construction of the World Trade Center and looks like something from a futuristic movie set, complete with sweeping marble staircase and 16 imported, swaying California palm trees.

It's also one of the best places to see some of downtown's most innovative free entertainment, with a year-round

Sculpture next to US Custom House; Trinity church tombstones.

series of special events that range from jazz trios to visiting circuses to avant-garde performance art.

There's a variety of upscale shops to explore here as well as in the neighboring **Courtyard**. Plus, a mouthwatering selection of restaurants that run the gamut from inexpensive New York deli to classic French or new American cuisine.

During spring, summer and early fall, concerts and performances also take place on the adjoining **Plaza**, a riverside park with a small marina and a terminal where ferries ply the river to and from Hoboken. Walk south along the water, past an ironwrought fence inscribed with the first lines of two odes to urban life (by poets Frank O'Hara and Walt Whitman), and you're at the start of a mile-and-a-half-long **Esplanade**. In cold or rainy weather, a stroll here has its own lonely mystique, but on a sunny summer's day you may feel as if you are in an entirely different city.

Stop off for a look at pocket parks decorated with whimsical environmental sculptures like Ned Smyth's unique *Upper Room*, tucked in between the river-view apartment buildings, or relax on one of the benches and gaze out across the Hudson.

At **South Cove**, the promenade curves around into an oriental-looking rock garden where a spiral ramp serves as a lookout point, with a great view of the Statue of Liberty through recently-planted pine trees.

New York's **Holocaust Museum** is slated to open nearby, as is a new park and path connecting this stretch of waterfront with Battery Park.

Power complex: Since 1910 New York has honored everyone from Teddy Roosevelt to Nelson Mandela with ticker tape parades which tend to conclude at **City Hall**. At the junction of Broadway and Park Row, this French Renaissance cum Federal-style edifice has been the seat of city government since DeWitt Clinton was mayor in 1812, and was co-designed by French **The Winter Garden.**

architect Joseph François Mangin, the man responsible for the Place de la Concorde in Paris. Open to the public on weekdays (there's a collection of historical portraits in the **Governor's Room**), it's surrounded by **City Hall Park**, a tree-shaded former common.

This park has played a role throughout history: as the site of public executions, as grounds for almshouses for the poor, and as the location of a British prison for captured Revolutionary soldiers. It is also where Alexander Hamilton led a protest against the tea tax in 1774, and where, two years later, George Washington and his troops heard the Declaration of Independence for the first time.

A statue of journalist and newspaper editor Horace Greeley stands nearby, an appropriate location since **Park Row** was known as "Newspaper Row" from the mid-19th to the early-20th centuries, when most of the city's newspapers were published within scooping distance of municipal scandals. (The

Fulton Fish Market.

Pace University building across from the park was the original headquarters of the *New York Times*.)

North on Centre Street, **Foley Square** is named for a famous behind-the-scenes Tammany Hall politician. It's also the site of such civic structures as the 1936 Cass Gilbert-designed **US Courthouse**, and the adjacent **County Courthouse**, where New Yorkers are summoned for jury duty selection.

Near Foley Square on Centre Street is the enormous **Municipal Building**, an ornate 1914 McKim, Mead and White confection where, at the second-floor civil wedding chapel, you can tie the knot in about five minutes.

Not far away, the grim-looking Metropolitan Correctional Center (a federal detention facility) is between Park Row and Pearl Street, near the city's police headquarters at **One Police Plaza**, a sprawling orange complex built in 1973. You can join cops and federal agents for lunch at the Metropolitan Improvement Company on the corner of Madison and Pearl Streets, or walk back through City Hall Park to join city employees and local politicians at Ellen's Café Bar and Bakeshop on Broadway, which is run by a former "Miss Subways."

For one of the best views of the **East River** and downtown Manhattan, walk down Frankfort Street or along Park Row. Both lead to the **pedestrian walkway** on the **Brooklyn Bridge**, the world's very first suspension bridge and still one of the most striking. Built between 1867 and 1883, it spans the East River from City Hall to Brooklyn's Cadman Plaza.

South Street Seaport: Walk east from Broadway along **Fulton Street** where, before the Brooklyn Bridge was built, ferries carried New Yorkers across the East River from the Fulton Street pier. In the mid-1800s, this was the center of New York maritime commerce, where spices from China, rum from the West Indies and whale oil from the Atlantic were bought and sold; where ships were

built, and where sailors thronged and enjoyed the seedy red light district.

All that ended after the American Civil War, and the old port fell into a decline that lasted right up to the mid-1970s. The change occurred when the **South Street Museum** joined forces with the Rouse Company in order to create **South Street Seaport**, a 12-block "museum without walls."

Near the **Titanic Memorial Lighthouse** at the corner of Fulton and Water Streets, **Schermerhorn Row** is a block of restored 19th-century warehouses built by a successful local merchant. They are the last surviving Federal commercial buildings in the whole city. The **Museum Visitor Center** here sells tickets for tours and exhibitions, as well as Seaport Line harbor cruises.

Across Fulton Street, **Cannon's Walk** is a shop-lined passageway on the Front Street side of Museum Block. The **Seaport Museum Gallery** is on the other side, just next to a 19th-century printing shop.

Don't confuse the **Fulton Market** building on Front Street with the **Fulton Fish Market** just behind it on South Street. The former is a three-story atrium filled with take-out food, boutiques and stylish restaurants, while the latter – in the shadows beneath the FDR Drive – is the country's largest wholesale fish market. Started in 1831 (and at its present locale since about 1909), it's one of the city's oldest continuously operating businesses. If you get there during working hours (midnight to 9am) you'll see burly men in rubber boots selling huge piles of fish to buyers. The Seaport Museum runs 6am tours here twice a month from approximately April to October.

You can also tour the ***Peking***, a four-masted sailing barque, and the ***Ambrose***, last of the city's lightships. Both are part of the museum's collection of historic ships.

Dog fights: In 1985, when construction workers were excavating the foundation for an office tower on Water Street,

Battery Park Independence celebration.

they discovered the remains of a merchant ship sunk as landfill between 1746 and 1755. (Part of the ship was recovered intact and sent to a Virginia maritime museum.) **Water Street**, lined by bars and brothels catering to a sea-going clientele, used to run along the river's edge before landfill schemes shifted it two blocks inland.

A relic of those days is the **Captain Rose House** at No. 73, once known as Kit Burn's Sportsman's Hall. Up to 500 spectators at a time flocked here to bet on bloodthirsty dog fights – even dog and rat fights. Although Manhattan's third-oldest, the house was never given individual landmark status. However, it's now owned by the city's department of Housing Preservation and Development and will hopefully be restored.

The red-light district is long gone, so these days office workers looking for a good time head for **Pier 17**, a three-story pavilion where bars and restaurants are packed with three-piece-suited employees from nearby buildings (on weekday evenings) and hordes of visiting New Jerseyites (on weekends). There's usually a crowd enthusiastically trying the latest gadget at The Sharper Image, checking out the latest foul-weather gear at The Weather Store, or sampling the ethnic delicacies of the third-floor food market.

During the summer, there are free evening concerts on **Pier 16**, which is also where, March through November, the graceful sloop *Pioneer* and a fleet of sturdy, ferry-like vessels depart on day and evening cruises.

Back to Battery Park: Several blocks south of the Seaport area – past **Gouverneur's Lane** and **Old Slip**, a filled-in 18th-century dock, there's a small park where stranded sailors once congregated. The **Vietnam Veterans Memorial**, a 14-ft-high monument erected by the city in 1985, now stands here at the foot of a brick amphitheater. Made of green glass etched with excerpts of letters written to and from soldiers serving in Vietnam ("I often

South Street Seaport.

wonder if what we're fighting for is worth a human life," reads one), it's eerily illuminated at night.

Not far away, ferries leave for **Governor's Island** from the Beaux-Arts-style **Battery Maritime Building**, built in 1909. Most recently a Coast Guard facility, Governor's Island is only occasionally open to the public. But anyone can take the **Staten Island** ferry from the terminal building at the end of Whitehall Street, beyond Battery Park. The 25-minute cruise to Staten Island not only offers impressive views of the Statue of Liberty but is still the cheapest ride in town (there's a short wait at the other end before you reboard for the trip back to Manhattan).

Boats leave Battery Park, not only for Staten Island, but also to the **Statue of Liberty** and Ellis Island. Known as the "Island of Tears" during the 32-year period it served as the immigrants' gateway to the United States, **Ellis Island** is the city's museum-of-the-melting pot, a national park that details the often-wrenching stories of the millions who passed through here en route to new lives in the New World. At least 40 percent of America's population has at least one ancestor who entered the country via Ellis Island between 1892 and 1924; 1,285,349 immigrants arrived in 1907 alone.

The main building took six years and $156 million to restore, and was reopened to the public, along with the rest of the island, in September 1990. Exhibits give insights into the country's immigration history and the process of immigration itself. Many potential settlers were turned away from New York on grounds of poor health, or for other reasons, and transported back to their countries of origin.

Outside the museum, there's a promenade that offers great views looking out towards the Statue of Liberty and the lower Manhattan skyline. Not far away is the over 600-foot-long **American Immigrant Wall of Honor**, which is covered with 480,000 names.

Hands across the sea.

THE STATUE OF LIBERTY

"I looked at that statue with a sense of bewilderment, half doubting its reality. Looming shadowy through the mist, it brought silence to the decks of the *Florida*. This symbol of America – this enormous expression of what we had all been taught was the inner meaning of this new country we were coming to – inspired awe in the hopeful immigrants." Like millions of other immigrants, Italian-born writer Edward Corsi's first glimpse of America was the heroic figure of the Statue of Liberty standing on tiny Liberty Island, her "beacon-hand" thrust skyward bearing a torch to light the way, the shackles of despotism broken at her feet.

It might sound corny to modern ears, but to the countless masses who sailed into New York Harbor – so many of them desperately poor and oppressed – the Statue of Liberty really was the "Mother of Exiles." Emma Lazarus's famous poem, written to raise money for the statue's pedestal, still captures its promise to the world.

Give me your tired, your poor,
Your huddled masses yearning to breathe free,
The wretched refuse of your teeming shore.
Send these, the homeless, tempest-tost to me,
I lift my lamp beside the golden door.

Today, the nation's preoccupation with leaky borders and illegal aliens injects more than a little irony into the poem, but the sentiment is no less true, and somewhere in America's heart, the words still reflect the best in a country and city built by immigrants.

Of course, the Statue of Liberty is itself an immigrant. In 1865 Edouard-René Lefèbvre de Laboulaye, a French intellectual, politician and admirer of America, made an off-hand suggestion to a young sculptor by the name of Auguste Bartholdi for a monument honoring French and American brotherhood.

Bartholdi seized the idea, seeing in it the perfect opportunity to indulge a longstanding interest in colossal statuary. It took more than eight years for the project to crystallize, but by 1874 enough money had been donated by the French people to begin construction. Gustave Eiffel, who later built the Eiffel Tower, designed the ingenious framework which supports the thin copper skin, hammered to less than an eighth of an inch thick but still weighing over 90 tons. In America, newspaper publisher Joseph Pulitzer began his fund-raising campaign for the statue's base, accepting everything from a nickel to $250 from more than 120,000 contributors. In 1885, Bartholdi's *Liberty Enlightening the World* was dismantled and shipped to the United States. It was formally dedicated in a ceremony on Bedloe's Island on October 28, 1886.

Since its renovation in 1986, the statue has attracted well over a million tourists a year. In this age of high-tech wizardry and 20-second attention spans, it's still a stirring and uncanny sight, made almost unreal by its enormous size.

The big attraction, of course, is climbing to the top, which is a wonderful idea if you're in decent physical condition and don't mind waiting in line for at least an hour or two. This is one of the world's greatest tourist attractions, after all, and if you're going to schlepp all the way out to Liberty Island it seems only right to get your money's worth.

But discretion being the better part of valor, there are a few things you should keep in mind before making an assault on the summit. For one thing, the only way up to the statue's crown is a narrow spiral staircase many stories high, which means you'll not only be exhausted, but you'll be dizzier than a dervish. One decidedly unAmerican aspect is that there's no air conditioning either – which is no big deal on a cool day but is absolute hell on a hot one, especially when there are hundreds of people pressed inside. Temperatures in excess of 100°F (38°C) are not uncommon. Needless to say, people with heart conditions or other medical problems should forget about even trying.

For those who stay behind, there are two exhibits well worth visiting at the base of the statue and good views from the top of the pedestal. Tickets for the Circle Line ferry to Liberty Island are sold at Castle Clinton in Battery Park. Depending on the time of the year, the ferry departs every 45 minutes or every hour. ■

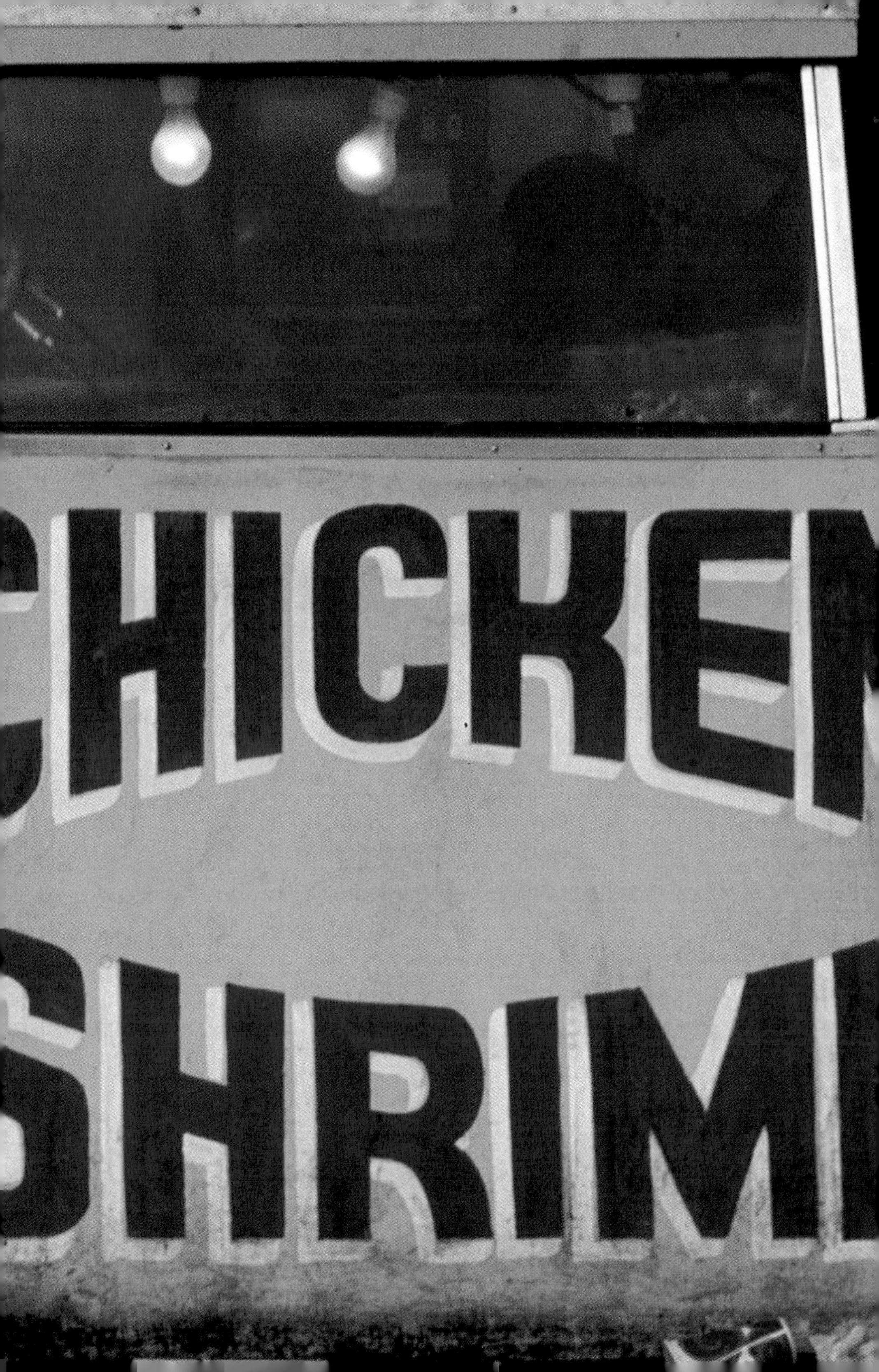
CHICKEN
SHRIM

THE OUTER BOROUGHS

The Manhattanite's nightmare is falling asleep on the subway as it dives beneath the East River (or worse, as it rumbles up to the Bronx), missing the last stop in Manhattan and ending up in the outer boroughs. Visitors panic at the idea of vacant lots, discount furniture stores, suburbia, terminal boredom. They turn to the subway token attendant, pleading, "Help! Are we anywhere near the Bronx Zoo yet?"

If *you* suffer this fear, you might be cured by a visit. Brooklyn, Queens, the Bronx, Staten Island: these are the four outer boroughs. All are more interesting than they appear, and easier to reach than you might imagine.

Ethnic environs: The key word in the boroughs is "neighborhood." Neighborhoods change. They overlap. They are also an ethnic delight. You can stroll through Middle Eastern shops that stock frankincense and myrrh. You can order your pasta in Italian; order your *kasha* in Yiddish.

The cultures clash, but that's nothing new. In 17th-century New York City, the Dutch fought their British neighbors. The Puritans frowned at the German Jews. The Chinese frightened the Europeans, then moved away from the Haitians. Hasidic Jews clashed with black Americans. Times change, problems with neighbors don't.

Some of these new neighbors are "upscale young Americans" in search of affordable rents. As the popularity and the price of Manhattan soars, the new generation is turning to former industrial zones, like **Long Island City** in Queens, **St George** in Staten Island, and **Fulton Ferry** in Brooklyn. Co-ops flourish where warehouses once thrived. Burnt-out buildings have become boutiques. Artists and lawyers have moved in on the river rats. And real estate values have tripled.

Amid the new is the older side of the boroughs: the boulevards, parks and palazzos built as grand civic projects at the turn of the century. Architects like Frederick Law Olmsted and Calvert Vaux found open space in the outer boroughs that was unavailable in Midtown. With sweeping gestures, they decked the boroughs with buildings that were inspired by Paris.

Until the population swelled after World War II, the boroughs had a pleasant suburban image: agreeable housing, easy access to the "City" and a special civic pride. Moving out to the boroughs meant moving *up*, especially if your point of departure was a tenement on the Lower East Side. As we said earlier, things change.

BROOKLYN: The 70 square miles on the southeast tip of Long Island encompass the most populous borough of New York City, Brooklyn. Its development commenced in the 1600s, when the Dutch bought Gowanus, then a Canarsie Indian village (now a sagging expressway), and the land they called Breukelen was

farmed and settled. The Dutch soon edged out the Canarsies.

In the mid-18th century, Long Island farmers made frequent ferry trips across the river to sell off surplus fruits and vegetables. In the 1790s, Brooklyn Heights began to expand, due in part to a plague of yellow fever. The high, dry bluffs of Brooklyn were an escape from the unhealthy city. At the same time, Brooklyn was becoming a popular summer home for financiers who would then use the ferry to get to their offices on Wall Street.

Today, a scenic way to escape from Manhattan is via the **Brooklyn Bridge**. A stroll across the walkway will lead you to Fulton Ferry, where cobblestone streets are coming back to life after lying dormant for decades. It was here at the Ferry that the borough set up up its first mass transit to Wall Street. In 1814, Robert Fulton's steam ferry, the *Nassau*, replaced the East River rowboats, flat sailboats and vessels powered by horses on treadmills. Brooklyn became an incorporated city in 1834, with a population close to 30,000.

A hub of homes and businesses grew up around the new docks. The area bustled with life until 1883, when the Brooklyn Bridge was built, then slid into obsolescence. Soon after, the city of Brooklyn was incorporated into New York City – and the hub became a slum. Now, new restaurants and shops have appeared; there are concerts and dance performances at **Empire-Fulton Ferry State Park**, and you can listen to chamber music on a converted barge moored nearby.

Around the bend to the east is the old **Brooklyn Navy Yard**, where abandoned warehouses have been turned into lofts. On the other side of the Ferry, the housing market has always been hot. **Brooklyn Heights**, where streets are lined with narrow rowhouses, brownstones change hands for a million dollars each.

A stroll through the Heights is extremely pleasant. Each block is iced **Pretzels.**

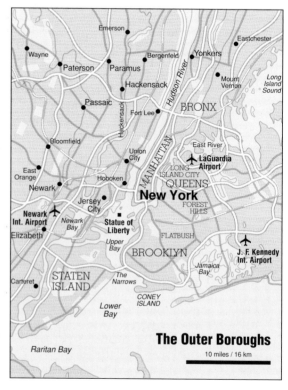

The Outer Boroughs

10 miles / 16 km

with wrought-iron flourishes, stained-glass windows and stone busts and trims. On the corner of **Willow Street and Middagh** is the oldest wooden house in the district, dating back to 1824. During the Civil War, the **Plymouth Congregational Church** on **Orange Street** served as an underground railroad station, while Henry Ward Beecher (Harriet Beecher Stowe's brother) preached abolitionism to the congregation.

Many streets in the Heights, like Middagh and Hicks, take the names of the neighborhood's 19th-century gentry. Five, however, are named after the flora of the period – **Pineapple**, **Cranberry**, **Orange**, **Poplar** and **Willow Streets**. It's rumored that the streets were christened by one of the Mistresses Middagh, who refused to consider street names of the neighbors she detested. It's more likely, however, that the names were chosen by the Heights' early developers.

The high life. The surrounding streets of Brooklyn Heights (**Grace Court Alley** mews, **Hicks** and **Remsen**), plus neighboring sections of **Carroll Gardens** and **Cobble Hill**, make up Brooklyn's heart of brownstones. Brownstone itself is iron oxide, too soft for structural use but suitable for facades. The buildings are skinny walk-ups built wall-to-wall with the houses next door. Their particular design, when they were first built in the 1800s, was meant to conserve heat and retard fire.

"Young urban professionals" of the 19th century frequently settled into Brooklyn brownstones, which were popular homes for newlyweds. Today, the narrow buildings and quiet streets are still popular – the Heights are just minutes from Wall Street by subway. A few single-family mansions remain, but most brownstones have been divided into smaller apartments.

The **Brooklyn Historical Society** includes a mini-museum on the ground floor of its landmark Heights building, located at 128 Pierrepont Street and

Clinton. Browse around and enjoy its rich mix of Dodgers baseball memorabilia, scholarly exhibits, maritime artifacts and Coney Island exhibitionism. Farther east, on Willoughby Street, the Brooklyn Arts & Culture Association Downtown Cultural Center, better known as **BACA Downtown**, offers ongoing theater, art and music events and workshops.

Along the river edge of the Heights is the **Promenade**. This much-used and appreciated walkway overlooks the East River, the Brooklyn Bridge and Manhattan. Far to the south, off the "toe" of lower Manhattan and on the way to Staten Island by ferry, lies **Governor's Island**. Known as Nooten Island in Dutch colonial days, it's been a home for New York's first governors, a quarantine station, and a training facility for the US Coast Guard.

At the foot of Brooklyn Heights is the **Civic Center**, with its Greek Revival Borough Hall. From here, follow Court Street to Atlantic Avenue's **Middle**

Eastern Bazaar. The shops on Atlantic, between Court and Henry, are bulging with imported spices, dried fruits, olives and *halvah*. Some bakeries cook their filo pastries in coal burning ovens, and the Middle Eastern restaurants are worth visiting. As Atlantic Avenue approaches the river, the Mid-East shares the sidewalk with a growing antique district. The shops have plenty of interesting stock (Victorian, Art Deco, 1930s, 1940s), and are usually open on weekends if not every weekday.

Another Brooklyn street which is a bazaar of ethnic enticements is **Court Street**. It begins at Cadman Plaza and travels, as the crow flies, through four Brooklyn neighborhoods – the Heights, Cobble Hill, Carroll Gardens and Red Hook. Many Italian establishments line Court Street, offering soft and hard imported cheeses, best-quality olive oils, freshly pressed pasta, baby artichokes, Italian broccoli and rich coffees. A hint of the earlier character of the street, when it bustled with immigrants from Galicia in the northwest of Spain, can be found in the shops selling wonderful Spanish foods.

To the east, where Atlantic meets **Flatbush Avenue**, things get pretty lowdown and dirty. But there is a high point at this junction, the monumental **Williamsburgh Savings Bank**, one of the tallest buildings in Brooklyn. Nearby on **Lafayette Street** is the innovative **Brooklyn Academy of Music (BAM)**, where the performance spectrum has been known to include multimedia maestro Laurie Anderson, Martha Clarke's performance art and the music of composer Philip Glass. BAM's latest addition is the beautifully restored **Majestic Theatre**, located just a few blocks from the main building.

Beyond Flatbush Avenue, Atlantic stretches into the triangle known as **Bed-Stuy**. The old neighborhoods of Bedford and Stuyvesant are infamous for their urban problems, though the district is beginning to show new signs of life. In **Crown Heights**, Hasidic

The Brooklyn Botanical Garden.

Jews and West Indian blacks are building communities worlds apart, but only doorsteps away.

Ebbets Field is no longer the site of Dodger baseball miracles, but **Tompkins Park** remains, and the acres of renovated homes make this one of the largest minority home-owning communities in the whole of New York.

Even farther east is **Brownsville**. Before World War II, this was a mainly Jewish slum. According to local talk, the corner candy store on **Livonia Avenue** served as headquarters for Murder Inc., the notorious gangster ring of the 1930s. For a Brownsville classic, check out Alfred Kazin's book called *A Walker in the City*.

Orientally oriented: The thoroughfare of eastern Brooklyn is **Eastern Parkway**. It runs through Bed-Stuy to Prospect Park, passing the **Brooklyn Public Library** and the marvelous **Brooklyn Museum**, whose Egyptian collection is the best outside of Cairo and London. The museum also boasts an unusual outdoor sculpture garden of New York building ornaments. Next door, at the surprisingly pastoral 50-acre **Brooklyn Botanic Garden**, the Japanese gardens alone are worth a visit. Founded in 1899, the **Brooklyn Children's Museum**, at 145 Brooklyn Avenue, is the oldest children's museum in America and very much a hands-on learning experience. There are thousands of interesting artifacts to wonder at here, and almost as many buttons and knobs to play with.

The huge roundabout at the western end of the Parkway is **Grand Army Plaza**. The **Soldiers' and Sailors' Memorial Arch** provides formal entrance to the 526 acres which make up Prospect Park. The park, plaza and boulevards were all designed by Frederick Law Olmsted and Calvert Vaux. The Plaza is their most literal tribute to Paris – an Arc de Triomphe at the focal point of the borough.

The Japanese Gardens. **Prospect Park** is considered to be Olmsted and Vaux's best work, even better, perhaps, than Central Park. Dreamily roam through the park's romantic regions: the **Long Meadow**, the **Vale of Cashmere** and the **Rose Garden**, or ride the antique carousel. The park also contains sports fields, tennis courts, a boating lake, and a zoo/wildlife conservation center which is geared toward children. Information is available in the renovated 1907 Beaux Arts boathouse.

In an eastern corner of the park, off Flatbush Avenue at Empire Boulevard, the **Lefferts Homestead** is a two-story, eight-room house that was built between 1777 and 1783. For visitors, it offers valuable insights into 18th-century colonial life. There are interactive exhibits especially designed for children, along with several rooms which have been restored to their original early American appearance.

The neighborhood of **Park Slope** runs along Prospect Park's western border. Though many of the Victorian rowhouses have been divided up into

apartments (not quite as expensive as Brooklyn Heights), most of them remain well-kept. From **Prospect Park West**, turn down Montgomery Place or Carroll Street. The shopping street, **Seventh Avenue**, is two blocks down from the park. Along the way, on **Montgomery Place**, there's a Roman arch, a Greek pediment and Chinese double arches – all in one building. Down the street, look for iridescent bricks framing peacock windows.

At **117 Carroll Street**, there's a flurry of architectural styles on the exterior and a tale of mystery within. According to Brooklyn lore, four servants died while trapped in the building's elevator. Now, a century or so later, the pitiful voices of the starving prisoners are said still to echo at night. Before leaving Park Slope entirely, be sure to check out the Venetian-style palazzo with an American Indian motif, located at **25 Eighth Avenue**.

Unlike Park Slope's rowhouses, the homes in **Prospect Park South** are de-tached; huge gables nearly touch those of the houses next door. Stroll down and around **Albemarle Road** to see copies of a Swiss chalet, a Spanish galleon, and even a southern plantation.

Flatbush's best boulevard is **Ocean Parkway**, just to the west. It passes residential **Gravesend**, founded in the 1600s by the widowed Lady Deborah Moody and named for her home in Britain. Lady Moody was both the first woman settlement founder, and the first founder to guarantee religious freedom with a written law.

Coney Island: South, on the coast, lies Coney Island, which is not actually an island, but a peninsula. At the eastern tip, the community of **Seagate** has a guarded entrance, but no apparent protection against encroaching shabbiness. The wealthier but uninspiring **Manhattan Beach** is at the other end of the boardwalk. The **Aquarium for Wildlife Conservation**, more familiarly known as the New York Aquarium, is located in-between, at West 8th Street

Island attractions.

and Surf Avenue. Recently overhauled, with a new outdoor theater for sea-lion performances, this metropolitan home for ocean life is one of the borough's most popular attractions.

The famous name of **Coney Island** really belongs to what was once Brooklyn's premier vacation center. New Yorkers have been escaping to Coney Island ever since the summers of the 1840s and in greater numbers after 1875, when the train connected the beach with the city. Garish hotels, little beach homes, the old Brighton Race Track and amusement parks were all erected; Dreamland (burned down in 1911), Luna Park (ditto in 1939) and Steeplechase (which was demolished by developer Donald Trump's father in 1964) were among them.

But now, most of the holiday bungalows have been claimed by urban decay and replaced by public housing. In summer, the remnants of the amusement parks seem to sag under the weight of the crowds. Off season, the games are locked up and guarded by stalking dogs. The wintry beach is as desolate as a vacant lot.

All is not lost. You can still get **Nathan's famous hot dogs**, at the stand on Surf and Stillwell, where fans insist the mass-produced sausages were invented in 1916. The grills sizzle up to 1,500 dogs an hour on a hot summer's day. You can still tempt fate and hang on for dear life aboard the Cyclone, the grand-dad of roller coasters, with its 3,000 feet of wooden track and cars speeding down it at 68 mph.

More importantly, the 1990s might well see the revitalization of Coney Island. There are plans to rebuild Steeplechase Park as a three-tier amusement center, which includes 14 theaters and 65 attractions, as well as a sports complex which will seat 14,000 people. Private developers, too, have realized the potential of the island, only 25 miles from the heart of Manhattan. New, single-family dwellings have been built, and changed hands rapidly. Attendance

Rear window.

at the Aquarium, for instance, has doubled since the mid-1980s.

"A whole new generation is starting to come out here," said a spokesman for the Aquarium, speaking to the *New York Times*. "They don't know what Coney Island was, or anything about its decline."

Things look promising: Farther east on the boardwalk is **Brighton Beach**, which for many years was an enclave of elderly Jews. As Coney Island slid into decay, Brighton's buildings stood like forts along the coast, waiting for crime to crack through the walls, and for time to wash out their district.

But in the mid-1970s, a wave of immigrants, mostly Soviet Jews, began moving into Brighton Beach, which soon became known as "Little Odessa." Today, their children – teenagers with rosy cheeks and leather jackets – hang out under the subway "El," or elevated train tracks, while authentic Russian restaurants, bookshops, markets and other businesses have infused the old

neighborhood with a renewed sense of vitality. You can even dance the night away at a series of exuberant nightspots on **Brighton Beach Avenue**.

Just north of Brighton is **Sheepshead Bay**, where the fishing boats are docked. You can buy fresh fish off the boats, or order it off the menu at one of the many restaurants. You can also charter a boat and captain, and bring home your own catch of the day. The boats leave early (and are expensive), so it is a good idea to stop by the day before and ask around for the best price.

QUEENS: The area in Queens which at one time was a swamp and then became "Corona Garbage Dump," ended up as the glamorous grounds of the 1939 and 1964 World's Fairs. The reconstruction work done for the fairs transformed the marshy land, and it was then renamed the rather more elegant **Flushing Meadows-Corona Park**.

In 1939, while visitors poured into Queens for the fair, the rest of the borough was also in transition. Countless commuters wanted new suburban homes, and the population quadrupled. When the Queensbridge Houses, just north of the **Queensboro Bridge**, were built for middle-class families, they became the country's biggest public housing development of the time.

The World's Fairs were located at **Northern Boulevard** and **Grand Central Parkway**. Relics of the events include the **Panorama of the City of New York**, a miniature replica of the city constructed in painstaking detail. It's on display at the **Queens Museum of Art**, in what was 1964's New York City Pavilion. Various other reminders of the fairs include the great steel globe called the **Unisphere**, and the **World's Fair Marina**.

Another landmark of Flushing Meadows – Corona Park is the USTA **National Tennis Center**, the site of the annual US Open. Not to mention **Shea Stadium**, the Mets' home, just beyond the subway station, with its capacity to seat 55,000 cheering baseball fans. The

The mighty Cyclone.

park also has lots of open spaces. There are paths for biking, running and strolling; a **skating rink**; **botanical gardens** with one of the largest rose gardens in the northeast (8,000 rosebushes); and a new zoo/wildlife conservation center.

Many people assume the most generous stretches of land in Queens belong to **JFK** and **LaGuardia airports**. These terminals with their long runways *are* huge, but more impressive acreage actually remains undeveloped: nearly a quarter of the borough has been preserved as parkland.

Alley Pond Environmental Center, near the northeastern border, offers tours of wilderness trails and exhibits of natural history. To the south, the **Jamaica Bay Wildlife Refuge** is a home for more than 300 species of birds and little mammals. The park is just south of the JFK runways, but the birds seem to like their jetpowered cousins. Nature tours and trail walks are offered.

Along the southern strip of Queens, **the Rockaways** form the biggest municipal beach in the country. To the east is **Far Rockaway**, where family homes are set back from the beach. To the west, in **Neponsit** and in **Belle Harbor**, old mansions cling to the bygone splendor of ritzy Rockaway days when wealthy New Yorkers vacationed here.

Neighboring **Jacob Riis Park**, part of the Gateway National Recreation Area which straddles New York and New Jersey, offers free admission as well as empty dunes on weekdays (although summer weekends can be as crowded as a lunchtime elevator). The fence near Neponsit's border marks the (unofficial) nude district.

An aging industrial section, **Long Island City**, was discovered in the early 1980s by artists searching for workspace. One celebrated result is **P.S. 1**, a museum and art center located in the once decrepit Public School 1, on 21st Street. Another is the **Isamu Noguchi Garden Museum** on Vernon Boulevard, not far from the giant sculpture works in the Socrates Sculpture Park.

Boarded-up boardwalk.

Movies and mortgages: Astoria, which borders Long Island City, is a modest section of small apartment buildings and semi-detached homes but has gained a new reputation as a center for New York's film industry. The motion picture business here dates back to the 1920s. The Marx Brothers and Gloria Swanson were among those working at what was then Lasky Studios. Now the flourishing **Kaufman Astoria Studios** occupy the old site, as well as many surrounding blocks. Films and commercials are rolling again.

One of New York's newer attractions is the **American Museum of the Moving Image**, located at 35th Avenue and 36th Street. It is the only museum in the United States devoted to the art, history, technique and technology of motion pictures, television and video. The museum attempts to probe the media of moving-images and to explain their impact on contemporary society.

Anyone who has been to London's Museum of the Moving Image, on the banks of the River Thames, will be disappointed by its American counterpart. Britain's MOMI is a multi-level, multi-media extravaganza, where actors dressed in period costume escort visitors through a galaxy of electronic wizardry. It's high-tech, global, and compulsively entertaining. Queen's AMOMI is low-key. Many of its exhibits are static (i.e. consisting of photographs or costumes); but the demonstrations tend to be diverting if unchallenging and the premises are tiny enough to cover in an hour's visit (although renovation is still taking place, and more galleries may open.) The contrast between the two similarly-named museums is overwhelming.

To the layperson's eye, this seems to be a marketing – rather than a consumer – error on the part of AMOMI. The museum began as the Astoria Motion Picture and Television Foundation, established in 1977 to save the Astoria Studios from demolition. In this regard, it has a pleasing, archival feel. By select-

AMOMI's
Tut's Fever.

ing the grand-sounding title "American Museum of the Moving Image," expectations rise. The museum was not helped by the fact that it opened the same year as London's MOMI, inviting further comparisons. To travel to Queens just for a day out here is to court disappointment.

If, however, you come armed with the knowledge that AMOMI has little pretensions beyond that of a neighborhood museum, then a visit can be very pleasant. The staff are unfailingly polite and helpful, the exhibits are fun, and artist Red Grooms' indoor theater, called **Tut's Fever**, is a dazzling display of cinematic whimsy.

Farther along, the **36th Street bridge** is also known as **Roosevelt Island Bridge**, as it leads to tiny **Roosevelt Island** in the middle of the East River. Although it lies only about 300 yards from the soggy shores of Queens, technically the island belongs to the borough of Manhattan. Roosevelt Island is covered in the "Upper East Side" chapter of this book (*page 171*).

Astoria prides itself on main drags like **Steinway Street** and **Broadway**, which are lined with Greek delis, Italian bakeries and Oriental markets. Despite the movie stars working nearby, the side streets remain reasonably quiet. Kids (Vietnamese, Latin American *et al*) play driveway basketball and pick-up soccer. Men lounge in lawnchairs not far away.

Another landmark of Long Island City is **Sunnyside Gardens**. It was just a swamp until the 1920s, when city planners gave the site new life as a working class housing development. Sunnyside Gardens was a good effort, with innovative plans. But in the 1930s, many homeowners could not make their mortgage payments. As evictions appeared in mailboxes, the Sunnysiders took action. They barricaded their doors and bombarded the sheriffs with flour and pepper. But Depression conditions couldn't be sandbagged. Nearly two-thirds of the original residents in Sunny-

side Gardens lost their homes following gloomy foreclosure.

The classiest garden apartments were designed for **Forest Hills**, a section of Queens inspired by English "Garden Cities." Planning commenced in 1906 with an endowment for low-cost housing. But in 1923, when the project was only half completed, a group of residents took over the management and began vetting newcomers. The district turned fashionable, and called itself the "lawn tennis capital of the western hemisphere." The grass courts of the **West Side Tennis Club** formerly hosted the US Open.

There are several modest communities in Queens. **Flushing** is packed with history, and perked up by its "**Little Asia**." Before the postwar building boom, the area was a quiet place with clapboard and shingle houses. The district's claim to history centers on a strong tradition of religious freedom. It is home to one of the biggest Hindu temples in North America, located on

Bowne Street. It was also an important center for Quakers.

The **Quaker Meeting House**, built in 1696, at Northern Boulevard and Linden Place, is the oldest house of worship in New York City. Nearby is the "Shrine to Religious Freedom," the historic **Bowne House**, on Bowne Street near 37th. In 1661, John Bowne, the Quaker leader, supposedly bought the land for eight strings of wampum. It is now a **museum**.

For a change of pace, a day at the racetrack should not be overlooked. The well-known race at **Belmont Park**, the world's largest thoroughbred track, is the Belmont Stakes, the third jewel of the triple crown. Important events at **Aqueduct** are the Wood Memorial and the Turf Classic, both significant races of their kind.

STATEN ISLAND: Once upon a time in New York, there was an island where roads were paved with oyster shells, where yachts stood guard by resort hotels, where proper European-style fin-

ishing schools were founded, and where Americans first played tennis.

Could this place be Staten Island, the smallest and least known borough? To most New Yorkers, the island is only an aging pier where the famous ferry goes. The ferry is a well-loved bargain: the excursion from South Ferry (near Battery Park in Manhattan) includes a view of the Statue of Liberty and the Manhattan skyline, and runs well into the evening. As the poet Edna St Vincent Millay wrote: "We were very tired, we were very merry – we had gone back and forth all night on the ferry." Most people only come for the ride, but, in fact, it's worth disembarking on Staten Island itself.

Staten Island's oversimplified image is of a once-pastoral place gone suburban. Until the 1830s, it remained a quiet settlement of fishing and farming villages. About that time, the beach became trendy. A literary crowd arrived, along with a second crowd with enough money to build mansions. Island indus-

Staten Island living.

try picked up steam and thrived well into the 20th century. But the area fell into dire straits during the Great Depression. Since then, many old landmarks have slipped into disrepair.

The ferry lands in the town of **St George**, where nearby attractions include the Staten Island Institute of Arts & Sciences. Located in a dignified 1918 building, it contains a variety of local historical exhibits.

Snug Harbor Cultural Center, west of St George, has also awakened to a new life. It opened in 1831 as Sailors' Snug Harbor, a home for retired seamen. Now its 80 acres of ponds, wetlands and woodlands are a haven for the arts and nature. The main buildings are Greek Revival landmarks. Neptune, tridents, parrots and ships still decorate the **Main Hall** interior, just as they did when the building served as quarters for the old sailors.

Outside, close to the **old gazebo**, Snug Harbor has held an impressive range of concerts and performances.

Historic Richmond Town.

Other parts of the renovation house the **Veterans Memorial Hall**, **Newhouse Gallery**, **botanical gardens**, and the **Staten Island Children's Museum**.

East of the ferry landing is the village of **Stapleton**, which centers on **Stapleton Park**. A colorful antique and restaurant row now extends southeast on **Bay Street**.

Some residents come down to Bay Street from their perch on the island's six hills: **Fort**, **Ward**, **Grymes**, **Emerson**, **Todt** and **Lighthouse**. Stately mansions with breathtaking views stand on the ridge of **Todt Hill**, the highest point south of Maine along the eastern seaboard.

From Stapleton, take a taxi up **Signal Hill**, a narrow hairpin lane. Along the way, alpine homes peek out of the cliff, half hidden by rocks and trees. At the top, beyond the super views from the ridge, you will enter the core of the island. Called the **Greenbelt**, this verdant slice of trees and meadows – more than 2,000 acres of contiguous parkland – is the result of a civic plan that tightly controls or prohibits development.

The Greenbelt includes **High Rock Park Conservation Center** (a refuge which was rescued from high-rise development plans) and **Latourette Park and Golf Course**. Around the bend, on **Lighthouse Hill**, is an idyllic corner imported from the Himalayas. The **Jacques Marchais Museum of Tibetan Art** includes two monastic-style stone buildings, a lotus pond and terraced garden. Inside, paintings, bronze figures and artifacts make up a small but fine collection.

Historic Richmond Town, on the southern tip of the Greenbelt, is an historical village depicting three centuries of life on Staten Island. Its 26 landmark buildings include the **Voorleezer's House** (*circa* 1695), the oldest American elementary school, and the **Historic Museum**, a first-class exhibition of the island's past. Demonstrations of traditional crafts are often held in the village. While in the Richmondtown area, take a stroll past the **William Cass house**, at 48 Manor Court. This Frank Lloyd Wright designed building, one in only three in New York City, has recently been given official landmark status.

From Richmondtown, **Amboy Road** leads down to **Tottenville**. It's difficult to believe that this tranquil spot is still part of New York City. Tiny stores squat near the corner of Amboy Road and **Sleight Avenue**, which wouldn't be out of place in upstate New York. People stroll through the neighborhood, or ride horses on the little main streets. The landmark of Tottenville is the **Conference House**, or **Billopp House**, at the end of **Hylan Boulevard**. This was the site of Benjamin Franklin's meeting in 1776 with the British commander, Admiral Lord Howe, in an attempt to prevent the American Revolution. The meeting failed, and war was inevitable.

When the boulevard reaches **Great Kills Park**, follow the entrance road through fields of swamp grass to the beach. Behind a spit of land are marinas;

across the water are views of Brooklyn and Manhattan's World Trade Center.

Several of the island's best easterly views include the **Verrazano Narrows Bridge**, built in 1964 as the longest suspension bridge in the world. The Verrazano connects Staten Island to Brooklyn and, often criticized, is known as the island's great change-maker. The traffic that poured across its span brought Staten Island's fastest and most uncontrolled boom in construction, especially inland.

While new building is still underway, better and more thoughtful planning – like that which resulted in the Greenbelt area – has become the rule rather than the exception. And though Staten Island may still be the city's smallest borough, its wealth of cultural and scenic attractions are helping ensure that it's no longer the least-known.

THE BRONX: In 1641, a Scandinavian named Jonas Bronk bought 500 acres of the New World from Indian natives. He and his family built their home on virgin **Colonial farming.**

land. The area was remote and lonely, so they began to throw parties for their friends. The Indian land was called Keskekeck then, but the name was changed by Manhattanites who would say to their neighbors, "Where are you going on Saturday night?"

"Up to the Bronks. And you?"

The tale is debatable. Nevertheless, the Bronx did begin with Jonas, and in the beginning it was virgin forest. In most sections of today's Bronx, idyllic woods seem inconceivable, but there is one place where the hemlock forest remains untouched: the 250-acre **New York Botanical Garden**.

The **Bronx River Gorge**, within the woods, is best reached from its arched stone footbridge. The buildings on the gardens' grounds include the historic **Lorillard Snuff Mill**, saved by its snack bar incarnation, and, most importantly, the **Enid A. Haupt Conservatory**, a crystal palace of grand proportions built in 1901 and currently undergoing extensive renovations.

The **Bronx Zoo**, though recently renamed **The International Wildlife Conservation Park**, is still the country's largest urban zoo – and still shares **Bronx Park** with the Botanical Gardens. The most decorative way to enter is through the **Paul Rainey Memorial Gate**, topped with Art Deco bronze casts of animals. Inside, one of the most popular exhibits is the **World of Birds**, which features spacious, climate-controlled habitats. The **World of Darkness** (nocturnal animals) and the **Aquatic Bird House** are also good modern additions. There's a pleasant **Children's Zoo**, a worthwhile monorail ride through Wild Asia, and African Plains with moats to keep the big cats away from their prey (that means you).

The zoo is at the geographic heart of the Bronx, but its nostalgic and architectural heart may well be the old **Grand Concourse**. This Paris-inspired boulevard began as a "speedway" across rural hills. As the industrial borough grew, the Concourse achieved a

The Verrazano Narrows Bridge.

classy role as the Park Avenue of the Bronx. Its Art Deco apartments remain, though few retain their luxury status. The area is not a safe place after dark, so make sure you are not alone here at night. The Bronx County Building, south at 165th Street, houses the **Bronx Museum of the Arts**. The museum features exhibitions of contemporary art, including sculpture, graphics, paints and photography.

North of the Grand Concourse at **Kingsbridge Road**, poet **Edgar Allan Poe's** small, shingled **cottage** squats among high-rise housing. Poe moved here in 1846 hoping the country air would be good for his consumptive wife, who was also his 13-year-old cousin. But she died at an early age, leaving Poe frayed and destitute; the haunting poem *Annabel Lee* is a reflection of the poet's distress. The house is now a museum.

Little Italy: The Little Italy of the Bronx is in **Belmont**. Its markets on **Arthur Avenue**, near the fork of Cres-

cent and East 187th Street, teem with people who can sometimes be seen nibbling the cured meats, appetizers, and freshly baked pastries for which the area is known. It is also a great place for restaurants. For ethnic research, try the **Enrico Fermi Center**, the country's first Italian-American library. The staff, of course, speak Italian and will help with most queries.

West of the Concourse, **Bronx Community College**'s most famous landmark is the **Hall of Fame**, which wraps around Gould Memorial Library. The library's great copper dome was known by scholars as The Great Green Nipple of Knowledge. There are seven campuses throughout the Bronx, including **Fordham University**, **Lehman College** and the **Albert Einstein College of Medicine**. The most impressive landmark at Fordham is the chapel, which has fine stained-glass windows.

Above University Heights is **Riverdale**, in the hilly northwest. It's hard to believe this is the Bronx. The curvy roads are lined with mansions – and a drive down Sycamore Avenue to West 249th Street brings you to **Wave Hill,** a once-private estate with public gardens overlooking the Hudson.

Not far away is **Van Cortlandt Park**, with stables, tennis courts and acres of playing fields. On weekends, West Indians play rounds of cricket here and a league of waiters from the neighborhood's Irish pubs and restaurants has soccer games between meals. The **Van Cortlandt Mansion Museum** overlooks the park's lake. The rooms are furnished for the public as they were for colonial gentry.

Swampy Corner: Another isolated section of the Bronx is the eastern corner where swampy land extends into Long Island South. The place to aim for is City Island. On the way, the highway passes near Co-op City, a sprawling, brown-towered housing development that rises from the lowlands like a huge urban beehive and includes schools, shops, and about 50,000 inhabitants.

The Bronx Zoo.

278

Pelham Bay Park, farther east, is one of the city's largest recreation areas and includes **Orchard Beach**, a popular summer destination created in 1936 by the Department of Parks, which imported tons of fine white sand from the Rockaways and Long Island. There are nature trails, riding stables, and a public golf course here as well.

Past Orchard Beach, the road reaches **City Island**, the borough's slice of New England quaintness. Accessible by car, city bus, or by boat, this 230-acre island off the northeast Bronx in Long Island Sound has remained quietly detached from the rest of the city.

The first industry on City Island, in the 1830s, was the Solar Salt Works, which marketed salt from evaporated sea water. Then oystering became big business, only to be replaced by shipbuilding; the boatyards along **City Island Avenue** once yielded masterworks like *Intrepid*, the 1968 winner of the America's Cup Race.

This main avenue sports other attractions too: fishing gear emporiums, several seafood restaurants and the **North Wind Undersea Museum**, a quirky little place where you can gawk at exhibits of marine life, vintage diving gear and other nautical curiosities. Farther along the avenue is stately **Grace Church**, this building being a fine example of Gothic Revival architecture.

Behind the church you'll find quiet, peaceful side streets lined with weathered bungalows and cottages; even a few large, fading Victorian mansions that still have their original stained-glass windows in front, and overgrown gardens out back.

Urban decay: The opposite end of the borough – in both location and reputation – is the **South Bronx**. Its best-known landmark is baseball's **Yankee Stadium**, known as The House That Ruth Built. Actually, the nickname is backwards. This is the house built for Ruth. Its shortened right field was designed for player Babe Ruth's special home-run record.

Other baseball stars associated with the stadium include Lou Gehrig, Micky Mantle and Joe DiMaggio; all told, more world championship flags and American League pennants have flown over Yankee Stadium than any other baseball field in the country. In the 1970s, as the neighborhood suffered financial thirst, $100 million was pumped into rebuilding the stadium; in the 1990s, its future is uncertain.

To some extent, the urban blight around the stadium has lessened. The **Hunts Point Market** (wholesale fruit, vegetables and meat) moved here from Manhattan in the 1960s and 1970s, breathing life into the area.

On the wreckage of what was once Charlotte Street, ranch-style homes have been built. The heroes are the families who've moved in, determined to salvage their neighborhood. Even here, where the district's problems are at their worst, to a venturing tourist this northern borough can prove it has new breath in its antique lungs.

Time to be tough.

INSIGHT GUIDES
Travel Tips

FOR THOSE
WITH MORE THAN
A PASSING INTEREST
IN TIME...

Before you put your name down for a Patek Philippe watch *fig. 1*, there are a few basic things you might like to know, without knowing exactly whom to ask. In addressing such issues as accuracy, reliability and value for money, we would like to demonstrate why the watch we will make for you will be quite unlike any other watch currently produced.

"Punctuality", Louis XVIII was fond of saying, "is the politeness of kings."

We believe that in the matter of punctuality, we can rise to the occasion by making you a mechanical timepiece that will keep its rendezvous with the Gregorian calendar at the end of every century, omitting the leap-years in 2100, 2200 and 2300 and recording them in 2000 and 2400 *fig. 2*. Nevertheless, such a watch does need the occasional adjustment. Every 3333 years and 122 days you should remember to set it forward one day to the true time of the celestial clock. We suspect, however, that you are simply content to observe the politeness of kings. Be assured, therefore, that when you order your watch, we will be exploring for you the physical—if not the metaphysical—limits of precision.

Does everything have to depend on how much?

Consider, if you will, the motives of collectors who set record prices at auction to acquire a Patek Philippe. They may be paying for rarity, for looks or for micromechanical ingenuity. But we believe that behind each $500,000-plus

bid is the conviction that a Patek Philippe, even if 50 years old or older, can be expected to work perfectly for future generations.

In case your ambitions to own a Patek Philippe are somewhat discouraged by the scale of the sacrifice involved, may we hasten to point out that the watch we will make for you today will certainly be a technical improvement on the Pateks bought at auction? In keeping with our tradition of inventing new mechanical solutions for greater reliability and better time-keeping, we will bring to your watch innovations *fig. 3* inconceivable to our watchmakers who created the supreme wristwatches of 50 years ago *fig. 4*. At the same time, we will of course do our utmost to avoid placing undue strain on your financial resources.

Can it really be mine?

May we turn your thoughts to the day you take delivery of your watch? Sealed within its case is your watchmaker's tribute to the mysterious process of time. He has decorated each wheel with a chamfer carved into its hub and polished into a shining circle. Delicate ribbing flows over the plates and bridges of gold and rare alloys. Millimetric surfaces are bevelled and burnished to exactitudes measured in microns. Rubies are transformed into jewels that triumph over friction. And after many months—or even years—of work, your watchmaker stamps a small badge into the mainbridge of your watch. The Geneva Seal—the highest possible attestation of fine watchmaking *fig. 5*.

Looks that speak of inner grace *fig. 6.*

When you order your watch, you will no doubt like its outward appearance to reflect the harmony and elegance of the movement within. You may therefore find it helpful to know that we are uniquely able to cater for any special decorative needs you might like to express. For example, our engravers will delight in conjuring a subtle play of light and shadow on the gold case-back of one of our rare pocket-watches *fig. 7*. If you bring us your favourite picture, our enamellers will reproduce it in a brilliant miniature of hair-breadth detail *fig. 8*. The perfect execution of a double hobnail pattern on the bezel of a wristwatch is the pride of our casemakers and the satisfaction of our designers, while our chainsmiths will weave for you a rich brocade in gold *figs. 9 & 10*. May we also recommend the artistry of our goldsmiths and the experience of our lapidaries in the selection and setting of the finest gemstones? *figs. 11 & 12.*

How to enjoy your watch before you own it.

As you will appreciate, the very nature of our watches imposes a limit on the number we can make available. (The four Calibre 89 time-pieces we are now making will take up to nine years to complete). We cannot therefore promise instant gratification, but while you look forward to the day on which you take delivery of your Patek Philippe *fig. 13*, you will have the pleasure of reflecting that time is a universal and everlasting commodity, freely available to be enjoyed by all.

Should you require information on any particular Patek Philippe watch, or even on watchmaking in general, we would be delighted to reply to your letter of enquiry. And if you send us

fig. 1: The classic face of Patek Philippe.

fig. 4: Complicated wristwatches circa 1930 (left) and 1990. The golden age of watchmaking will always be with us.

fig. 6: Your pleasure in owning a Patek Philippe is the purpose of those who made it for you.

fig. 9: Harmony of design is executed in a work of simplicity and perfection in a lady's Calatrava wristwatch.

fig. 10: The chainsmith's hands impart strength and delicacy to a tracery of gold.

fig. 2: One of the 33 complications of the Calibre 89 astronomical clock-watch is a satellite wheel that completes one revolution every 400 years.

fig. 5: The Geneva Seal is awarded only to watches which achieve the standards of horological purity laid down in the laws of Geneva. These rules define the supreme quality of watchmaking.

fig. 7: Arabesques come to life on a gold case-back.

fig. 8: An artist working six hours a day takes about four months to complete a miniature in enamel on the case of a pocket-watch.

fig. 11: Circles in gold: symbols of perfection in the making.

fig. 12: The test of a master lapidary is his ability to express the splendour of precious gemstones.

PATEK PHILIPPE
GENEVE

fig. 13: The discreet sign of those who value their time.

fig. 3: Recognized as the most advanced mechanical regulating device to date, Patek Philippe's Gyromax balance wheel demonstrates the equivalence of simplicity and precision.

your card marked "book catalogue" we shall post you a catalogue of our publications. Patek Philippe, 41 rue du Rhône, 1204 Geneva, Switzerland, Tel. +41 22/310 03 66.

THOMAS COOK
MasterCard
TRAVELLERS CHEQUES...

...HOLIDAY ESSENTIALS

Travel money from the travel experts

THOMAS COOK MASTERCARD TRAVELLERS CHEQUES ARE
WIDELY AVAILABLE THROUGHOUT THE WORLD.

Getting Acquainted

The Place

Area: New York City lies in the southeast corner of New York State at the mouth of the Hudson River. It covers about 368 square miles (953 sq km).

Geography: Greater New York is divided into five boroughs – Manhattan, the Bronx, Queens, Brooklyn and Staten Island. Manhattan is the second-smallest (after Staten Island) but most densely populated, with 1,488,000 people crammed onto an island 13 miles long and not quite two miles wide.

Population: 7,323,000 (Greater New York).

Nickname: The Big Apple.

Religion: Christian, Jewish, Moslem, Buddhist, Hindu plus various others also represented.

Time Zone: Eastern Standard Time (EST); five hours behind London; one hour ahead of Chicago; three hours ahead of California.

Currency: US dollars and cents.

Weights and measures:
The US uses the Imperial system of weights and measures.
Metric is rarely used. Below is a conversion chart.
1 inch = 2.54 centimeters
1 foot = 30.48 centimeters
1 mile = 1.609 kilometers
1 quart = 1.136 liters
1 ounce = 28.4 grams
1 pound = .453 kilograms
1 yard = .9144 meters

Electricity: 110 volts.

International Dialing Code: (1).

Local Dialing Codes: 212 for Manhattan; 718 for Brooklyn, Staten Island, Queens, and the Bronx.

Climate

New York's climate is fairly unpredictable, which is to say that sometimes rain or snow can come as a surprise. Still, weather reports are usually reliable. Summer temperatures are normally in the mid-70° to mid-80°s F range (13–29°C) with frequent heat waves accompanied by uncomfortable humidity, when the mercury might top 100°F. September and October often usher in a balmy, dry "Indian summer," filling the parks and office plazas with sun-worshippers. In winter, temperatures can drop as low as 10 or 15°F (–12 or –9°C) but, except for January and February, usually stay above freezing point. Raincoats are advised year-round and except for casual wandering and sightseeing, dress can be somewhat formal. As regards the amount of precipitation that falls in New York in a typical year, the average annual rainfall is 44 inches (112 cm) as well as 29 inches (74 cm) of snow that falls over the same time period.

Economy

New York City is the world's foremost financial center (the New York Stock Exchange, Commodity Exchange, etc. are all located here). It holds a leading position in the retail and wholesale trades, manufacturing, fashion, art and the service industries. However, the economy has slowed down since the boom time of the 1980s, approaching (but not yet reaching) the recession levels of the 1970s. Job layoffs and the continued exodus of major corporations to the more bucolic pastures of New Jersey, Westchester and Connecticut have contributed to the current slump. Like everything else, however, what goes down eventually comes back up.

Government

New York City was first incorporated as a city in 1653 and expanded as "Greater New York" in 1898 (when it grew to include the outer boroughs). The city is governed by a mayor and a strong city council – recently made even stronger since the US Supreme Court ruled that the city's Board of Estimate (which was composed of the presidents of each borough, the mayor and the city comptroller) was unconstitutional. The biggest shake-up in local government since the Greater City of New York was created gives the council control over the municipal budget as well as zoning and land use.

Culture and Customs

New York is a fast-paced town whose residents are possessed of a restless energy that legend says is necessary for survival. Few people seem to have time for anything not on their mental schedule, and even asking for directions in the street is best done with an awareness of this, ideally while moving at the same pace and in the same direction as the informant.

New Yorkers have persuaded themselves that living at breakneck speed, always under pressure, is stimulating and is what gives them their edge and makes Manhattan the center of the universe (which all New Yorkers believe implicitly). It may also explain why few people choose to live out their latter years in the city, if, indeed, they survive long enough to make that choice.

The city is undeniably stimulating and exciting not only for the wealth of its social and cultural pleasures but also because of its fascinating and truly varied, almost 24-hour street life. Its multifarious neighborhoods, segueing from one to another, offer boundless diversions to the eye and ear. A casual stroll in almost any direction rewards the explorer with guaranteed serendipity. Rockefeller Plaza at lunchtime, SoHo's West Broadway on Saturday, Central Park on Sunday, or Washington Square on any summer weekend will provide as much entertainment as the best Broadway show.

Fascinating Facts

Big: The first elephant to set foot in North America did so in New York City – on April 13, 1796.

Bigger: The largest meteorite ever to hit the Earth weighs in at 34 tons, and is displayed at the American Museum of Natural History on Central Park West.

Longest: Originally an Indian trail, Broadway continues well beyond the city's boundaries; as the Albany Post Road, it goes all the way to the state capital – a distance of 175 miles.

Wildlife: The first flea circus in the US made its debut in New York City in 1835.

Waterlogged: It takes an average of seven hours and 15 minutes to swim around the island of Manhattan, barring unforeseen weather (or hospital stays).

Saintly city: Two of the United States' officially canonized saints lived in New York City (one was even born here); a third passed through on his way upstate.

Heavy music: What may be the only concrete piano in existence lives in the Museum of the American Piano on West 58th Street.

Urban parking: The 26,000-acre Gateway National Recreation Area, headquartered in Brooklyn's Floyd Bennett Field, is the largest US national park located in a major metropolitan area.

Quick change artists: Radio City's Rockettes make an average of seven costume changes during the annual gala Easter Show.

Let there be light: The average Times Square neon bulb lasts for 2½ years.

Planning the Trip

Visas and Passports

A passport, a passport-size photograph, a visitor's visa, evidence of intent to leave the United States after your visit and, depending upon your country of origin, an international vaccination certificate, are required for entry into the United States by most foreign nationals. Visitors from the United Kingdom staying less than 90 days no longer need a visa. Vaccination certificate requirements vary, but proof of immunization against smallpox or cholera may be necessary.

Canadian and Mexican citizens, as well as British residents of Canada and Bermuda, are normally exempt from these requirements but it is always wise to check for specific regulations on international travel in your home country.

Customs

For a breakdown of customs allowances write to US Customs Service, PO Box 7407, Washington, DC 20044. Tel: 202-927 6724.

Meat or meat products, illegal drugs, seeds, plants, fruits and firearms are among the prohibited goods. Do not bring in any of these or any duty-free goods which are worth more than $400 (returning Americans) or $100 (foreign travelers). Visitors over 21 are allowed to bring in 200 cigarettes, 3 lbs of tobacco or 50 cigars and one liter of alcohol.

Gift exemption

A non resident may claim, as free of duty and internal revenue tax, articles up to $100 in value for use as gifts for other persons, if you will remain in the United States for at least 72 hours and the gifts accompany you. This $100 gift exemption or any part of it can be claimed only once every six months. You may include 100 cigars within this gift exemption. However, alcoholic beverages may not be included in the gift exemption. *Make sure you do not have your articles gift-wrapped, as they must be available for customs inspection.*

If you are not entitled to the $100 gift exemption, you may bring in articles up to $25 in value free of duty for your personal or household use. You may include any of the following: 50 cigarettes, 10 cigars, 150 milliliters of alcoholic beverages, or 150 milliliters of alcoholic perfume or proportionate amounts. If any of these limits are exceeded or if the total amount of all dutiable articles exceeds $25, no exemption can be applied.

Articles bought in "duty-free" shops in foreign countries are subject to US Customs duty and restrictions but may be included in your exemption.

Extension of Stay

Non-US citizens should contact the US Immigration and Naturalization Service at 425 I. St, NW, Washington, DC 20536. Tel: 202-514 4316.

American medical services are extremely expensive. Always travel with full and comprehensive travel insurance to cover any emergencies.

The dollar comes in denominations from $1 through $5, $10, $20, $50, $100 and up. It is always green, although bearing the head of different presidents. There is a two-dollar bill, although it is considered unlucky and is rarely seen. Coins begin with the penny (1¢) and ascend through the nickel (5¢), dime (10¢), quarter (25¢), half-dollar (50¢) and the infrequent one-dollar coin, which is unpopular as it closely resembles a quarter.

American visitors

Credit cards are accepted almost everywhere, although not all cards at all places. They can also be used to withdraw money at ATMs (automatic teller machines) marked with the corresponding stickers (i.e. Visa, Mastercard, American Express, etc.). Out of state bank cards work, too, provided you find out what the corresponding system in New York is before you leave home.

Overseas visitors

Although New York used to act like a backward nation when it came to dealing with foreign currency, today there are numerous outlets for exchange (although a check not written in dollars can still take weeks to clear).

A few banks still charge a fee to change traveler's checks unless you have an account there, although traveler's checks (as long as they are in dollar amounts) are accepted in most hotels and good restaurants so long as they are accompanied by proper identification. Keep your passport handy.

It is advisable to acquire enough dollars at one of the airport banks or currency exchanges to last for a day or two at least. Once in Manhattan, money can be exchanged on weekdays at one of the branches of **Thomas Cook Currency Exchange** (29 Broadway, 41 East 42nd St, and 630 Fifth Ave. Tel: 757 6915). **Thomas Cook**'s office at 160 East 53rd Street (Tel:

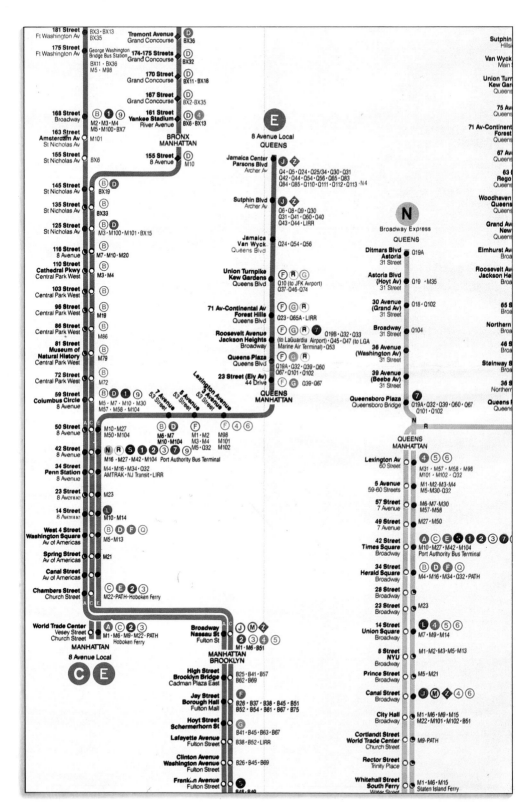

755 9780) also sells and cashes traveler's checks; also at **American Express** (374 Park Ave. Tel: 421 8240) plus other branches around town and **Chemical Bank** (277 Park Ave. Tel: 935 9935) and numerous other branches.

Among foreign exchange centers offering full services are the **Ruesch International** at 608 Fifth Ave, tel: 977 2700, the **People's Foreign Exchange** at 500 Fifth Ave, tel: 391 5270 and **Harold Reuter & Co**, in Grand Central Station, tel: 661 7600.

Banks that deal with international money transactions include **Chemical**, **Chase Manhattan**, **Citibank** and **Westminster Bank USA**. Check the telephone book for the addresses of different branches.

Public Holidays

As with other countries in the world, the United States has gradually shifted most of its public holidays to the Monday closest to the actual dates, thus creating a number of three-day weekends throughout the year. Holidays that are celebrated no matter what day on which they fall are:
Christmas, **New Year's Day**, **Thanksgiving** (last Thursday in Nov).
Election Day (day following first Monday in November, every four years).
Independence Day (July 4).

Other holidays are:
Martin Luther King Jr's Birthday (Jan 15).
President's Day commemorating Lincoln and Washington (Feb, 3rd Monday).
St Patrick's Day (Mar 17).
Memorial Day (May, last Monday).
Labor Day (Sept, first Monday).
Yom Kippur and **Rosh Hashanah** (both in Sept).
Columbus Day (Oct, 2nd Monday).
Veterans Day (Nov 11).

Getting There

Unless otherwise stated, all telephone numbers are preceded by the area code (212).

By Air

East of Manhattan on Long Island, New York's two major airports, **John F. Kennedy International** and **LaGuardia**, are respectively 15 and 8 miles from the city, with driving time from Kennedy estimated at just under one hour. In practice, heavy traffic can sometimes double this. Most charters and domestic flights and some international flights use LaGuardia. New York's third airport, **Newark**, is actually in New Jersey and, although slightly more distant, is often faster to reach to and from Manhattan.

By Sea

Stretching along the Hudson River from 48th to 52nd Streets in Manhattan, the Passenger Ship Terminal has customs facilities, baggage handling, rooftop parking and bus connections to Midtown, all in a spacious, air-conditioned building.

By Rail

Trains arrive and depart from Manhattan's two railroad terminals: **Grand Central** at Park Avenue and 42nd St, and **Pennsylvania Station** at Seventh Avenue and 33rd Street. City buses stop outside each terminal and each sits atop a subway station. Amtrak information, tel: 582 6875 or (toll-free) 1-800-872 7245.

By Road

From the south, the **New Jersey Turnpike** leads into lower Manhattan via the Holland Tunnel or Lincoln Tunnel (Midtown) and offers access farther north via the George Washington Bridge, across which traffic from the west also enters the city off the Bergen-Passaic Expressway. From the northwest, the **New York State Thruway** connects with the Henry Hudson Parkway leading into northern Manhattan. Driving in from the Long Island airports, access is via the Midtown Tunnel or (also from the New England Thruway) across the Triborough Bridge and down Manhattan's East River Drive. The city's main bus terminal, the **Port Authority**, sits atop two subway lines and is serviced by long distance bus (including Greyhound) as well as several local commuter lines. City buses stop outside. A modern, air-conditioned terminal with shops and facilities, it tends, like most bus stations, to attract its share of riffraff and lowlife. Although well-policed, it is not the sort of place to trust strangers or to leave bags unguarded.

Special Facilities

Children

Most of the activities that adults would take part in are likely to appeal to children as well, especially the Circle Line boat trip around Manhattan, Macy's Thanksgiving Day parade and July 4 fireworks display, the Guinness World Records exhibit, and the Staten Island ferry. There are wonderful children's zoos in Central Park and at both the Bronx and Staten Island. And some supposedly adult activities, such as visiting the Fulton Fish Market at six o'clock in the morning, might be more popular with children than with their parents. Small Journeys, tel: 874 7300, specializes in educational tours and sites of special interest to the younger set. And Central Park has an entire children's district that includes the Conservatory Water, Fifth Avenue at 72nd Street, where weekend crowds race their model boats; and the statues of Alice In Wonderland, Mother Goose and other fairy tale figures are always swarming with kids.

The Children's Museum of Manhattan, 212 West 83rd St, tel: 721 1234, encourages participation and there are similar hands-on museums at Snug Harbor in Staten Island, tel: 718-273 2060 and in Brooklyn at 145 Brooklyn Ave, tel: 718-735 4400. You may want to consider also the Fire Department museum, 278 Spring St, tel: 691 1303; the dazzling Liberty Science Center (just across the Hudson River, in New Jersey), tel: 201-200 1000; and the South Street Seaport's Children's Center, tel: 669 9400.

There are hundreds of exotic fish for kids to wonder at in the New York Aquarium, West 8th St and Surf Ave, Coney Island, tel: 718-265 3474 (FISH); and there are playgrounds in Central Park, Washington Square Park, at West 74th Street and Riverside Drive, and in Yorkville at Second Avenue and 93rd Street.

Consult weekly listings in local papers or magazines for a full list of children's theater events. Among the more established troupes are:
The Paper Bag Players, 50 Riverside Dr. Tel: 362 0431.
Gramercy Puppet Theater, 123 Waverly Pl. Tel: 254 9074.
The Little People's Theatre, 39 Grove St. Tel: 765 9540.

Gays

The Gay and Lesbian Switchboard, tel: 777 1800, exists specifically to provide information to gay men and women about all aspects of gay life in New York including recommendations of bars, restaurants, accommodations, legal counselling, etc. The Gay and Lesbian Visitor Center, 135 West 20th St, tel: 463 9030, is another helpful organisation. Many bookshops (such as the Gay & Lesbian Bookstore, 584 Hudson St, tel: 989 4850) stock the *Gay Yellow Pages*, along with various other useful publications.

Disabled

Information about rights, facilities, etc from the Mayor's Office for People with Disabilities, 52 Chambers Street, Room 206, New York, NY 10007, tel: 788 2830.

Students

Columbia University, tel: 854 1754, operates an International Students Office to give advice on visas and other documents; the university also has an Information and Visitors Service, tel: 854 2845, which publishes a weekly calendar of events at the university. Similar information services are offered by Hunter College, 695 Park Ave, tel: 772 4000, and New York University's Office of Student Affairs, Loeb Student Center, 566 La Guardia Pl., tel: 998 4900, where there's a lounge and basement dining room, plus free literature about student activities.

Useful Addresses

The New York Convention & Visitors Bureau, 2 Columbus Circle, New York, NY 10019, tel: 397 8222, has brochures and information about all the five boroughs, with the emphasis on Manhattan.

The Greater Harlem Chamber of Commerce, 1 West 125th St, New York, NY 10027, tel: 427 7200, is a useful source of information about specific events and landmarks in Harlem. There's also:

The Bronx Council on the Arts, 1738 Hone Ave, NY 10461. Tel: 718-931 9500.

The Bronx Tourism Council, 880 River Ave, NY 10452. Tel: 718-590 3518.

The Fund for the Borough of Brooklyn,

16 Court St, Brooklyn, NY 11201. Tel: 718-855 7882.

The Queen's Council on the Arts, 161-04 Jamaica Ave, Queens, NY 11432. Tel: 718-291 1100 or 718-291 ARTS.

The Staten Island Borough President's Office, Borough Hall, Staten Island, NY 10301. Tel: 718-816 2005.

Tour Operators

Maps and literature can be obtained during the week from the New York City Convention & Visitors' Bureau at Two Columbus Circle at the intersection of Eighth Ave and 59th St. Tel: 397 8222.

Ask for a copy of the Big Apple Visitors' Guide, a comprehensive listing of activities and tours. Among the most popular tours are those operated by **American Sightseeing International/ Short Line** and **Gray Line New York Tours**, tel: 397 2620 (all the regular sites); New York Apple Tours, tel: 201-947 4000; 1-800-876 9868 (double-decker buses, with hop-on, hop-off itineraries); and **Circle Line**, tel: 563 3200, which offers cruises up the Hudson River to West Point and back, and operates boats encircling Manhattan island.

Also, there are dozens of specialized tours such as **Harlem Spirituals Inc.**, tel: 757 0425, with its Sunday Morning Gospel Tour; **Manhattan Passport**, tel: 861 2746, which specializes in cultural and entertainment activities; **Big Onion Walking Tours**, tel: 439 1090 and **Sidewalks of New York**, tel: 517 0201, for tours with neighbourhood or historical themes; **Spirit Cruises**, tel: 727 2789, for moonlit cruises with dining and dancing; and **Seaport Liberty Cruises**, tel: 630 8888, for harbor trips departing from South Street Seaport; and **Island Helicopter Tours**, tel: 564 9290, offering spectacular aerial views.

Here are some others:

Art Horizons International, tel: 969 9410. Visits galleries, museums, and artists in their studio lofts.

Backstage on Broadway, tel: 575 8065. Tours that explain the intimate workings of the Broadway theaters.

Brownstone Tours. Tel: 718-875 9084. Visits Brooklyn brownstone houses.

Citywalks, tel: 989 2456. Specializes in downtown Manhattan.

Municipal Art Society, tel: 935 3960. The city's architectural highlights, including Grand Central Station.

Shopping Tours of New York, tel: 877 5820. Buying spree, by limo.

The **Lower East Side Tenement Museum** at 97 Orchard St, tel: 431 0233, offers walking tours on Sundays, which take you through a neighborhood rich with turn-of-the-century immigrant history, led by well-informed local historians. Other special events are offered year-round; call for a current schedule.

Another view of the immigrant experience is provided by the **Chinatown History Museum**, 70 Mulberry St (second floor), tel: 619 4785, which sponsors walks around one of the city's most fascinating ethnic enclaves.

You can explore the city's music underground with the **Rock and Roll Tour of New York**, tel: 807 ROCK, a guided bus excursion to sites that have been made famous by contemporary rock stars (Saturday departures from the Hard Rock Café on West 57th St).

The **Urban Park Rangers** lead nature walks and hikes in parks throughout the five boroughs; they also conduct a wide variety of wildlife workshops and events. Tel: 427 4040 for details; or 1-800-201 7275 on weekends and evenings.

Buildings around which tours are conducted are **Carnegie Hall** (Tel: 247 7800); **Gracie Mansion** (Tel: 570 4751); **Lincoln Center** (Tel: 875 5350) including the **Metropolitan Opera**; **National Broadcasting Company** (Tel: 664 7174); **Radio City Music Hall** (Tel: 632 4041); **Rockefeller Center** (Tel: 632 4000); the **United Nations** (Tel: 963 7713); **Grand Central Station** (Tel: 935 3960). The South Street Seaport Museum (Tel: 669 9416) runs a few 6am tours of the **Fulton Fish Market** from April–October.

Travel Packages

Package tours operated both by hotels and tour operators are listed in a comprehensive Tour Package Directory, with a map locating all hotels mentioned, available free from the New York Convention & Visitors Bureau. They range from basic two-night stays with titles such as "The Bare Bones" or "Super Saver" to seven-night "Big Apple Deluxe" packages that include guided tours of Lincoln Center and the opera, a yacht dinner cruise and a helicopter flight above Manhattan. There's a package, in short, for all budgets and all tastes. They can be booked either through a travel agent or directly from the hotels or tour operators listed.

Touring Out of Town

Trips to **Atlantic City**, the major gambling mecca of the East Coast, leave throughout the day from pick-up points around town. Passengers are dropped off at the various Atlantic City hotels and sometimes there are fare reductions or free gambling chips offered. Call Gray Line, tel: 397 2600, for schedules and information.

In winter, the Scandinavian Ski & Sports Shop (Tel: 757 8524) offers day trips to **Hunter Mountain** on Wed, Sat and Sun, departure time 7am; also weekend excursions to Vermont. Both ski rentals and lift tickets are included in the package price. Amtrak (1-800-872-7245) offers occasional day trips upstate, including excursions to Saratoga Springs during the summer horseracing season and also along the Hudson River for fall foliage sightseeing.

The **Catskill Mountains** is a popular year-round vacation destination for New Yorkers, with ski resorts as well as farms, health spas and year-round luxury resorts. You can call 1-800-882 CATS for specific information on the area, or get an all-over picture of upstate attractions by writing to request an "I Love New York" travel guide from the New York State Division of Tourism, 1 Commerce Plaza, Albany, NY 12245, or call 1-800-I LOVE NY (456 8369).

In summertime, New Yorkers love to get out of town, preferably to the **Hamptons** or **Fire Island** but sometimes just to **Jones Beach** (Tel: 516-785 1600), a great stretch of sand and surf relatively close to the city. All these places are on **Long Island** to the east, serviced by the Long Island Railroad (tel: 718-217 LIRR) from Pennsylvania Station with crowded trains that nevertheless usually arrive faster than driving on the congested highways. (There are also limousines, helicopter and jitney bus services to the Hamptons. Telephone the Long Island Convention & Visitors Bureau at 1-800-441 4601 for details.)

The **Hamptons towns** are pretty, with interesting shops and cute restaurants, but nearby **Sag Harbor** and **Shelter Island** are just as scenic and much quieter. Day-trippers in search of less exclusive beach ambiance are better advised to visit Fire Island, to which ferries run from Bayshore (Tel: 516-665 3600) across to **Ocean Beach**, the most popular community; from Sayville (Tel: 516-589 0810) and Patchogue (Tel: 516-475 1665). There are some guest houses on Fire Island but rarely enough rooms in summer.

Other popular spots to visit are the old whaling town of **Mystic**, Connecticut, where Mystic Seaport (Tel: 203-572 0711) is the country's largest maritime museum; and the town of **New Hope**, Pennsylvania (Tel: 215-862 5880), an artists' and writers' colony with smalltown ambiance and barge rides on the Delaware canal. Both are within a two-hour drive of Manhattan and have numerous quaint inns and bed-and-breakfasts.

Embassies and Consulates

Australia, 636 Fifth Ave. Tel: 245 4000.
Austria, 950 Third Ave. Tel: 737 6400.
The Bahamas, 767 Third Ave. Tel: 421 6420.
Bangladesh, 821 UN Plaza. Tel: 867 3434.
Barbados, 800 Second Ave. Tel: 867 8435.
Belgium, 50 Rockefeller Plaza. Tel: 586 5110.
Bolivia, 211 East 43rd St. Tel: 687 0530.
Brazil, 630 Fifth Ave. Tel: 757 3080.
Canada, 1251 Avenue of the Americas. Tel: 596 1700.
Costa Rica, 80 Wall St, Suite 1117. Tel: 425 2620.
Denmark, 825 Third Ave. Tel: 223 4545.
Finland, 380 Madison Ave. Tel: 573 6007.
France, 934 Fifth Ave. Tel: 606 3600.
Germany, 460 Park Ave. Tel: 308 8700.
Greece, 69 East 79th St. Tel: 988 5500.
Ireland, 345 Park Ave. Tel: 319 2555.
Israel, 800 Second Ave. Tel: 351 5200.
Italy, 690 Park Ave. Tel: 737 9100.
Jamaica, 767 Third Ave. Tel: 935 9000.

Japan, 299 Park Ave. Tel: 371 8222.
Malta, 249 East 35th St. Tel: 725 2345.
Mexico, 8 East 41st St. Tel: 689 0456.
The Netherlands, 1 Rockefeller Plaza. Tel: 246 1429.
New Zealand, 1 UN Plaza. Tel: 826 1960.
Norway, 825 Third Ave. Tel: 421 7333.
Portugal, 630 Fifth Ave. Tel: 246 4580.
Russia, 9 East 91st St. Tel: 348 0926.
Saudi Arabia, 866 UN Plaza. Tel: 752 2740.
South Africa, 333 East 38th St. Tel: 213 4880.
Spain, 150 East 58th St. Tel: 355 4080.
Sweden, One Dag Hammerskjold Plaza. Tel: 751 5900.
Switzerland, 665 Fifth Ave. Tel: 758 2560.
Trinidad and Tobago, 420 Lexington Ave. Tel: 682 7272.
United Kingdom, 845 Third Ave. Tel: 745 0202.
Venezuela, 7 East 51st St. Tel: 826 1660.

Practical Tips

Business Hours

New Yorkers work long and hard in a city where this is generally seen to be an advantage. Normal business hours are 9am–5 or 6pm but shops, particularly, tend to stay open much later – especially in the main parts of town. Needless to say, there is no close-down at lunchtime, which for many stores is the busiest time of day. Some shops are open on Sundays. Banking hours are nominally 9am–3pm but increasingly, banks are opening as early as 8am and staying open into the late afternoon or early evening hours.

Most New Yorkers in the service industries (restaurants, hotels, transportation) regard tips as a God-given right, not just a pleasant gratuity. The fact is, many people rely on tips to make up for what are often poor hourly salaries. Therefore, unless service is truly horrendous, you can figure on tipping everyone from bellmen and porters (usually 50¢ a bag; or $1 if only one bag); to hotel doormen ($1, especially if they hail you a cab); hotel maids ($1 a day, left in your room when you check out), rest room attendents (at least 25¢) and room-service waiters (approximately 15 percent of the bill). In restaurants, the best way to figure out the tip is to double the tax (which adds up to a little more than 15 percent; add a dollar or two if service is great). In taxis, it's reasonable to tip 15 percent of the total fare, with a 25¢ minimum.

Religious Services
MIDTOWN

Central Synagogue, 123 East 55th St, at Lexington Ave. The city's oldest synagogue in continuous use.
St Patrick's Cathedral, Fifth Ave, between 50th and 51st Streets. The city's most famous Catholic church.
St Peter's Lutheran Church, 619 Lexington Ave, at East 54th St. Jazz eucharists on Sunday afternoons.
Fifth Avenue Presbyterian Church, 705 Fifth Ave, at West 55th St. Frequent Sunday concerts.
Marble Collegiate Church, Fifth Ave and West 29th St. Former pastor Dr Norman Vincent Peale put this 1854 Dutch Reform church on the map.

UPPER EAST SIDE

St Nicholas Russian Orthodox Cathedral, 15 East 97th St. Built in 1902; traditional Russian Orthodox.
Temple Emanu-el, 840 Fifth Ave at East 65th St. Built in 1929, the world's largest Reform temple.
The Mosque of New York, Third Ave and East 96th St. New York's newest mosque, catering to all Muslims.

UPPER WEST SIDE

Riverside Church, 490 Riverside Drive at West 122nd St. Interdenominational; features the world's largest carillon and bell.

Islamic Center of New York, 1 Riverside Drive at West 72nd St. Muslim center.
Buddhist Church of New York, 332 Riverside Drive at West 105th St. Zen meditations are held here.
Cathedral of St John the Divine, Amsterdam Avenue and West 112th St. The world's largest Gothic cathedral offers weekly concerts and special events, as well as religious services.

HARLEM

Canaan Baptist Church, 132 West 116th St. Tel: 866 0302. One of the best places to hear soul-stirring music.
Abyssinnian Baptist Church, 132 West 138th St. Former church of Adam Clayton Powell, Jr and an integral part of Harlem's religious and political history.
Mother A.M.E. Zion Church, 140–146 West 137th St. The city's first African-American church, established in 1796.
St Philip's Episcopal Church, 208 West 134th St. Since 1818 has played a key role in the religious, political and economic life of the city's African-American community.

THE VILLAGES/LOWER MANHATTAN

Grace Church, 802 Broadway at East 10th St. Designed by James Renwick, this Gothic Revival Episcopal church was also the site of Tom Thumb's wedding in 1864.
John Street Methodist Church, 44 John St. The "mother church" of American Methodism, built in 1841.
Trinity Church, Broadway and Wall St. The city's oldest Episcopal parish (Alexander Hamilton is buried in the graveyard); frequent concerts and special events.

THE OUTER BOROUGHS

Friends Meeting House, 137–16 Northern Blvd, Flushing, Queens. The oldest house of worship in New York City, built in 1694.

Media

The internationally-known *New York Times* is the paper of choice for most well-informed readers, with its bulky Sunday edition listing virtually everything of consequence. On a daily basis, three tabloids compete for the rest of the audience: the *New York Post*, famed for its garish headlines and downmarket appeal; and the *Daily News* which until outsold (by the *Los Angeles Times* and *New York Times*), boasted of having the largest daily circulation of any newspaper in America. The weekly *Village Voice* is most valuable for its comprehensive listings and classified ads, while a small but feisty competitor, the *New York Press*, is one of the best of the many free weeklies to be found around town.

Television

Free tickets are occasionally available for shows produced here by the three major networks: **ABC**, 77 West 66th St. Tel: 456 3537, **CBS**, 51 West 52nd St. Tel: 975 2476 and **NBC**, 30 Rockefeller Plaza. Tel: 664 2333 but not for programs by the Public Broadcasting System (PBS). These can be picked up on channels 7, 2, 4 and 13 respectively on the VHF band. There are three additional local stations WNYW (5), WPIX (11), WOR (9) as well as about a dozen UHF stations, some of which broadcast in Spanish and other languages.

At present four cable companies – under the umbrella of Time Warner – offer a wide variety of basic cable channels, although the exact number differs from borough to borough. Most major hotels offer cable in their guests' rooms and some of the Manhattan public access programs (particularly late at night) are as sexually explicit as you're likely to see anywhere in the world. Not necessarily admirable, but certainly something to tell the folks about back home.

Postal Services

Manhattan's main post office on Eighth Avenue between 31st and 33rd Street is open 24 hours a day for stamps, express mail and certified mail. For information, tel: 967 8585.

Telecoms

For complaints, dial 811; wrong number refunds, dial 211; and the current time, dial 976 1616.

Manhattan numbers all have the same 212 prefix; Brooklyn, Queens, Staten Island and the Bronx numbers are prefixed by 718. This and other area codes must be preceded by 1 when direct dialing from Manhattan.

For information about Manhattan numbers dial 411; for information about other numbers dial 1, then the area code, then 555 1212. For international calls dial 011 (the international access code), then the country code, city code and local number. For more information on international dialing call this toll-free number: 1-800-874 4000. (Numbers prefixed with 800 are free.)

Telephones accepting credit cards can be found in major centers as Grand Central and Pennsylvania stations, plus most major hotels offer telex and fax services. Faxes can also be sent from most of the copy and printing shops found around the city, as well as the now-ubiquitous Mail Boxes Etc. outlets.

Emergencies
Security and Crime

Like any major city, but perhaps even more than most, New York is not a place to take any risks with your life or your belongings. Miscreants whose lives are devoted to exploiting the unwary will be quick to seize advantage of your bewilderment, so adopt the typical New Yorker's guise of looking street-smart and aware at all times. Ostentatious displays of jewelry or wealth invite muggers; foolhardy excursions into deserted regions (such as Central Park) at night are equally unwise. And although the subways are not as dangerous as their reputation, they are not a safe place for women traveling alone late at night. Once having passed through the turnstile, stay within sight – or at least within shouting range – of a token booth. Don't stand on the edge of the platform unless you are sure about the people standing near to you. In emergencies, dial 911 for police, fire or ambulance.

Useful telephone numbers:
Police, fire or **ambulance**, tel: 911.
Deaf Emergency Line, tel: 1-800-342 4357 (police, fire, ambulance).
Sex Crimes Report Line, tel: 267 7273.
Alcoholics Anonymous, tel: 683 3900.
Suicide Prevention HelpLine, tel: 532 2400.

Downtown police precincts:
(Call for non-emergencies only; otherwise dial 911).
1st, 16 Ericsson Place (West Canal Street). Tel: 334 0611.
5th, 19 Elizabeth St (Chinatown). Tel: 334 0711.
6th, 233 West 10th St (Greenwich Village). Tel: 741 4811.
7th, 19 Pitt St (Lower East Side). Tel: 477 7311.
9th, 321 East 5th St. Tel: 477 7811.
10th, 230 West 20th St. Tel: 741 8211.
13th, 230 East 21st St. Tel: 477 7411.
17th, 167 East 51st St. Tel: 826 3211.
Midtown South, 375 West 35th St. Tel: 239 9811.
Midtown North, 524 West 42nd St. Tel: 760 8300.

Uptown police precincts:
19th, 312 East 94th St. Tel: 860 1550.
20th, 120 West 82nd St. Tel: 580 6411.
Central Park, Transverse Road at 86th St. Tel: 570 4820.
23rd, 164 East 102nd St. Tel: 860 6411.
24th, 151 West 100th St. Tel: 678 1811.
25th, 120 East 119th St. Tel: 860 6511.
28th, 2271 Eighth Ave (near 123rd St). Tel: 678 1611.
30th, 451 West 151st St. Tel: 690 8811.
32nd, 250 West 135th St. Tel: 690 6311.
34th, 4295 Broadway. Tel: 927 9711.

Loss of Belongings

Your chances of retrieving lost property are not high, but the occasional public-spirited individual may turn items in to the nearest police precinct. To inquire about items left on public transportation, tel: 718-625 6200. Items left in taxis, tel: 840 4734.

Lost or stolen credit cards:
American Express, tel: 1-800-528 4800.
Visa, tel: 1-800-227 6800.
Carte Blanche/Diners Club, tel: 1-800-525 9135.
MasterCard, tel: 1-800-826 2181. All 800 calls are free of charge.

Medical Services

Useful telephone numbers:
On-call doctors, tel: 718-238 2100.
Dental emergency, tel: 679 3966 (after 8pm, tel: 679 4172).
Kaufman's Pharmacy, 50th St and Lexington Ave, tel: 755 2266, is open 24 hours a day every day of the week.

Hospitals with emergency rooms:
Medical services are very expensive in this country. Are you insured?

Midtown/downtown
Bellevue Hospital, First Ave and East 27th St. Tel: 561 4141.
NYU Medical Center, 550 First Ave at 33rd St. Tel: 263 7300.
Cabrini Medical Center, Third Ave and East 20th St. Tel: 995 6000.
Beth Israel Medical Center, First Ave at East 16th St. Tel: 420 2000.
St Vincent's Hospital, Seventh Ave at 11th St. Tel: 604 7000.

Uptown
Columbia Presbyterian Medical Center, 622 West 168th St. Tel: 305 2500.
Harlem Hospital, 506 Lenox Ave. Tel: 491 1234.
Mount Sinai Hospital, Fifth Ave and East 100th St. Tel: 241 6500.
Lenox Hill Hospital, 77th St and Park Ave. Tel: 434 2000.
New York Hospital, York Avenue and East 70th St. Tel: 746 5454.

Getting Around
On Arrival
Orientation

Most of the city's best-known hotels as well as offices, the Broadway theater district and major shops are concentrated in the Midtown area, which runs from about 30th St north to Central Park at 60th St. Generally, even-numbered streets have one-way eastbound traffic; odd-numbered streets, westbound traffic. There are very few exceptions. Most avenues are one-way, either north or south, the major exception being Park Ave which is wide enough for two-way traffic north of 44th St.

Buses do not run on Park Ave but do run on most other avenues as well as on major cross-streets (also two-way): Houston, 14th, 23rd, 34th, 42nd, 57th, 66th, 86th, 116th, 125th and a few others. Subway trains cross town at 14th and 42nd St but there is no north–south line east of Lexington Ave or west of Eighth Ave and Broadway above 59th St.

Recommended Maps

Most good book stores sell a variety of New York maps, with possibly the largest selection being at Hagstrom Map & Travel Center, 57 West 43rd St, tel: 398 1222, which is a subsidiary of one of the country's biggest mapmakers, the American Map Corporation. Another good source is the Rand McNally Map & Travel Store, 150 East 52nd St. Tel: 758 7488.

Maps are included in the free tourist magazines available in most hotel lobbies, but tend to be selectively incomplete. Ditto with the literature offered by the Convention & Visitors Bureau, with the exception of the pull-out map in their Big Apple Travel Planning Guide, which keys in major landmarks, and includes a subway map.

Airport/City

Carey Airport Express operates buses (under $15) from both **JFK** and **LaGuardia** air terminals to six Manhattan drop-off points, including one opposite Grand Central Station. Taxis are metered ($30-$40 from Kennedy; $22-$25 from LaGuardia) but the fare from the airport in Newark, New Jersey (about $40) includes a $10 surcharge. Bridge and tunnel tolls are extra.

Unsuspecting visitors straight off an airplane are often besieged by private taxi drivers offering rides into the city at inflated prices. The more naïve you look, the higher the price quoted. The vehicle on offer may turn out to be sumptuous: an air-conditioned limo with deep carpets and a good sound system, but it's best to resist temptation. Most drivers are, in their own fashion, reputable enough – out to make a buck, not interfere with your life. But it can be an unnerving experience traveling a little-known route with

an unfamiliar, unregistered driver, even if you've negotiated a reasonable price. Unless you have great savvy and a keen sense of direction, it's best to stick to the official taxi stands.

Helicopter service between Newark, LaGuardia and JFK and the 34th Street Heliport in Manhattan is run by New York Helicopter, tel: 1-800-645 3494.

New Jersey Transit and Olympia Trails Coach Service operate regular express buses between **Newark** airport and Manhattan, the former to the Port Authority Bus Terminal at 8th Avenue and 41st Street, the latter to Penn Station, the World Trade Center and Grand Central Station. Minibus services from all three airports to major Manhattan hotels is provided by Gray Line Air Shuttle, tel: 315 3006, at fares averaging $13 to $20 a person.

The cheapest route from JFK to the city is via Green Bus Lines to the Lefferts Boulevard subway station (from which A trains run to Brooklyn, lower Manhattan and the west side) or to the Kew Gardens-Union Turnpike station (E and F trains to Queens and mid-Manhattan). From LaGuardia, the Triboro Coach Corporation operates the Q-33 bus to the 74th Street subway station in Jackson Heights, Queens, from which various trains run to Manhattan.

Many airlines maintain a joint Airlines Ticket Office at 100 East 42nd Street. Tel: 986 0888.

Public Transportation

Subway trains run on a 24-hour basis; so do buses, but less frequently after midnight. Information on either by dialing 718-330 1234.

Taxis, all metered, cruise the streets randomly and must be hailed. One fare covers all passengers up to four (five in a few of the larger cabs). Call 840 4734 for lost property in taxis; 221 8294 to make a complaint. After 8pm there is a fifty cent surcharge on all taxi rides. For out-of-town trips the fare doubles once outside the city limits.

Private Transportation
By Car

Driving around Manhattan is not much fun although, should the need arise, there is a generous range of firms

available at all airports from which cars can be rented. You must be at least 21 years old, have a valid driver's license and at least one major credit card to rent a car. Be sure that you are properly insured for both collision and liability. Insurance is usually not included in the base rental fee. You may already be insured by your own insurance or credit-card company. It is also a good idea to inquire about an unlimited mileage package. If not, you may well be charged extra per mile over a given limit.

Rental fees vary depending on the time of year, how far in advance you book your rental, and if you travel on weekdays or weekends. Inquire about any discounts or benefits you may be eligible for, including corporate, credit card or frequent flyer programs.

Alamo	
US	(800) 327-9633
International	+1-305-522 0000
Avis	
US	(800) 331-1212
International	+1-918-664 4600
Budget	
US	(800) 527-0700
International	+1-214-404 7600
Dollar	
US	(800) 800-4000
International	+1-813-877 5507
Enterprise	
US	(800) 325-8007
International	+1-314-781 8232
Hertz	
US	(800) 654-3131
International	+1-405-749 4424
National	
US	(800) 227-7368
International	+1-612-830 2345
Thrifty	
US	(800) 331-4200
International	+1-918-669 2499

By Limousine

If you can afford the extravagance of this, the ultimate luxury in road transportation, contact one of the private car companies for a limousine at your beck and call. These include:

Carey Limousine, tel: 599 1222.
Smith Limousine, tel: 247 0711.
Dav-El Limousines Inc., tel: 645 4242.
Gotham Limousines Inc., 527 West 36th St, tel: 868 8860.

Where to Stay

The old adage that New York has more of everything than virtually anywhere on earth is only a slight exaggeration when it comes to hotel accommodations. The following list is hardly exhaustive, but rather represents a sampling of the best hotels in Manhattan in the moderate to luxury price range, plus a few inexpensive "characters." Most are Midtown, with a few farther afield.

When making reservations, ask specifically about special rates and "package deals," especially for weekend stays. Telephone reservations staffs in America are notorious for quoting only the most expensive rates, but many hotels offer an ever-changing variety of discounts and promotions. You are well advised to book your room by credit card and secure a guaranteed late arrival, in the foreseeable circumstance that your flight is interminably stacked up over the airport or your 30-minute limo ride from the airport turns into a 2-hour nightmare of traffic jams. New York City is the last place on earth you want to find yourself stranded without a hotel room. The 800 telephone numbers are toll-free reservations switchboards.

In addition to standard hotels, we have included a short list of "suite hotels" and bed & breakfast accommodation. The former are basically apartments, available from a few nights up to rates by the month. The latter are modeled on those in the United Kingdom and Europe. As with B&Bs everywhere, reservations should be made as far in advance as possible.

A subjective rating system follows, which is **based on current prices**:
$$$$ = Top of the line
$$$ = Upscale
$$ = Reasonable
$ = Least expensive

Hotels
Midtown

The Algonquin, $$$ 59 West 44th St. Tel: 840 6800; 1-800-548 0345. Once a haven for the Round Table (New York's version of the Bloomsbury literary set), still a favorite of the theater set, the Algonquin retains an atmosphere of sedate, oak-panelled, turn-of-the-century charm. Clubby and Victorian in demeanor, civilized in its treatment of guests, and right in the heart of the Broadway theater district.

Doral Court, $$ 130 East 39th St. Tel: 685 1100; 1-800-624 0607. Sister hotel to the Doral Inn (there are four Doral hotels in Manhattan, and guests at one can use the facilities of the others), this is a small, bright, modern hotel where service is friendly, especially in the lobby-level Courtyard Café and Bar. Its location on a quiet side street, close to Midtown business, shopping and transportation (like Grand Central Station) is also a plus.

The Doral Inn, $$ Lexington Ave at 44th St. Tel: 755 1200; 1-800-223 5823. Ironically known for its fine view of the majestic Waldorf Astoria across the street, yet clean, comfortable, and affordable, if somewhat heavily trafficked by tourists and airline staff.

The Drake Hotel, $$$ 440 Park Ave at 56th St. Tel: 421 0900; 1-800-372 5369. A huge Swiss-owned model of decorum and efficiency, much favored by corporate executives for its clean, hushed, boardroom atmosphere. Very large and very modern rooms.

The Essex House-Hotel Nikko, $$$ 160 Central Park South. Tel: 247 0300; 1-800-NIKKO US. A multi-million dollar upgrade has transformed this once-staid 1930s landmark-on-the-park into an ultra-luxury property with a health spa, Japanese restaurant and fully equipped business center, among other amenities.

Hotel Beverley, $$ 125 East 50th St. Tel: 753 2700. This recently renovated establishment, over 60 years old, is the kind of place only frequent travelers to New York know about. With its comfortable and reasonably-priced suites that come equipped with kitchenettes (some also with views of the neighboring Waldorf Hotel), you can see why. There are also a restaurant, beauty salon, barber and 24-hour pharmacy on the premises.

Hotel Inter-Continental, $$$ 111 East 48th St. Tel: 755 5900. Opened in the 1920s as The Barclay, this hotel blends executive-class efficiency with majestic spaces and a full range of pampering services. Public rooms include two fine restaurants, a clothier, and a luxury gift shop.

New York Palace, $$$$ 455 Madison Ave at 50th St. Tel: 888 7000; 1-800-221 4982. A grandiose monument to lavish, American-style pomp and excess, recently purchased by the Sultan of Brunei. Appointed in a style that can only be called post-Modern Rococo, all gilt and marble and floral splashes, the Palace has a meticulous regime of flawlessly detailed service that can make the average guest feel like an imperial Pasha. In its brashly high-style way it's very New York.

The New York Hilton, $$$ 1335 Avenue of the Americas. Tel: 586 7000; 1-800-HILTONS. A Hilton: huge, modern, impersonal but consistent.

Omni Berkshire Place, $$$ 21 East 52nd St. Tel: 753 5800; 1-800-THE-OMNI. Though it's been acquired by the Omni chain, the Berkshire retains its old-fashioned grace and Continental attention to personal services. Known by some frequent guests as "a junior Plaza," it is comfortable and comforting, a tastefully appointed oasis of calm and dignity right in the heart of the Midtown shopping and business bustle.

The Paramount, $$ 235 West 46th St (between Broadway and Eighth Ave). Tel: 764 5500; 1-800-225 7474. A definitive New York fashion statement (and the third in Ian Schrager's roster of chic hotels). The Paramount's high design rooms and public spaces dazzle and amaze. Designed by Philippe Starck, they also attract hordes of the "hip unrich," who come here to enjoy such extraordinary amenities as beds with headboards made of reproductions of famous paintings, a fitness club, a supervised playroom for children, an elegant restaurant and The Whiskey, a trendsetting small bar. Rooms are small but well-, even futuristically-equipped.

Le Parker Meridien, $$$ 119 West 56th St. Tel: 245 5000; 1-800-543 4300. Part of the internationally known French chain, modern, airy, with an excellent restaurant.

The Peninsula, $$$ 700 Fifth Ave at 55th St. Tel: 247 2200; 1-800-262 4967. Gracious, continental in its services, with a fine health club and spa, in a prime location.

The Plaza, $$$$ Fifth Ave at 59th St. Tel: 759 3000; 1-800-759 3000. Once the grandest of New York's grand hotels, the venerable Plaza recently underwent a loving restoration that refurbished its Edwardian splendor to dazzling splendor. Then it was purchased by billionaire developer Donald Trump, who poured millions of dollars more into it – not that this was needed. The rooms are furnished with fine antiques; the high ceilings decorated with charming murals; and the service as close to Olde World elegance as you'll find in America. The Plaza also features the Oak Bar and the Edwardian Room, two of Old Money's favorite before-and-after theater spots.

Renaissance Hotel, $$ Two Times Square. Tel: 765 7676; 1-800-682 9222. A recent star of the new, improved Times Square. Rooms include such high-tech innovations as large-screen TVs and two phone lines. Very convenient for theaters, restaurants and Midtown business.

The Ritz-Carlton, $$$$ 112 Central Park South. Tel: 757 1900; 1-800-241 3333. It is often remarked that if you removed a baronial country mansion from the South of England to Central Park South, you'd have something like the Ritz-Carlton. Tweedy, refined, and comfortable without being overly elegant or plush, it is favored by the international corporate elite and Old Money.

The Royalton, $$$ 44 West 44th St. Tel: 869 4400; 1-800-635 9013. A chic, ultra-exclusive, and ultramodern creation of Ian Schrager of Studio 54 disco fame, with the same jet set clientele. Every line and appointment from the lobby to the lavatories is as boldly, coldly futuristic as the set of a science fiction film, complete with state-of-the-art video and stereo gadgetry. Yet the Royalton bends over backwards to provide the scurrying, "can-do" pampering expected by its clientele of Beautiful People and Beautiful People-watchers. Convenient to the theater district.

The Sherry-Netherland, $$$ 781 Fifth Ave at 59th St. Tel: 355 2800. With the Pierre and the Plaza, the Sherry-Netherland completes a triumvirate of truly grand luxury hotels all within a mint's toss from one another. This majestic empress of hotels has earned such a faithful club of visitors that reservations must be had well in advance. Grandly expansive spaces, both public and in the rooms and suites, with royal treatment to match.

St Moritz, $$ 50 Central Park South. Tel: 755 5800. Extraordinarily old-fashioned in a way some people find utterly charming and others rather stodgy, St Moritz is the maiden aunt of Midtown hotels. Small, quiet, unassuming and comfy as an overstuffed armchair, it does boast a pleasant outdoor café, and an even more pleasant address just across from Central Park – yet near enough to Midtown shopping, business and theaters.

St Regis, $$$ 2 East 55th St. Tel: 753 4500. A grand Edwardian wedding cake of a building, filigreed and charmingly muralled (by the likes of Maxfield Parrish), the St Regis is a magnet for somewhat older, moneyed guests who appreciate the ambience of a more regal age than ours. The convenient location doesn't hurt, either.

UN Plaza-Park Hyatt, $$$ One United Nations Plaza. Tel: 758 1234; 1-800-233 1234. The clientele for this bustling, bravely moderne establishment is obvious. Although its location is inconvenient for some visitors, others appreciate its busy atmosphere of international intrigue and deal brokering, as UN representatives and staffs from many nations meet in its heroically proportioned lobby and dine at the aptly-named Ambassador Grill. Besides the sight seeing, benefits to non-ambassadorial guests include rooms with glorious views of Manhattan's skyline and the East River, and a fine set of fitness and recreation rooms including tennis courts and swimming pool.

The Waldorf-Astoria, $$$ 50th St and Park Ave. Tel: 355 3000. The most famous hotel in New York during its gilded heydays in the 1930s and 1940s, with a sweeping pre-War panache recently restored to something one feels must be very like its early glory. The grand look of the lobby and public spaces is something like H.G. Wells's heroic view of the future, and something like Cecil B. DeMille's view of Cleopatra's Egypt, and never fails to lift the visitor's spirits. The rooms are less grand but with a gracious charm that somehow eludes many younger establishments. The location is very convenient to Midtown shopping, as well as theater and business.

Upper East Side

The Carlyle, $$$$ 35 East 76th St. Tel: 744 1600. Posh, reserved, and serene in its elegance, The Carlyle remains one of the city's most highly acclaimed luxury hotels. The appointments are exquisite, the furnishings antique, and the service formal.

The Pierre, $$$$ 2 East 61st St. Tel: 838 8000; 1-800-743 7734. Justly renowned as one of New York's finest luxury hotels, with a fabulous pedigree of guests that goes back to its opening in the early 1930s. (It's now run by the Four Seasons luxury chain.) The location at Fifth Avenue and 61st Street is perfect for those intent on business or Midtown shopping and there is also a lovely view of Central Park. Rooms are large and elegant; service is quietly efficient and top flight; dining in the Café Pierre or tea in the beautiful Rotunda are among the city's most civilized offerings.

Hotel Plaza Athenee, $$$$ 37 East 64th St. Tel: 734 9100; 1-800-447 8800. Another Francophile's delight, very pretty and also very elegant.

Hotel Wales, $$ 1295 Madison Ave (at 92nd St). Tel: 876 6000; 1-800-428 5252. Once a shabby but personable hostelry known for its low rates and splendid views of Central Park, today the Wales still has those views, but has been successfully transformed into a cozy oasis of affordable luxury. Its location in the upmarket Carnegie Hill neighborhood, close to Museum Mile, chic little restaurants and Madison Avenue boutiques (as well as Central Park) is an added plus – and you can feast on the best breakfast in New York, at the eastside branch of Sarabeth's Kitchen on the ground floor. The hotel's tea salon is the setting for complimentary light breakfasts, afternoon teas and chamber music concerts.

Hotel Westbury, $$$ 15 East 69th St. Tel: 535 2000; 1-800-321 1569. Owned by Britain's Forte Hotels, which has imported a sense of London's severe graces and discreet comforts.

Hotel Beacon, $ 2130 Broadway at 75th St. Tel: 800-572 4969. This hotel within an apartment building with full-time residents is the hip place to stay in the Upper West Side. Each room has a kitchenette with coffee-maker, full refrigerator, stove and sink. Suites, with a separate bedroom, can fit four.

Hotel Excelsior, $ 45 West 81st St. Tel: 362 9200. Another old-fashioned hotel, which dates from the 1920s. Located on a pleasant block between Central Park West and Columbus Avenue's myriad shopping opportunities, this is a good place to stay for folks with simple needs. As an added bonus, there's a great old neighborhood coffee shop on the premises. Kitchenettes and weekly rates available.

The Milburn, $ 242 West 76th St. Tel: 362 1006. On a quiet side street a short walk from Lincoln Center, this 16-floor hotel offers recently refurbished rooms with color television, kitchenettes and 24-hour concierge service.

Radisson Empire Hotel, $$ 44 West 63rd St. Tel: 265 7400. You can roll out of bed and into Lincoln Center if you stay here, which makes this recently renovated 77-year-old hotel a favorite with visiting culture mavens, as well as those looking for comfort at reasonable rates. You can also walk to Central Park, the Museum of Natural History and other major attractions.

Chelsea/Gramercy Park/ Murray Hill

The Chelsea Hotel, $$ 222 West 23rd St. Tel: 243 3700. A landmark of bohemian decadence, home to beatnik poets, then Warhol drag queens, then Sid Vicious, and now... some of all of the above. For the young and adventurous, a stay at the Chelsea can be part of a ritual pilgrimage to all that is hip in lower Manhattan, as redolent with arty history as the West Village streets and the Lower East Side punk clubs. For other visitors, the Chelsea is just a dowdy, dim, and rather decrepit address, with lackadaisical service, a questionable ambience and an inconvenient location.

Gramercy Park Hotel, $$ 2 Lexington Ave at 21st St. Tel: 475-4320; 1-800-221-4083. Gramercy Park is an astonishing pocket of *fin de siècle* calm and greenery located between (but at a discreet distance from) the busy Manhattan districts. There's even a Victorian park, with squirrels cavorting in enormous old trees. The Gramercy Park Hotel, therefore, is favored by visitors who seek to relax when they return after a hard day and night in New York. Antique and genteel as a dowager princess, not plush but comfy, and moderate in price.

Morgans, $$$ 237 Madison Ave at 37th St. Tel: 686 0300; 1-800-334 3408. Another fantasy brainchild of Studio 54's Ian Schrager, Morgans may be the most fashionable temporary address in Manhattan, an ultra-exclusive, ultramodern enclave of the international jet set and millionaire celebrities. The operant words are minimalist and discreet: everything in stark grays, black and white, and so understated it doesn't even call itself a hotel or hang a sign over the door. The service, meanwhile, is extraordinarily pampering; it is said there is *nothing* the staff won't do for guests. Make reservations well in advance.

Greenwich Village

Washington Square Hotel, $ 103 Waverly Pl. Tel: 777 9515; 1-800-222 0418. Close to a century old, this historic hotel offers a unique Village locale, right off Washington Square Park, as well as small but cheerful rooms that tend to be popular with young, overseas visitors. In a former incarnation, this was the seedy Hotel Earle, where – among other things – Papa John wrote the 1960s rock song *California Dreamin'*.

Lower Manhattan

Holiday Inn Downtown, $$ 138 Lafayette St. Tel: 966 8898; 1-800-HOLIDAY. In a renovated historic building on the borders of Chinatown, Little Italy and SoHo, this hotel offers reasonably priced accommodations within walking distance of downtown's restaurants and clubs.

Millenium Hilton, $$$ 55 Church St. Tel: 693 2001; 1-800-835 2220. The sleekest of lower Manhattan's hotels: a modern, streamlined monument to corporate efficiency. Excellent restaurant, service, and views.

New York Marriott Financial Center, $$ 85 West St. Tel: 385 4900; 1-800-242 8685. One of the three Marriotts in New York and adjacent to the World Financial Center's shops, restaurants and business headquarters.

New York Vista Hotel, $$$ Three World Trade Center. Tel: 938 9100; 1-800-258 2505. Like the rest of the WTC, everything at the Vista is designed for executive class efficiency, deploying a full range of services for business patrons. The rooms are spacious and airy, and the view from any angle is spectacular, whether it's of the Statue of Liberty, Wall Street or the Hudson River waterfront. In addition, it's convenient for the fine restaurants of TriBeCa.

Suite Hotels and Bed & Breakfasts

Manhattan East Suite Hotels, $$ Tel: 465 3600; 1-800-ME-SUITE. The concept is akin to renting an apartment on a nightly, weekly, or monthly basis. Accommodations range from one-room "guest rooms" without kitchen (but with refrigerator) to two-person studios and 1- or 2-bedroom suites with kitchens. More "homey" than a hotel, they may be ideal for experienced travelers who won't miss room service, or for small families. Manhattan East currently operates nearly 2,000 such suites at nine locations from 31st Street up to 76th Street.

Chelsea Inn, $ 46 West 17th St. Tel: 645 8989; 1-800-777 8215. Casual, student-style accommodations include studios and 2-bedroom suites with kitchens, for short- or long-term stays.

Off SoHo Suites, $ 11 Rivington St. Tel: 353 0860; 1-800-OFF-SOHO. Though geographically more Lower East Side than SoHo, the suites here are clean and comfortable, and include TV and fully-equipped kitchens. Attracts a casually hip, mostly overseas clientele.

City Lights Bed & Breakfast Ltd, $ Tel: 737 7049. An agency that lists B&Bs, studios, suites, and short-term apartments in locations around the city. Other agencies: **B&B Network of New York**, tel: 645 8134 and **Urban Ventures**, tel: 594 5650.

Youth Hostels

For the young or those on a budget, the newly-renovated **New York International Youth Hostel**, 891 Amsterdam Ave at West 103rd St. Tel: 932 2300, offers dormitory-style accommodation at extremely low prices. Foreigners can stay for a week, whether or not they are members. There's a charge for linens, and a self-service kitchen and laundromat as well as a cafeteria.

Eating Out

There are literally thousands of restaurants in New York, of all sizes, types, specialties and qualities. The following does not even begin to hint at an "exhaustive" list. We cite here some of the best, those we recommend with few or even no qualms at all – enough to keep any visitor busy and happily dining for a few weeks' stay. Some famous restaurants are included because they are merely pilgrimage sites for tourists, and not to mention them would be an oversight. But we cannot wholeheartedly recommend them for dining because we ourselves feel they are overrated.

To the dismay of travel guide editors, restaurants bloom and fade, appear and disappear with startling abruptness. Changes in management, chefs or just decor can, seemingly overnight, make or break a restaurant. We have tried to list consistent, long-running successes, but no one can issue guarantees.

In order to calculate the tip, most New Yorkers simply double the sales tax shown on the bill, leaving a tip of about 17 percent at the current rate. In restaurants with captains, it is customary to leave an additional 5 percent. In most instances, we indicate which restaurants accept major credit cards, and others that accept only American Express or none at all. Your best bet is to ask when you call to make reservations.

Reservations are often necessary and almost always recommended; at the top of the line establishments, such as the Four Seasons and the River Café, they may be required as much as two weeks in advance. Of course, not all holders of reservations appear at their appointed hour, so you can take the chance of standing on line. Although many New Yorkers are uncharacteristically stoic about this form of punishment, it can be a tedious and nerve-racking experience, and doesn't add anything to the enjoyment of dining.

NOTE: Some New York restaurants close on Sundays, and a few close altogether in August. Another reason to call ahead.

Restaurants

Eating establishments of all types are mentioned throughout the main body of this book, but listed below is a selection of restaurants particularly worth seeking out.

Midtown

TOP OF THE LINE

The Four Seasons, 99 East 52nd St. Tel: 754 9494. A Manhattan favorite, though the cuisine does not always live up to its reputation as one of *the* restaurants in New York. But the restaurant is remarkable, partly for its moderne decor, all marble and copper and New York-style swagger. Partly it's the clientele in the famous Grill Room cutting fantasy deals over their scotches and bourbons, their New Orleans-style shrimp and meaty crabcakes. And partly it's the fantasy setting of the Pool Room, with its grand marble pool and palm trees. The menu changes with the seasons of the year (hence the name) and is wildly eclectic, with the roast duck and grilled fish often cited as favorites. Very popular, so make your reservations two weeks in advance. All major credit cards. Dinner: Mon–Thurs 5–9.30pm, Fri–Sat 5–11.30pm (Grill Room Mon–Sat 5–11.30 p.m.)

Le Bernardin, 155 West 51st St. Tel: 489 1515. One of the city's most elite establishments, offering excellent dining for a clientele of powerful corporate and financial leaders. Known for the delicacy of its seafood, from its pearly oyster and sea urchin appetizers to its variety of fresh ocean catch prepared in light wine sauces. The atmosphere and service are quite formal and a bit aloof, which is somehow fitting; more conducive to settling business than to romantic trysts. All major credit cards. Reservations necessary. Dinner: Mon–Sat 6–10.15pm.

La Cote Basque, 60 West 55th St. Tel: 688 6525. More outstanding French cuisine in a lovely setting. The prices are high, but worth it. Well-located to theaters. Dinner: Mon–Fri 6–10.30pm, Sat till 11pm.

Le Perigord, 405 East 52nd St (between First Ave and the East River). Tel: 755 6244. Another formal, old-world French restaurant with staying power – and first-class, classic cuisine. All major credit cards. Reservations required. Dinner: Mon–Fri 5.15–10.30pm, Sat until 11pm.

Lutece, 249 East 50th (between Second and Third Avenues). Tel: 752 2225. Once considered to be the best French restaurant in New York, Lutece has been sold by chef/owner Andre Soltner and the kitchen is now under the supervision of a former chef from Le Bernardin. You'll still need to book in advance to dine in this pretty townhouse, however, where the atmosphere is intimate and surprisingly friendly, considering the *haute* reputation. Accepts major credit cards. Reservations for dinner accepted. Open: Mon–Sat 6–10pm.

UPSCALE

China Grill, 60 West 53rd St. Tel: 333 7788. Pricey, nouvelle-Orientale, in a spacious, dim-lit interior that stretches to the 54th Street side of the CBS building. An extremely popular lunch and dinner hangout for media-types. Major credit cards accepted. Reservations recommended.

The Russian Tea Room, 150 West 57th St. Tel: 265 0947. Never known for its menu yet a thoroughly unique New York institution, the Russian Tea Room is a *must* for those who don't mind paying a high price for the chance to spy on film celebrities, Broadway stars and well-heeled "characters". The decor is eccentric and dining is in effect an excuse for sightseeing. It's best to stay with basic fare such as the Chicken Kiev, borscht and blinis. The cholesterol-conscious should beware: everything here is soaked in enough butter and cream sauce to float the Russian Navy. It's as expensive as a Broadway show, but quite possibly more entertaining. Just to say you've seen it, go for lunch, which will cost less than dinner. Now serves uniquely Russian afternoon teas; there's also an upstairs cabaret. Reservations recommended. All major credit cards. Lunch/dinner/tea: Mon–Fri 11.30 am–midnight, Sat–Sun from 11am.

San Domenico, 240 Central Park South at Columbus Circle. Tel: 265 5959. One of the most highly-rated Italian restaurants in the city, this magnet at Central Park South offers unusual Bolognese fare, especially the variety of Northern Italian pastas and the extremely large wine list. A fine place to take a large party, but not for an intimately romantic meal. Reservations required. All major credit cards. Dinner: Mon–Sat 5.30–11.30pm, Sun 4–10pm.

"21", 21 West 52nd St. Tel: 582 7200. A clubby, playpen for the business elite that is more a sightseers' pilgrimage than an unforgettable dining experience. Open till midnight Mon–Sat (closed Sundays.)

Billy's, 948 First Ave at 52nd St. Tel: 753 1870. Red-checked tablecloths and old-timey waiters give this upscale neighborhood hangout, which opened in 1870, a "real New York" feeling. The menu includes specials like corned beef and cabbage; open seven days for lunch and dinner. All major credit cards.

Café Un Deux Trois, 123 West 44th St. Tel: 354 4148. A before-and-after theater favorite, which features casual French-bistro-type fare in a bustling former hotel lobby. A fun place. Open late, every day.

Jezebel, 630 Ninth Ave at 45th St. Tel: 582 1045. Convenient to the theater district, this is one of the city's most atmospheric restaurants, with soul food served beneath fringed lamps and hanging antique lace dresses. Most major credit cards. Open for dinner every night.

Oyster Bar, lower level, Grand Central Station. Tel: 490 6650. A New York institution and a must for seafood lovers. The best fresh oysters and clam chowder in town, and you can sit at a counter or sit down in the dining room or salon. Most major credit cards. Open during the day, and evenings.

The Palm, 837 Second Ave (between 44th and 45th Streets). Tel: 687 2953. Sawdust on the floor, waiters who've been here at least a century, and steaks and more steaks are the

hallmark of this former speakeasy. A bit pricey. Most major credit cards.

Rosa Mexicano, 1063 First Ave at 58th St. Tel: 753 7407. Perhaps the most authentic Mexican fare in New York, scarcely resembling the greasy, gloppy messes passed off on the unsuspecting by gringo cooks in so many South o' the Border theme restaurants. Start at the lively bar, with an excellent margarita. The traditional Mexican main courses are delivered with admirable restraint – this is *not* fire-breathing "Tex-Mex," though you can pepper it to taste. The professional and friendly staff are accustomed to explaining the finer points of the menu. Reservations recommended. All major credit cards. Dinner: daily 5–midnight.

Rusty Staub's, 575 Fifth Ave at 47th St. Tel: 682 1000. Hearty, real American food like barbecued ribs and a surprisingly extensive wine list are the draw cards of this popular Midtown restaurant and bar, owned by a former baseball player. American Express. Open for lunch and dinner daily.

Sardi's, 234 West 44th St. Tel: 221 8440. Recommended for sightseeing, this once-glamorous, more recently touristy theater district bar & grill is again under its original ownership. Go for drinks only: Mon–Thur 11.30am–12.30pm, Fri–Sat till 1am, Sun noon–11pm.

Smith & Wollensky, 201 East 49th St. Tel: 753 1530. Another bustling, efficient steakhouse where portions are gigantic. A good wine list here, too. Accepts most major credit cards. Open for lunch and dinner weekdays, just dinner on weekends.

Sparks Steakhouse, 210 East 46th St. Tel: 687 4855. The granddaddy of New York steakhouses, Sparks is burly, boisterous, and unabashedly American. Not for the painfully shy, but a great spot to see successful New Yorkers having fun the old-fashioned way: loud and fast, whether they're drinking whiskey and telling jokes at the smoky bar or consuming huge steaks cooked to precision and placed between their elbows by the tirelessly brisk staff. Do not be misled by the high spirits, however: dinner is not particularly cheap, and reservations are needed. All major credit cards. Dinner: Mon–Thur 5–11pm, Fri–Sat till 11.30.

Carnegie Deli, 854 Seventh Ave at 55th St. Tel: 757 2245. A pilgrimage site in the heart of Midtown, this is one of New York's most famous Jewish delicatessens, where a corned beef sandwich is a must. Very crowded at lunch time, but open from 6–4am every day.

Upper East Side/Upper West Side

Café des Artistes, 1 West 67th St, off Central Park West. Tel: 877 3500. Romance is in the air at this elegant French restaurant, decorated by murals of naked nymphs. Most major credit cards. Open: Mon–Sat noon–midnight, Sun to 11pm.

Le Cirque, 58 East 65th St. Tel: 794 9292. Very elegant French restaurant where celebrities of the late Jackie Onassis caliber hobnob. Make reservations far in advance. Dinner: Mon–Sat 6–10.30pm.

Primavera, 1578 First Ave at 82nd St. Tel: 861 8608. Primavera attracts a tweedy, well-heeled crowd of Upper East Side regulars with its refined atmosphere similar to a private men's club. It is therefore a rather formal experience, which some visitors find soothing and others off-putting. The kitchen is best known for standard pasta entrees handled with a minimum of frills or fanciful gestures. It's rarely spectacular, but then spectacle would be frowned upon here. Here again, one pays to sup among the city's power brokers. Reservations a must. All major credit cards. Dinner: Mon–Sat 5.30-midnight, Sun from 5pm.

Café Luxembourg, 200 West 70th St. Tel: 873 7411. Well-established, once impossibly trendy Upper West Side eatery where the French-American menu has a definitive *nouvelle* slant – and the occasional local celebrity-sighting makes for a satisfying night out. All major credit cards. Reservations required. Dinner, plus Sunday brunch.

Elaine's, 1703 Second Ave between 88th and 89th Streets. Tel: 534 8103. Mentioned for its celebrity-watching potential.

Tavern On The Green, Central Park West at 67th St. Tel: 873 3200. The Tavern is perhaps more liked for its festive atmosphere and sightseeing opportunities than for its menu, though the kitchen has been on the mend over the last few years. An enormous faux-palace sprawled among the greenery of Central Park, it has the lovably daffy scale and good-natured brio of an airport terminal designed by Lewis Carroll. (It is said to serve more dinners than any other restaurant in the US. Watch the dizzying bustle of waiters serving a few hundred tables and you'll believe it.) The menu, though improved, can still be hit-or-miss; the lamb and veal are recommended. All major credit cards. Reservations recommended. Dinner: daily 5.30–midnight.

Wilkinson's Seafood Café, 1573 York Ave between 83rd and 84th Streets. Tel: 535 5454. A congenial Upper East Side favorite known more for its wonderful atmosphere than its food, though the fried calamari and broiled swordfish are recommended. All major credit cards. Dinner: Mon–Fri 6–10.30pm, Sat to 11pm, Sun 5.30–9pm.

REASONABLE

Jim McMullen, 1341 Third Ave between 76th and 77th Streets. Tel: 861 4700. A celebrity (models, sports figures, actors) hangout that also attracts folks from the neighborhood. American Express, MasterCard, Visa. Lunch and dinner daily.

Museum Café, 366 Columbus Ave at 77th St. Tel: 799 0150. One of the original Yuppie restaurants in the neighborhood, and still packing them in. Most major credit cards. Open: daily for lunch and dinner.

Pamir, 1437 Second Ave between 74th and 75th Streets. Tel: 734 3791. The best Afghan cuisine in New York.

Harlem

UPSCALE

The Terrace, 400 West 119th St. Tel: 666 9490. It's a bit of a taxi ride out of most visitors' way, and it's located in Columbia University at Morningside Drive, better known for 1960s controversy than fine dining. But it's a wonderful sort of eagle's nest 14 stories above street level, with a magnificent view of the Hudson River and Manhattan's famous skyscrapers. On a clear evening, especially in spring or fall, one can almost forget to eat for ogling the beautiful lights. The atmosphere is quite formal, so expect to dress up a bit (there's after-dinner dancing on Friday nights). The cuisine is equally elegant, with French/Mediterranean offerings like Panache of Maine Lobster with Cumin Couscous. Major credit cards. Reservations necessary. Dinner: Tue–Sat 6–10pm.

INEXPENSIVE

La Famille, 2017 Fifth Ave. Tel: 289 6899. Tasty food in a cozy atmosphere.

Sylvia's, 328 Malcolm X Boulevard (Lenox Ave). Tel: 996 0660. Hearty, home-cooked meals and a favorite New York destination for Sunday brunch with a soulfood flavor.

Wilson's Bakery and Restaurant, 1980 Amsterdam Ave. Tel: 923 9821. Especially good for breakfasts and pastries.

Copeland's, 549 West 145th St. Tel: 234 2356. A well-known favorite.

The Villages/Chelsea/ Union Square

UPSCALE

Periyali, 35 West 20th St. Tel: 463 7890. A fine Greek restaurant in Chelsea. The long wooden bar and dining areas are appointed with an eye to spare lines and bare walls. The meals are similarly straightforward: the expected variations on lamb, moussaka, calamari, and baklava, all treated with a respect for natural tastes and subtleties. Service is friendly, the atmosphere casual but refined. American Express, Visa, Mastercard only. Reservations required. Dinner: Mon–Thur 6–11pm, till 11.30pm Fri–Sat.

Provence, 38 MacDougal St. Tel: 475 7500. A warm, romantic restaurant with Southern French food. Very popular. Open: lunch and dinner daily.

Union Square Café, 21 East 16th St. Tel: 243 4020. Some of the friendliest service in New York and some of the most interesting cuisine attracts a hip, young crowd, many of whom work for nearby publishing houses. Innovative California/Mediterranean influenced cuisine. Most major credit cards. Open: daily, lunch and dinner.

REASONABLE

Chelsea Commons, 463 W 24th St (at 10th Avenue). Tel: 929 9424. In front it's a downhome pub; in the middle room, a jazz piano-bar; and out back, in season, one of the most delightful little courtyard bistros in Manhattan, with small trees dappling aged brick walls that shut out virtually all the noise, bustle and smells of the city. The mood is extraordinarily relaxed, to the point where you may have to wave vigorously to get your waiter's notice but in Manhattan, such pleasurable lethargy is a rare commodity. The menu is tiny, though lately they've been experimenting in summertime with steamed crabs "Maryland style," a peppery (and messy) delicacy which can only be appreciated with pints of good ale. Kitchen open: daily till 1am, bar till 4am.

Indochine, 430 Lafayette St. Tel: 505 5111. A Vietnamese-Cambodian restaurant which is situated near Washington Square, much improved now that the fashion models have moved on to other spots. Trendy. Dinner: daily 6pm–12.30am.

Japonica, 100 University Place at 12th St. Tel: 243 7752. A fine, not-too-fancy downtown Japanese restaurant. Dinner served Mon–Thur 5–11pm, till 11.30 Fri–Sun.

Knickerbocker, 33 University Place. Tel: 228-8490. A bar and restaurant that epitomizes New York; dark wood panelling, and – after 9.30pm – cool, traditional jazz. A great place for steak or just a burger. All major credit cards. Lunch and dinner daily.

Il Mulino, 86 West 3rd St between Thompson and Sullivan Streets. Tel: 673 3783. The large portions, variety of pastas and almost smothering service make this Greenwich Village institution a favorite of New Yorkers, so reservations well in advance are a must. Come prepared to eat well; from the instant you sit down and are confronted with plates of cold meats and fresh-baked breads, to the piping hot fusilli with truffles, to the stunningly thick veal chops, Il Mulino desires that you be filled up for at least 24 hours. Not the fanciest Italian establishment in the city, but perhaps one of the friendliest and most loved. Dinner: Mon–Sat, 5–11.30pm.

Taka, 61 Grove St. Tel: 242 3699. A tiny, often busy, and very authentic

Japanese sushi and sashimi restaurant in the West Village. Dinner: Tue–Sun 5pm–midnight.

INEXPENSIVE

America, 9 East 18th St between Fifth Ave and Broadway. Tel: 505 2110. Huge. Noisy. Fun. With one of the largest selections of regional American food in the world, some of which may remind you of the meals you once had in school cafeterias. However, it's a definite experience. American Express, Mastercard, Visa. Open: daily from 11.30am–midnight.

Cedar Tavern, 82 University Pl. between 11th and 12th Streets. Tel: 929 9089. Once famous as a hangout for poets and Abstract Expressionist painters, this dark yet chummy restaurant-pub is still a favorite with downtown New Yorkers. Regulars are a diverse lot: business people and office workers rub elbows with students and professors from nearby NYU. The beautifully carved bar from which it derives its name features pints of Guinness and fine bartenders. A large back room and smaller rooftop terrace serve hearty American grub such as hamburgers and roast beef sandwiches, with daily specials a bit more adventurous. A fine spot to withdraw from the city's hurly-burly and relax. Most major credit cards. Open: Mon–Thur and Sun till midnight, Fri–Sat till 3.30am.

Florent, 69 Gansevoort St, near Greenwich St. Tel: 989 5779. Situated deep in the heart of the meat-packing district, this 24-hour stainless-steel café serves everything from escargot to onion soup. The clientele is also interesting.

Lower East Side/Chinatown/ Little Italy/SoHo

UPSCALE

Raoul's Restaurant, 180 Prince St. Tel: 966 3518. A sleek, dark French bistro in SoHo, elegant and trendy, with a satisfying menu and a small garden. Most major credit cards.

REASONABLE

Canton, 45 Division St near the Bowery. Tel: 226 4441. A pleasant, midsize space patrolled by polite staff. Best known for seafood, it's also expensive by Chinatown standards; be sure to inquire the price of any seasonal dishes before ordering. No credit cards. Dinner: daily 5–9.30pm.

Patrissy's, 98 Kenmare St at Lafayette St. Tel: 226 8854. Although much of Little Italy is overcrowded, overpriced and overrated, Patrissy's is worth the trip. Situated on the northern outskirts of the area, well away from the most congested streets and sidewalks, this quietly elegant, mildly formal hideaway has good service and appetizers. For entrees, try the gigantic veal chop or gnocchi. All major credit cards. Reservations suggested. Dinner: daily 6pm–midnight.

INEXPENSIVE

Broome Street Bar, 363 West Broadway at Broome St. Tel: 925 2086. When you've had enough of the stylish snobberies and outrageous prices of SoHo, nip over to this old-timey pub-restaurant and relax. It's not exactly a hideaway, and when hordes of shoppers descend on SoHo generally, Kenn & Bob's can catch the overflow. But from mid-afternoon through early evening, weekends as well as weekdays, it's a relatively quiet treat, with a well-stocked bar and a large number of small tables where you can loll over American-style pub grub (burgers, quiche, thick Reuben sandwiches of corn beef and sauerkraut). No reservations or credit cards. Kitchen open: daily till 11pm.

Excellent Dumpling House, 111 Lafayette (just below Canal St). Tel: 219 0212. Chinatown is a colorful, bustling little world within a world. You can certainly have bad and expensive meals here, but you can also find some of the best and most authentic Chinese dining experiences outside the Orient itself. The Excellent Dumpling House is aptly named: unpretentious, unadorned and on the outskirts of Chinatown proper, it is nevertheless always packed with locals and devoted visitors who love its no-nonsense atmosphere, its reasonable prices, and its stellar dumplings (especially the vegetable dumplings, steamed or fried). No reservations, but there's sometimes a short wait on line; it's best for mid-afternoon lunch. No credit cards. Open: daily 11am–9pm.

Katz's Deli, 205 East Houston St at Ludlow St. Tel: 254 2246. An authentic Lower East Side delicatessen which means no fancy decor, a bit of grease and grime, and enormous corned beef sandwiches. Try it for lunch, between 11am and 4pm. No credit cards.

Thailand, 106 Bayard St. Tel: 349 3132. This is one of the early pioneers of Thai food in New York, and the food is quite good. The total lack of atmosphere is offset by the kitschy decor – ask if you can be seated in one of the "pagodas". They'll spice your meal extra-hot if you ask; a specialty is the frog sauteed with spicy garlic sauce. The shrimp and chili salads and the coconut curries are also winners. Order a premium Singha Beer to cool you down. All major credit cards. Dinner: daily 6pm–midnight.

TriBeCa/Lower Manhattan

UPSCALE

Bouley, 165 Duane St between Hudson and Greenwich Streets. Tel: 608 3852. Never mind the warehouses across the street; inside, this spot is startlingly beautiful. David Bouley, who earned his fans at nearby Montrachet, opened this elegantly decorated bit of Provence in 1987. Considered by some to be to the best restaurant in New York, Bouley draws large crowds of trendsetters to TriBeCa with its creative and sometimes whimsical nouvelle French interpretations; the black bass, breast of pigeon, sauteed scallops and vegetable souffles are highly regarded. All major credit cards. Dinner: Mon–Sat 5.30–11pm.

Chanterelle, 2 Harrison St at Hudson St. Tel: 966 6960. Another elegant, and very highly-regarded spot in TriBeCa, noted for its exquisite nouvelle French creations. Reservations recommended. Dinner: Tue–Sat 6.30–10.30pm.

Hudson River Club, Four World Financial Center at Vesey St. Tel: 786 1500. Views of the Hudson, this time from a formal setting overlooking the WFC's boat basin. This very proper (but still friendly) restaurant features innovative regional cuisine, including venison and rabbit. Desserts are splendid, too. Most major credit cards are accepted. Open: lunch Mon–Fri noon–2.30pm, dinner: Mon–Sat 5.30–10pm.

Montrachet, 239 West Broadway (below Canal). Tel: 219 2777. One of the very elegant, very trendy restaurants in TriBeCa. Light and inventive nouvelle

French cuisine and professional service warm up the somewhat frigid attitudes of the "Beautiful People" who frequent this spot. Make reservations. American Express only. Dinner: Mon–Sat 6–11pm.

TriBeCa Grill, 375 Greenwich St at Franklin St. Tel: 941 3900. Actor Robert DeNiro's trendy place-to-be-seen, serving upscale drinks and bistro fare at expensive prices. Make reservations well in advance. Dinner: daily 6–11pm.

Windows on the World, 107th Floor, One World Trade Center. Tel: 938 1111. Famed for its breathtaking views and pricey menu. A tourist attraction, sure, but worth the experience at least once. Call for current dining hours, or check local listings.

El Teddy's, 219 West Broadway between Franklin and White Streets. Tel: 941 7070. The exterior of this TriBeCa landmark features the Statue of Liberty sinking behind its facade. The interior decor looks like a Salvador Dali peyote dream of Mexico. But it's not just the fantasy design that consistently attracts a downtown mix of Wall Streeters, art dealers and well-heeled tourists. It's the inventive "nouvelle Mexican" cuisine; softshell crab tacos, duck and fig tacos, steak and salsa burritos, and gigantic, salty margaritas are the truly winning aspects of this moderately pricey mainstay. Unique. All cards accepted except Diners Club. Dinner: Mon–Thur 6–11pm, Fri–Sat till midnight.

INEXPENSIVE

Riverrun, 176 Franklin St. Tel: 966 3894. One of the earliest TriBeCa "pioneers," this combination of restaurant and pub attracts a hip, younger clientele with its limited American menu, friendly bartenders, and opportunities to star-gaze at "downtown" artists and visiting rock stars. For dinner, the Southern fried chicken and pork chops sauteed in hoisin sauce are tasty; for a bar snack, try the zesty barbecue chicken wings. Friendly and very casual. All major credit cards. Dinner: 6pm–midnight.

The Outer Boroughs

UPSCALE

Peter Luger, 178 Broadway. Tel: 718-387 7400. A Brooklyn landmark, this one near the Williamsburg Bridge. Preserving a gaslight-era charm, this family establishment has been in operation 100 years – ancient history by US standards. Steak, steak and more steak is the Victorian heart of the simple menu. Exposed wood beams, a smoky bar, and a clientele in which downhome Brooklynites rub elbows with business class interlopers from "The City" make for a loose, sometimes loud, and genuinely fun time. Reservations suggested. No credit cards. Dinner Mon–Thur and Sun 6–10pm, Fri till 11pm, Sat till 11.30pm.

The River Café, 1 Water Street (Cadman Plaza West). Tel: 718-522 5200. Make your reservations two weeks ahead if possible, because this barge restaurant, beautifully situated on the East River at the Brooklyn end of the Brooklyn Bridge, is justly famous for its spectacular view of lower Manhattan's skyscrapers. The superior American cuisine (steak and seafood, with fanciful desserts) lives up to its setting. New York rarely feels so romantic and beautiful as during a sunset dinner here. All major credit cards. Lunch Mon–Fri 12–2.30pm. Dinner: 6.30–11pm every night.

Water's Edge, 44th Drive at the East River Yacht Club. Tel: 718-482 0033. An example of New Yorkers' capacity to embrace paradox with total aplomb, the East River Yacht Club is a preserve for the moneyed sailboat crowd set right in the midst of the industrial waterfront of Queens. However, it does boast a sweeping view of the Manhattan skyline which is quite breathtaking at sunset. The cuisine is American "surf & turf" steaks and ocean catches like salmon and Dover sole, all handled with competence if not a great deal of flair. Diners Club and American Express only. Reservations are wise. Dinner: Mon–Sat 6–11pm.

REASONABLE

Clover Hill/Camille's, 272 Court St. Tel: 718-875 0895. A welcome addition to downtown Brooklyn, Clover Hill/Camille's menu tends towards creatively seasoned soups and salads, with a choice of heartier entrees. Bring your own wine or beer. No credit cards, either. Dinner: Tue–Thur 6–10pm, Fri and Sat 6–11pm, Sun 5–9pm.

INEXPENSIVE

Dominick's, 2335 Arthur Ave. Tel: 718-733 2807. Take a hike to the Bronx for this old-fashioned Italian eatery, where you share tables with other diners. No menu, no credit cards. A true New York experience.

Attractions

What to See and Do

Although much of the enjoyment of a New York visit is in merely strolling around and observing the sights, there are a large number of organized attractions. Since opening times may vary according to season, it's best to call the numbers provided before you visit. Unless listed under free admission or otherwise noted, most of these attractions charge admission.

Manhattan

Central Park Zoo/Wildlife Center, Fifth Ave and 64th St. Tel: 861 6030. Open: daily. Now has barless habitat displays.

Empire State Building, Fifth Ave and 34th St. Tel: 736 3100. Open: daily 9.30am–midnight. Observatories on 86th and 102nd floors.

Gracie Mansion, East End Ave at 88th St. Tel: 570 4751. Open: Wed 10am–4pm, reservations required. Official residence of New York's mayor.

Guinness World of Records, Empire State Building. Tel: 947 2335. Open: daily 9am–10pm. Lifesize displays, artifacts, videos.

Hayden Planetarium, Central Park West at 81st St. Tel: 769 5920. Open: daily, except Thanksgiving and Christmas. Black Light Gallery and spectacular laser shows.

The Old Merchant's House, 29 East 4th St. Tel: 777 1089. Open: Sun afternoons. New York the way it used to be, from trunks of old clothes to authentically-furnished rooms, all pre-served in a five-story house.

Theodore Roosevelt Birthplace, 28 East 20th St. Tel: 260 1616. Open: Wed–Sun 9am–5pm. Reconstructed home of the only New York-born Presi-dent. Exhibits, films.

Statue of Liberty, ferry information. Tel: 269 5755. The ferry to this na-tional monument departs every 45 minutes to an hour from lower Manhat-tan, depending on season.

World Trade Center Observation Deck, Two World Trade Center, Vesey and Liberty Streets. Tel: 435 7397. Open: daily. Great view on clear days and nights.

The Outer Boroughs

The **Bronx Heritage Trail**, call for ap-pointment at 718-881 8900. Self-guided tours of three historical houses including Edgar Allan Poe Cottage, *circa* 1812. This can also be visited in-dependently: East Kingsbridge Road and Grand Concourse.

Bronx Zoo (also known as The Interna-tional Wildlife Conservation Park), Fordham Rd and Pelham Pwy. Tel: 718-367 1010. Open: daily 10am–5pm. One of the country's largest urban zoos.

Historic Richmondtown, 441 Clarke Ave, Staten Island. Tel: 718-351 1617. Open: weekdays 10am–5pm, weekends 1–5pm. An historical recrea-tion of life the way it used to be, in buildings up to 250 years old.

New York Aquarium, Coney Island, Brooklyn. Tel: 718-265 FISH. Open: daily 10am–4.45pm. Exotic aquatic creatures, feeding, performances.

New York Botanical Garden, Southern Blvd, Bronx. Tel: 718-817 8700. Open: Tue–Sun 10am–6pm or 4pm, depend-ing on season. Walking trails, forest, gardens, floral exhibits.

New York Hall of Science, 47-01 111th St, Flushing Meadows, Queens. Tel: 718-699 0005. Open: Wed–Sun 10am–5pm. Hands-on science, tech-nology exhibits.

New York Transit Museum, Boerum Place and Schermerhorn St, Brooklyn. Tel: 718-330 3060. Open: Tue–Fri 10am–4pm, weekends 11am–4pm. Old subway cars and other transit memorabilia dating to 1903.

Queens Zoo/Wildlife Center, Flushing Meadow Park. Tel: 718-271 7761. Open: daily. The city's newest wildlife conservation center, with bears, wolves and other indigenous North American creatures.

Staten Island Zoo, 614 Broadway. Tel: 718-442 3101. Open: daily 10am–4.45pm. Renowned reptile collection plus mammals, birds, fish.

Wave Hill, 675 West 252nd St, Bronx. Tel: 718-549 3200. Tours Sun. Admis-sion: free on weekdays. Gardens, greenhouses, woodland walks, con-certs and a café at an estate overlook-ing the Hudson.

Manhattan

FREE ADMISSION

Belvedere Castle, in Central Park, 79th St. Tel: 772 0210. Nature exhib-its and educational programs.

City Hall, Broadway at Murray St. Tel: 788 3000. Open: Mon–Fri 10am–3.30pm. Historic and artistic exhibits.

Con Edison Energy Museum, 145 East 14th St. Tel: 460 6244. Open: Tue–Sat 10am–4pm. From Edison's experiments to the 21st century.

The Dairy, Central Park at 64th St east of carousel. Tel: 794 6564. Open: Tue–Sun 11am–4pm, Fri 1–4pm. Infor-mation about the park, plus exhibits.

Federal Hall National Memorial, 26 Wall St. Tel: 264 8711. Open: Mon–Fri 9am–5pm. Films, exhibits and con-certs at the site of Washington's inau-guration.

General Grant National Memorial, Riv-erside Dr and 122nd St. Tel: 666 1640. Open: Wed–Sun 9am–5pm. Tomb of Civil War general and 18th President Ulysses S. Grant.

New York Stock Exchange, 20 Broad St. Tel: 656 5167. Open: Mon–Fri 9.15am–4.15pm. Admission by free ticket only. Gallery overlooks trading floor.

New York Unearthed, 17 State St (at Pearl St). Tel: 363 9372. Open: Mon–Sat noon–6pm. Archaeological rem-nants of the city's past along with his-torical dioramas.

Rockefeller Center, 30 Rockefeller Plaza at concourse level. Tel: 632 4000. Self-guided walking tours, plus brochures in the lobby.

United Nations, 46th St and First Ave. Tel: 963 7713. Free tickets to General Assembly available before 10.30am and 3.30pm sessions.

The Outer Boroughs

FREE ADMISSION

Brooklyn Botanic Garden, 1000 Washington Ave. Tel: 718-622 4433. Open: Tue–Fri and weekends year-round.

Hall of Fame for Great Americans, Bronx Community College, University Ave and 181st St. Tel: 718-220 6003. Open: daily 10am–5pm. Statues of various presidents, statesmen, and artists.

Harbor Defense Museum, Fort Hamil-ton, Brooklyn. Tel: 718-630 4349. Open: Mon-Fri. Collection of coastal armament and history of the area's forts.

High Rock Park Conservation Center, 200 Nevada Ave, Staten Island. Tel: 718-667 2165. Open: daily 8am to sundown. Walking trails through wood-lands with streams and ponds.

Queens Botanical Garden, 43–50 Main St, Flushing. Tel: 718-886 3800. Open: Tue-Sun 10am–5pm. Rose col-lection, demonstration gardens, fruit trees, herb garden.

Queens County Farm Museum, 73–50 Little Neck Park, Floral Park. Tel: 718-347–FARM. Open: weekdays 9am–5pm, weekends noon–5pm. Historic farmhouse, animals, special events, tours.

Staten Island Botanical Garden, 1000 Richmond Terrace, Snug Harbor. Tel: 718-273 8200. Open: daily dawn-dusk. Includes ponds, lakes, tree walks and greenhouse collections.

Museums

Opening hours of museums often change depending on the season, so it's a good idea to telephone ahead before visiting. Major museums usu-ally charge an admission fee; some of the smaller ones do not.

Upper East Side

The largest group of major museums are located within a mile or two of each other just off Fifth Avenue on the upper East Side. Some of these museums offer free admission on Tuesday or other evenings and most offer a dis-count to students and senior citizens.

Cooper-Hewitt Museum, Fifth Ave and 91st St. Tel: 860 6868. The

Smithsonian Institution's national design collection. Open: Tue 10am–9pm, Wed–Sat 10am–5pm, Sun noon–5pm.

Frick Collection, 1 East 70th St. Tel: 288 0700. European masters from the 14th to 19th century. Open: Tue–Sat 10am–6pm, Sun 1–6pm.

Guggenheim Museum, Fifth Ave and 89th St. Tel: 423 3500. Modern painting and sculpture in newly-revamped building originally designed by Frank Lloyd Wright. Open: Fri–Wed 10am–8pm.

International Center of Photography, Fifth Ave and 94th St. Tel: 860 1777. Exclusively photographs. Open: Tue 11am–8pm, Wed–Sun 11am–6pm.

Jewish Museum, Fifth Ave and 92nd St. Tel: 423 3200. Devoted to Jewish art and culture. Open: Sun, Mon, Wed and Thur 11am–5.45pm, Tue 11am–8pm.

Metropolitan Museum of Art, Fifth Ave and 82nd St. Hundreds of famous masterpieces scan the history of world art; while the roof garden offers a grand view of the New York skyline. Open: Fri and Sat 9.30am–8.45pm, Tue–Thur and Sun 9.30am–5.15pm.

Museum of the City of New York, Fifth Ave and 103rd St, tel: 534 1672. The museum shows the city's history since its days as a Dutch trading post. Open: Wed–Sat 10am–5pm, Sun 1–5pm.

National Academy of Design, Fifth Ave and 89th St. Tel: 369 4880. Changing exhibitions and permanent collection. Open: Wed–Sun noon–5pm.

Whitney Museum of American Art, Madison Ave and 75th St. Tel: 570 3676. Concentrates primarily on 20th-century American art. Open: Wed, Fri, Sat and Sun 11am–6pm, Thur 1-8pm.

Midtown

American Craft Museum, 40 West 53rd St. Tel: 956 6047. Contemporary folk and craft art. Open: Tue 10am–8pm, Wed–Sun 10am–5pm.

Museum of Television & Radio, 25 West 52nd St. Tel: 621 6600. Radio and TV programs spanning 60 years. Open: Tue-Sun noon–6pm, Thur noon–8pm.

Museum of Modern Art, 11 West 53rd St. Tel: 708 9480. Changing exhibitions, daily film shows. Open: Fri–Tue 11am–6pm, Thur 11am–9pm.

Upper West Side

American Museum of Natural History, Central Park West at 79th St. Tel: 769 5100. Shows in its Naturemax Theater. Open: Mon, Tue, Thur and Sun 10am–5.45pm, all other days 10am–8.45pm.

Children's Museum of Manhattan, 212 West 83rd St. Tel: 721 1234. A lively addition to the city's roster of museums, it includes participatory exhibits. Open: Mon–Fri 1–5pm, weekends 11am–5pm.

New-York Historical Society, 170 Central Park West. Tel: 873 3400. A fascinating museum and research library devoted to arts, antiques, photos, manuscripts and artifacts. Open: call for hours.

Harlem

Black Fashion Museum, 155 West 126th St. Tel: 666 1320. Open: daily noon–8pm or by appointment.

The Cloisters, Fort Tryon Park. Tel: 923 3700. The Metropolitan Museum's collection of medieval art. Open: Tue–Sun 9.30am–4.45pm, till 5.15pm in summer.

El Museo del Barrio, 1230 Fifth Ave. Tel: 831 7272. Devoted to Puerto Rican and Latino art. Open: Wed–Sun 11am–5pm.

Schomburg Center for Research in Black Culture, 515 Lenox Ave at 135th St. Tel: 491 2200. Part of the NY Public Library, the Schomburg is a research source with various documents and artifacts on the African-American experience.

Studio Museum in Harlem, 144 West 125th St. Tel: 864 4500. Contemporary African-American artists. Open: Wed–Fri 10am–5pm, weekends 1–6pm.

More Manhattan Museums

The Abigail Adams Smith Museum, 421 East 61st St. Tel: 838 6878. A converted 18th-century carriage house with authentic period rooms and historic memorabilia. Open: Mon–Fri noon–4 pm, Sun 1–5pm.

American Numismatic Society, Broadway at 155th St. Tel: 234 3130. Rare coins, gleaming medals, and decorations of all kinds. Open: Tue–Sat 9am–4.30 pm, Sun 1–4pm.

Asia Society, 725 Park Ave. Tel: 288 6400. Permanent collection, changing exhibits, bookstore. Open: Tue–Sat 11am–6pm, Sun noon–5pm.

China House Gallery, 125 East 65th St. Tel: 744 8181. Open: Mon-Sat 10am–5pm, Tue 10am-8pm.

Forbes Magazine Galleries, 60 Fifth Ave. Tel: 206 5548. Toy soldiers, Fabergé eggs. Open: Tue, Wed, Fri and Sat 10am–4pm.

George Gustav Heye Center of the National Museum of the American Indian, 1 Bowling Green. Tel: 668 6624. A unique display of Native American art and artifacts; part of a huge collection until recently housed in the former Indian museum on upper Broadway. Call for hours.

Hispanic Society of America, Broadway at 155th St. Tel: 926 2234. Art from Spain and Portugal. Open: Tue–Sat 10am–4.30pm, Sun 1–4pm.

Intrepid Sea-Air-Space Museum, naval history aboard World War II aircraft carrier moored at West 46th St in Hudson River. Tel: 245 0072. Open: Wed–Sun 10am–5pm in winter; daily in the summer.

Japan Society Gallery, 333 East 47th St. Tel: 752 0824. Exhibits from the Orient. Open: Tue–Sun 11am–5pm.

Lower East Side Tenement Museum, 97 Orchard St. Tel: 431 0233; 387 0341. Museum/gallery displaying exhibits on the lives of 19th-century immigrants.

Museum for African Art, 593 Broadway. Tel: 966 1313. Home of the Center for African Art; special exhibits. Open: Fri and Sat 11am–8pm, Sun, Wed and Thur 11am–6pm.

Museum of American Folk Art, Columbus Ave at 66th St. Tel: 595 9533. Lectures, workshops, special exhibits and a permanent exhibition. Open: Tue–Sun 11.30am–7.30pm.

Museum of the American Piano, 211 West 58th St. Tel: 246 4646. More than 40 early pianos, some restored to playing condition. Open: Tue–Fri 10am–4pm.

New Museum of Contemporary Art, 583 Broadway. Tel: 219 1222. Find out what's new on the art world horizon. Open: Wed, Thur and Sun noon–6pm, Fri–Sat noon–8pm.

NYC Fire Museum, 278 Spring St. Tel: 691 1303. Collection of fire department exhibits. Open: Tue–Sat 10am–4pm.

NYC Police Museum, 235 East 20th St. Tel: 477 9753. Police equipment and memorabilia. Open: weekdays 9am–2pm; call for an appointment.

Society of Illustrators, 128 East 63rd St. Tel: 838 2560. Founded in 1901, a museum of illustration history with archives of memorabilia, portraits, manuscripts and special exhibits. Open: weekdays (except Mon) 10am–5pm, Tue till 8pm.

South Street Seaport Museum, 207 Front St. Tel: 669 9424. A 12-block museum-without-walls that includes galleries, historic ships, films. Open: daily 10am–5pm.

Outside Manhattan

American Museum of the Moving Image, 35th Ave at 36th St, Astoria, Queens. Tel: 718-784 0077. Art, history and technology of movies, TV and video. Open: Tue–Fri 1–5pm, weekends 11am–6pm.

Bronx Museum of the Arts, 1040 Grand Concourse at 165th St. Tel: 781 6000. Changing exhibits. Open: Wed-Fri 10am–4.30pm, weekends 11am–4.30pm.

The Brooklyn Museum, 200 Eastern Pwy. Tel: 718-638 5000. Vast collection of Egyptian, primitive, European and American art. Open: Wed–Sun 10am–5pm.

Brooklyn Children's Museum, 145 Brooklyn Ave. Tel: 718-735 4400. Founded in 1899 as the first of its kind. Open: Wed-Mon 2pm–5pm.

Ellis Island Immigration Museum, Ellis Island. Tel: 363 3200 or 269 5755 (ferry information). A multi-million dollar restoration of the country's major immigrant gateway, with photographs, letters, artwork and other exhibits. Open: weekdays 9am–5pm, weekends 9am–6pm.

North Wind Undersea Museum, 610 City Island Ave, Bronx. Tel: 718-885 0701. Vintage diving equipment; exhibits and educational programs on marine life, the environment. Open: weekdays 10am–5pm, weekends noon–5pm.

P.S. 1 Museum, 46-01 21st St, Long Island City. Tel: 718-233 1440. Site-specific and other cutting-edge art exhibits. Open: Wed–Sun noon–6pm.

Queens Museum of Art, near Shea Stadium, Flushing Meadows-Corona Park. Tel: 718-592 5555. 20th-century art, lectures and a 9,000-square-foot model of New York City. Open: Tue–Fri 10am–5pm, weekends noon–5pm.

Snug Harbor Cultural Center, 1000 Richmond Terrace, Staten Island. Tel: 718-448 2500. Indoor/outdoor exhibits, in a park-like 19th-century haven for retired sailors. Galleries open Wed-Sun noon–5pm; grounds open dawn till dusk.

Statue of Liberty National Monument, Liberty Island. Tel: 363 3200. At the base of the statue, it tells the story of US immigration from 1600 onwards. Ferry leaves from Battery Park. Tel: 269 5755 for times.

Staten Island Institute of Arts & Sciences, 75 Stuyvesant Pl. Tel: 718-727 1135. History and culture of the city's smallest borough. Open: Mon–Sat 9am–5pm, Sun 1–5pm.

Tibetan Museum, 338 Lighthouse Ave, Staten Island. Tel: 718-987 3500. Jewel-like collection in a hillside setting.

Art Galleries

It's theoretically possible for somebody to wander down to SoHo on one's first Saturday in New York, get into casual conversation with one of the habitués at any art gallery opening and find themselves spending the evening at the best party of their life. Possible, but increasingly unlikely. When SoHo first saw a major influx of artists decades ago, they came because the decline in the area's light manufacturing companies meant that large spaces were virtually going begging. Perfect for conversion into artists' lofts and studios, and cheap too. Weekend partying became endemic; almost nobody has enough friends to fill 4,000 square feet of space and the unspoken rule was that if you heard about a party you were invited.

It was commonplace to climb three flights of creaking stairs on Greene Street or Walker and find yourself among three or four hundred revelers. The dedicated "party circuit" pioneers used to meet in Fanelli's or the Broome Street Bar early on Saturday evening to swap addresses. "Follow that couple carrying a bag of ice," was the advice of one veteran and invariably this led to an "open" party. Alas, concurrent with the boom in art prices, many artists became unable to pay the increasingly high rent for lofts.

Nevertheless, SoHo now boasts more galleries than ever, with many of the major ones on West Broadway (**Leo Castelli**, **O.K. Harris**, **Sonnabend**, the **Dia Center for the Arts**) and others on adjoining streets such as Greene (**John Weber**, **Phyllis Kind**, the **Pace Gallery**, **Sperone Westwater**), Prince (**Ward-Nasse**, **Louis K. Meisel**), Wooster (**Paula Cooper**), Broome (**SoHo 20**) and, increasingly, along lower Broadway (**Thread Waxing Space**, **P.P.O.W.**).

Over in the **East Village**, galleries spring up overnight and disappear just as quickly. Some of the best known have moved to Broadway below Houston Street, where Saturday is a favored opening day. Drop by the American Indian Community House Gallery at 708 Broadway, near 4th Street, the only Native American-owned gallery on the East Coast.

True art fans should consult the listings in the art section of the New York Times on Sunday or just go down to SoHo on Saturday afternoons, casually wandering in and out of galleries and happening on openings. Most galleries have a pile of free booklets which list all the shows around town. While in **SoHo** or nearby **TriBeCa** it's worth checking out the following places, most of which have some degree of artist participation:

AIR, 63 Crosby St. A women's art collective.

Alternative Museum, 594 Broadway, with a focus on social and political issues.

Artists Space, 38 Greene St. New trends, new artists, also performance art and daily visual screenings.

The Clocktower, 108 Leonard St. Artists and their studios, plus a gallery.

Franklin Furnace, 112 Franklin St. The printed word as art, etc.

New Museum of Contemporary Art, 583 Broadway. A seven-year continuous performance art project held in a side window every month.

Printed Matter, 77 Wooster St. Books on and for artists.

White Columns, 148 Christopher St (in the West Village).

Current listings are essential to save time when touring **Uptown** galleries – which tend to be stretched out along East 57th Street between Fifth Avenue and Park Avenue, on both sides of Madison Avenue and some side streets to the north. There are now well over 400 art galleries in the naked city.

Photography

A score of galleries around Manhattan are devoted to photography, including:
Camera Club of New York, 853 Broadway. Tel: 260 7077.
Greenberg Gallery, 120 Wooster St. Tel: 334 0010.
Neikrug, 224 East 68th St. Tel: 288 7741.
Witkin, 415 West Broadway. Tel: 925 5510.
Pace/MacGill, 32 East 57th St. Tel: 759 7999.
The International Center of Photography, Uptown, 1130 Fifth Ave. Tel: 860 1777 and Midtown, 1133 Sixth Ave. Tel: 768 4680.

Multi-Media

Performance art, multi-media presentations and various uncategorizable events are held at several spots around the city, including:
The Kitchen, 512 West 19th St. Tel: 255 5793.
LA MAMA, 74A East 4th St. Tel: 475 7710.
Franklin Furnace, 112 Franklin St. Tel: 925 4671.
P.S. 1, 46-01 21st St, Long Island City. Tel: 233 1440.
P.S. 122, 150 First Ave. Tel: 477 5829.
Dia Center for the Arts. Tel: 431 9232. **Symphony Space**, 2537 Broadway (at 95th St). Tel: 864 5400.
Events at these places tend to be listed in a variety of free publications usually found stacked in the foyers of most SoHo, TriBeCa, East Village and other galleries.

Poetry Readings

There are numerous literary and poetry readings which take place typically in bookstores, cafés and churches, including:

Downtown

Ear Inn, 326 Spring St. Tel: 226 9060.
Nuyorican Poets' Café, 236 East 3rd St. Tel: 505 8183.
Poetry Society of America, 15 Gramercy Park. Tel: 254-9628.
St Mark's Church, 2nd Ave and East 10th St. Tel: 674 0910.
Fez, at Time Café, 380 Lafayette St. Tel: 533 7000.

Uptown

Books & Co., 939 Madison Ave. Tel: 737 1450.
92nd Street YM-YWHA, 1395 Lexington Ave. Tel: 996 1100.
New York Public Library, Fifth Ave and 42nd St. Tel: 930 0571.

Concert Halls

Lincoln Center for the Performing Arts, Broadway and 64th Street, is the city's pre-eminent cultural center. It's home of America's oldest orchestra, the New York Philharmonic, which gives 200 concerts annually in both **Avery Fisher Hall** and nearby **Alice Tully Hall**, which also houses the Chamber Music Society. The New York City Opera and New York City Ballet both perform in the **New York State Theater**. Also in this complex are the **Vivian Beaumont Theater**, the **Julliard Music School**, an excellent **reference library** of music and the arts, and the **Metropolitan Opera House**, home of the Metropolitan Opera Company and the American Ballet Theater. Tours of Lincoln Center are offered daily between 10am and 5pm; for details, call 875 5350 or 875 5400.

New York's oldest joke concerns the tourist who asks how to get to **Carnegie Hall** and is told "Practice, practice." It's quicker to take the N or RR subway trains to 57th Street or cross 57th Street to Seventh Avenue by foot or the 28 bus to this century-old hall, where the world's greatest performers have appeared. For tour or ticket information, call 247 7800. Another major concert arena is **Merkin Hall**, 129 West 67th St. Tel: 362 8719. A welcome new addition outside Manhattan is the concert hall at the Aaron Copeland School of Music, at Queens College. Tel: 718-793 8080.

Dance and Opera

Amato Opera Company Theatre, 319 Bowery. Tel: 228 8200.
BAM Opera House, Brooklyn Academy of Music, 30 Lafayette Ave, Brooklyn. Tel: 718-636 4100.
Light Opera Company of Manhattan, Playhouse 91, 316 East 91st St. Tel: 831 2000.
Opera Orchestra of New York, 239 West 72nd St. Tel: 799 1982.
Two Village restaurants: **Asti**, 13

East 12th St. Tel: 741 9105 and **Bianchi & Margherita**, 186 West 4th St. Tel: 242 2756 both feature waiters and waitresses who double as opera singers.

There are numerous dance troupes in the city, like the **Martha Graham Dance Company**, the **Alvin Ailey American Dance Group**, and the **Dance Theater of Harlem**. Dance venues around town include:
Brooklyn Academy of Music, 30 Lafayette Ave, Brooklyn. Tel: 718-636 4100.
City Center, 131 West 55th St. Tel: 581 7907.
Dance Theater Workshop, 219 West 19th St. Tel: 924 0077.
Danspace, St Mark's Church, Second Ave at East 10th St. Tel: 674 8112.
The Joyce Theater, 175 Eighth Ave. Tel: 242 0800.
Wave Hill, 249th St and Independence Ave, Riverdale. Tel: 718-549 3200. Outdoor, site-specific performances (summer only).

Contemporary Music

Madison Square Garden, Seventh Ave between 31st and 33rd Streets. Tel: 465 6000 or 465 6741.
Radio City Music Hall, Sixth Ave and 50th St. Tel: 247 4777.
Symphony Space, 2537 Broadway. Tel: 864 5400.
Town Hall, 123 West 43rd St. Tel: 840 2824.
Beacon Theater, Broadway at 74th St. Tel: 496 7070.
Apollo Theater, 253 West 125th St. Tel: 749 5838.
And just out of town at:
Meadowlands Arena, East Rutherford, New Jersey. Tel: 201-935 3900.
Nassau Coliseum, Uniondale, Long Island. Tel: 516-794 9300.

Theaters

Very few Broadway theaters are actually on Broadway, although **the half-price ticket booth (TKTS)** where you can sometimes pick up seats for that night's performances is at Broadway and 47th Street, in Times Square. The line begins to form early but the wait is worth it, as full-priced Broadway tickets run to $65 a seat and more. There is another **TKTS booth** at Two World Trade Center. Otherwise there are numerous ticket brokers, many of whom can be contacted via hotel concierges. Again, the *New York Times* offers the best listings of what's playing where (also be sure to check *The New Yorker* and *New York* magazines), although no indication is given as to whether tickets will be available – for that you must call the theater.

The alternative to Broadway is off-Broadway, where performances scarcely differ in quality from the former category, albeit performed in smaller theaters. The vast majority of off-Broadway theaters, and indeed, the more experimental off-off-Broadway theaters, are downtown in the Greenwich Village area. Here you'll find the **Public Theater** complex – seven theaters in one building at 425 Lafayette St. Tel: 598 7150 – where *Hair* and *A Chorus Line* originated before being transferred to uptown venues. The **Theater for the New City** at 155 First Ave, tel: 254 1109, s one of many showplaces for new work by experimental theater artists.

A few blocks from Times Square, along West 42nd Street between Ninth and Tenth Avenues, a group of off-Broadway theaters have set themselves up as **Theater Row**. The most complete source for off and off-off Broadway listings is the *Village Voice*. Useful numbers for tickets and/or information are 765-ARTS (2787), a free 24-hour hotline; NYC/On Stage, tel: 768 1818 and The Broadway Line, tel: 563 2929.

Movies

As a general rule and with certain exceptions, first-run movies get their showing in Midtown cinemas, the largest of which are in the Times Square area with a group of others in the West 50s and East 50s and 60s. Others are on the Upper East Side, on East 34th Street near Third Avenue and in Greenwich Village. Newspapers and *The New Yorker* and *New York* magazine carry complete listings.

Movie theaters are dotted all over town with at least a score of venues devoted to revival, cult, experimental and genre films. The **French Institute**, 22 East 60th St, tel: 355 6160, and the **Japan Society**, 333 East 47th St, 752 0824, specialize in foreign language showings. Places such as **Cinema Village**, 22 East 12th St, tel: 924 3363; the **Film Forum**, 209 West Houston St, tel: 727 8110; **Anthology Film Archives,** 32 Second Ave, tel: 505 5181 and the **Walter Reade Theater** at Lincoln Center, tel: 875 5600, all specialize in vintage films or others of a special nature. The annual New York Film Festival also takes place at Lincoln Center every fall.

Diary of Events

It's just possible that there may be somebody somewhere who goes to New York for a rest. But it's certainly the least likely place to choose because in The Big Apple (the term originated among sports figures and jazz musicians in the 1920s) there's something happening 24 hours, every day of the year.

If you have time to plan your visit well ahead, write to the New York Convention & Visitors Bureau, Two Columbus Circle, New York, NY, 10019, for a free calendar of events or call 397 8222 when you arrive.

JANUARY

Horse-racing season (through April) opens at Aqueduct Racetrack, Queens.
National Boat Show, Jacob K. Javits Convention Center.
Greater New York International Auto Show, Coliseum.
Ice Capades, Madison Square Garden.
Metropolitan Opera season (to March) at Lincoln Center.
New York City Ballet at Lincoln Center (through February).
New York Philharmonic at Lincoln Center (to May).
Collegiate basketball at Madison Square Garden.
Chinese New Year (sometimes early February).

FEBRUARY

Black History month.
Flower show, New York Botanical Garden, Bronx.
Westminster Kennel Club dog show, Madison Square Garden.
National Antiques Show, Madison Square Garden.

MARCH

Cat Show, Madison Square Garden.
St Patrick's Day (March 17) and Greek Independence Day (March 25). Parades, both down Fifth Ave.
New York Flower Show, Pier 92 at 51st Street.
Spring Bulb Show, Brooklyn Botanic Garden.
Circus Animal Walk, Ringling Brothers, Barnum & Bailey Circus (about March 23).
Art Expo, Javits Convention Center.
New Directors Film Festival, Museum of Modern Art.

APRIL

Baseball season begins: New York Yankees and New York Mets.
Macy's Spring Flower Show.
Easter Parade on Fifth Avenue.
New York Black Expo, Pier 88.
New York City Ballet Season (to June) at Lincoln Center.

MAY

New York beaches open.
Black World Championship Rodeo, Harlem
Belmont Racetrack opens.
Solidarity Day parade, Fifth Avenue.
Armed Forces Day Parade, Fifth Avenue.
9th Avenue International Food Festival.
Martin Luther King Parade, Fifth Avenue.
Salute to Israel Parade, Fifth Avenue.
Ukrainian Festival, 7th Street and Second Ave.
Brooklyn Heights Promenade Art Show.
Memorial Day Parade, Broadway and 72nd St.

JUNE

Gay Pride Day Parade, Fifth Avenue.
Second Avenue Festival, 68th Street.
Free Metropolitan Opera concerts in parks of each borough.
Central Park South outdoor art show.
Snug Harbor Sculpture Festival (to October).

Puerto Rican Day Parade, Fifth Avenue.
Flag Day events, Fraunces Tavern Museum.
Flower Show (to October), New York Botanical Garden, Bronx.
JVC Jazz Festival throughout the city.
52nd Street Festival.
Feast of St Anthony, Little Italy.

JULY

Free Shakespeare in Central Park (to August) and in Brooklyn's Prospect Park.
Free concerts at South Street Seaport.
Free Museum of Modern Art Summergarden concerts.
Harbor Festival, parade, fireworks on July 4.
Feast of Mount Carmel, Bronx.
Washington Square Music festival.
New York City Opera, Lincoln Center.
Festival Italiana, Carmine Street.
American Indian Midsummer Pow Wow, Queens County Farm Museum.
New York Philharmonic free parks concerts (all boroughs, into August).
Serious Fun! Lincoln Center – innovative performances in music and dance.

AUGUST

Lincoln Center Out-of-Doors Festival.
Harlem Week.
Washington Square Music Festival.
Washington Square Art Show.
Third Avenue Summerfest.
Festival of the Americas, Sixth Avenue.
Richmond County Fair, Staten Island.

SEPTEMBER

US Open Tennis Championships, Queens.
Football season begins.
San Gennaro Festival, Little Italy.
New York Philharmonic season opens, Lincoln Center.
Third Avenue Fair.
"New York is Book Country" outdoor publishers' trade show, Fifth Avenue and 59th Street.
West Indian American Day Parade, Brooklyn.
Metropolitan Opera season (to May) opens, Lincoln Center.
UN General Assembly opens.
Schooner Regatta, South Street Seaport.
Columbus Avenue Festival.

OCTOBER

New York Rangers hockey season opens, Madison Square Garden.
Harvest Festival, Tibetan Museum, Staten Island.
Winter horse-racing season begins at Aqueduct race track, Queens.
Next Wave Festival at BAM, Brooklyn Academy of Music.
Big Apple Circus (to January), Lincoln Center.
Pulaski Day Parade, Fifth Avenue.
Hispanic Day Parade, Fifth Avenue.
Columbus Day Parade, Fifth Avenue.
Halloween Parade, Greenwich Village.

NOVEMBER

New York City Marathon, Staten Island to Central Park.
Macy's Thanksgiving Day Parade.
Christmas Star Show, Hayden Planetarium.
Christmas Holiday Spectacular, Radio City Music Hall.
New York City Ballet season opens.
Veterans' Day Parade, Fifth Avenue.
National Horse Show, Madison Square Garden.
Origami Christmas Tree, Museum of Natural History.

DECEMBER

Giant Christmas Tree, Rockefeller Center.
Giant Hanukkah Menora, Grand Army Plaza, Brooklyn.
The Nutcracker, New York City Ballet at Lincoln Center.
New Year's Eve celebrations in Times Square; fireworks in Central Park, Brooklyn's Prospect Park and at South Street Seaport.

Nightlife

Clubs appear and vanish in New York even more abruptly than restaurants. While flagships like the Village Vanguard and the Rainbow Room seem eternal, others, especially the ultra-chic discos and dance clubs, are more ephemeral, seeming to rise and fall literally overnight. Visitors are well advised to consult up-to-date listings in the weekly New Yorker magazine, New York magazine and the Village Voice before venturing out on the town.

The following represent a range of the best clubs, offering various types of live and recorded music as well as comedy, cabaret acts and even poetry

readings. Because cover charges, ticket prices, reservation policies and show times vary tremendously from club to club and act to act, you must call and ask for details. As a very loose rule of thumb, expect to spend $15 to $25 or more per person for featured "name acts," and $3 or more for a drink, though there is wide variation. Figure that in general, featured live acts won't commence before 9 or 10pm, though many of the jazz clubs have midday brunch music on weekends. Dance clubs don't wake up before midnight.

Dress codes are casual to punk chic in most of the jazz, rock, folk and eclectic music clubs listed below, as well as in the comedy clubs. The code is more dinner-jacket at the nightclub/cabarets. Dress is most crucial at the dance clubs, where being able to flash the latest in hip fashion can literally be the difference between getting in and getting snubbed by the doorman.

Jazz

THE VILLAGES

Blue Note, 131 West 3rd St. Tel: 475 8592. The West Village is home to the most famous jazz clubs in the country. First and foremost, there's the Blue Note, which has been packed virtually every night for years. The reason is simple: the club presents the very best of mainstream jazz and blues, from time-honored greats to more contemporary acts. Typically, the line-up here features such luminaries as the Modern Jazz Quartet, Etta James, Joe Williams, Betty Carter, the Count Basie Orchestra...the list goes on and on. For die-hard fans, there's a late-night session that jams until 4am, after the last set.

Village Vanguard, 178 Seventh Ave South. Tel: 255 4037. Born over half a century ago in a Greenwich Village basement, this flagship cut its teeth helping to launch fabulous talents like Miles Davis and John Coltrane. In its adulthood it hardly keeps up with the "vanguard" anymore, but rather presents the greats and near-greats of what is now the mainstream. Your heart won't race, but you may well tap your toes. Very charming and popular – to avoid disappointment call well in advance for reservations.

Sweet Basil, 88 Seventh Ave South. Tel: 242 1785. Another venerable West Village jazz spot, Sweet Basil tends to book acts that will rarely shock or challenge, but that do represent fine mainstream jazz. A supper club as well as music venue, Sweet Basil reserves Monday nights for Miles Evans and the Monday Night Orchestra, who explore the more eclectic compositions of the late, great Gil Evans.

Bradley's, 70 University Place. Tel: 228 6440. A tiny, intimate restaurant-bar-jazz club. The cover charge can be relatively steep (compared to the size of the rooms), but the atmosphere should please the really serious music-lovers.

Fat Tuesday's, 190 Third Ave at 17th St. Tel: 533 7902. A tame, tiny jazz club where the big name acts tend to be of the smoothest, most laid-back tradition. Mose Allison, Charlie Byrd and Les Paul, for instance, are among regular headliners here.

Zinno, 126 West 13th St. Tel: 924 5182. A pleasing café and supper club with a delightful outdoor garden, featuring unobtrusive jazz on the piano.

MIDTOWN

The Five Spot, 4 West 31st St. Tel: 631 0100. A fairly recent addition to the city's jazz club roster, and a good one. Features pricey dining and contemporary fusion and jazz in an ornately elegant ballroom setting.

Red Blazer Too, 349 West 46th St. Tel: 262 3112. A hefty dose of New Orleans-style jazz in comfortable, relaxed surroundings, plus dining and dancing.

UPPER WEST SIDE

Birdland, 2745 Broadway at 105th St. Tel: 749 2228. The Upper West Side's answer to the Village jazz scene, offering "live jazz and fine dining 7 days a week." The acts, while rarely big names, tend to be fine (often local) mainstream professionals. The clientele is a casual blend of Columbia U. students and aficionados.

Iridium, 44 West 63rd St. Tel: 582 2121. Some people find this venue, beneath the restaurant of the same name, strangley disorienting – the decor being Gaudí-esque in the extreme. But since it opened in early 1994, Iridium has also presented some of the

jazz world's most gifted denizens. Definitely worth checking out.

Rock, Folk, Funk & Dance

MIDTOWN

Rodeo Bar, 375 Third Ave at 27th St. Tel: 683 6500. Like the name says, this East Side neighborhood music bar has a kitschy Wild West theme, a correspondingly loose and lanky atmosphere, and (sometimes) live performances by "cowboy rock" bands like Asleep At The Wheel.

Roseland, 239 West 52nd St. Tel: 247 0200. Historically, a venue for traditional ballroom dancing; lately, an occasional venue for performances by alternative rock bands and other non-mainstream performers.

The Supper Club, 240 West 47th St. Tel: 921 1940. A romantic, violet-toned throwback to New York's heyday of the 1940s, with dining, dancing and, recently, onstage appearances by the likes of Bob Dylan and former Talking Head David Byrne.

THE VILLAGE/SOHO

The Bitter End, 149 Bleecker St. Tel: 673 7030. A Greenwich Village landmark, the Bitter End books an eclectic mishmash of folk, folk rock, soft rock, blues, some comedy and cabaret… whatever. A classic example of eternal bohemianism, it's very popular with young adult tourists and can be mobbed on weekend nights.

The Bottom Line, 15 West 4th St. Tel: 228 6300. A tiny, venerable, mostly folk music and blues venue in the heart of Greenwich Village. A word of warning: this club is very popular with the college crowd, who will line up outside a week in advance to purchase tickets. And once inside, it's a mad scramble for the best seats. Still, the intimacy of the space and the top-quality bookings make the struggle well worthwhile.

CBGB & OMFUG, 315 Bowery at Bleecker St. Tel: 982 4052. The club where punk started in America, still the quintessential punk venue, in effect a museum to the spirit of '77. A dark, gloomy cave in the midst of the Bowery's decrepitude, CBGB has a beaten-down anti-glamor that's quite charming if you can appreciate it. You won't have heard of any of the young bands, because CBGB remains one of

the most open venues for thousands of new "underground" groups with bad haircuts and names like Hide The Babies, False Virgins and Some Weird Sin. Worth the pilgrimage. Dress down as far as you can without being picked up on the streets for vagrancy, and enjoy the slumming.

Delia's, 197 East 3rd St. Tel: 254 9184. A tiny, surprisingly classy East Village place for dinner and dancing to contemporary music.

The Mercury Lounge, 217 East Houston St. Tel: 260 4700. Small and down-to-earth, with excellent acoustics, this club caters to the alternative-music crowd, and is one of the best of a slew of new Lower East Side hangouts along Houston and down Ludlow Street.

Sin-é, 122 St Mark's Place (just beyond Avenue A). Tel: 982 0370. Folk music, often with an Irish accent to it, in a hip, relaxed, café setting with no liquor license, but lots of laid-back atmosphere.

Webster Hall, 125 East 11th St. Tel: 353 1600. Another large club-of-the-moment that, due to its East Village locale, is a little less slick than most. Open Wednesdays to Saturdays from 10pm, it's popular with a young, black-clad crowd for all-night dancing to everything from rock and reggae to house and who knows; theme nights range from "runway parties" to psychedelia.

Wetlands, 161 Hudson St below Canal. Tel: 966 4225. This TriBeCa bar & club struggles to keep the spirit of the hippie era alive and gently grooving on good vibes. It's remarkably successful, considering it's in Manhattan. The weekly billings combine 60s-style rock bands (psychedelia, Grateful Dead sound-alikes, Led Zeppelin imitators) and acoustic folk music with reggae and a little jazz and funk. Very casual, of course, and a soothing switch from the more hard-edged and hard-hearted clubs. Peace, man.

CHELSEA/UNION SQUARE

Irving Plaza, 17 Irving Pl. Tel: 777 6800. A dilapidated hall that's gone through more than one incarnation, currently featuring everything from jazz and rock to X-rated performance art.

Limelight, 47 West 20th St (at Sixth Ave). Tel: 807 7850. A converted church with distinctly non-religious doings inside, and at this point –

over a decade after it opened – the longest-lasting dance-til-you-drop club in the city. Not for the faint-hearted.

Nell's, 246 West 14th St. Tel: 675 1567. A once notable dance club, Nell's trendsetting glory has faded, which is just as well for those who are not royalty or movie stars, because now you'll have an easier time getting in the door. The club still attracts some celebs, however.

Tramps, 45 West 21st St between 5th and 6th Avenues. Tel: 727 7788. A large, sleek Chelsea music club with a Bayou flair, regularly featuring the tops in cajun, zydeco, rock and Southern-fried boogie. No "attitude," much fun.

UPPER EAST SIDE

Manny's Car Wash, 1558 Third Ave. Tel: 369 2583. A welcome addition to the mostly nonexistent Upper East Side music scene, Manny's is another spot devoted to Chicago-style blues and urban rock. Sunday night jam sessions are free.

HARLEM

Apollo Theater, 253 West 125th St. Tel: 749 5838. A legendary showcase for all kinds of entertainment.

Cotton Club, 666 West 125th St at Westside Hwy. Tel: 663 7980. Yes, the Cotton Club, making a fair job of updating the spirit of Jazz Age Harlem for an urban contemporary audience. A dressed-to-the-nines crowd of hipsters comes for dinner and dancing to classy modern soul music.

Showman's Café, 2321 Eighth Ave. Tel: 864 8941. Tasty food and good music.

THE OUTER BOROUGHS

Lauterbach's, 335 Prospect Ave at Sixth Ave. Tel: 718-788-9140. The decor of this Brooklyn club is that of a punked-out, beaten-up bomb shelter, and the atmosphere is accordingly loose and downhome. The food is abominable. But if you're in or exploring Brooklyn and want to take in a rock club, this is the place to be, with up and coming bands cranking up lots of rowdy energy and noise.

NEW JERSEY

Maxwell's, 1039 Washington St, Hoboken, New Jersey. Tel: 201-798 4064. This successful club draws its share of young rock fans from The City

as well as from "Joisey" and regularly books the best of the underground and "independent label" rock bands. The music tends to be more adventurous and rambunctious than in the top-of-the-pops clubs. A word of caution: If you stay late, getting back across the Hudson to Manhattan can be an adventure, as taxis become not only scarce but expensive.

Avant-Garde

The Knitting Factory, 74 Leonard St, between Broadway and Church St. Tel: 219 3055 and 219 3006. Now relocated deep in the heart of TriBeCa, this eclectic avant-garde mecca – formerly on East Houston Street – is perhaps the best spot in the country for catching the next wave in experimental jazz, rock, poetry, and every possible combination of the same. Leading lights of New York's "downtown" music, like John Zorn, Elliot Sharp and the Lounge Lizards, are regulars, but the 7-nights-a-week bookings are far too adventurous and wide ranging to sum up in any single category. Dress down, because it's amazingly casual for such an "in" spot.

World Beat

S.O.B.'s, 204 Varick St at Houston St. Tel: 243 4940. The name of this SoHo restaurant and music club stands for "Sounds of Brazil," but it long ago expanded its repertoire to become the premiere club in the city for internationalist dance musics. One recent month's billings was a typically exhaustive world music tour: the contemporary samba of Brazilian singer Margareth Menezes; the West African funk band Les Amazones de Guinea; Jamaican reggae singer Alton Ellis; South African drummer Sipho Mabuse; the Bronx hip-hop of Afrika Bambaata; the Samoan rappers Boo-Yaa Tribe; and the salsa of Johnny Y. Ray. Call for dinner reservations, then dance the calories away.

Comedy and Cabaret

MIDTOWN

Caroline's Comedy Club, 1626 Broadway. Tel: 757 4100. A plush setting for Caroline's features a continuous roster of young comic hopefuls along with some of the biggest names in the "biz." An evening here can also be your

chance to laugh your way onto American television; some of the shows are videotaped for national cable TV consumption.

Danny's Grand Sea Palace, 346 West 46th St. Tel: 265 8130. A lively Thai restaurant with a piano bar and cabaret room. Show starts around 9pm.

Don't Tell Mama, 343 West 46th St. Tel: 757 0788. Very jolly, goodtimey spot, long favored by a theatrical crowd. In the front there's often a sing-along at the piano bar. The back room is a nonstop cabaret featuring comedians and torch singers. Don't bring your inhibitions.

Michael's Pub, 211 East 55th St. Tel: 758 2272. This Midtown restaurant and cabaret features a variety of top acts ranging from Broadway and TV stars to Big Band swing to jazz singers like Mel Torme to previews of Broadway musicals. The decor is inappropriately somber, but the atmosphere is comfortable, if a bit tweedy. Best known for Woody Allen's weekly stint.

The Oak Room, Algonquin Hotel, 59 West 44th St. Tel: 840 6800. A dark, intimate piano bar with great singers (Harry Connick Jr played here before he made it big).

Rainbow & Stars, 65th Floor, GE Building (30 Rockefeller Plaza). Tel: 632 5000. Traditional nightclub and cabaret acts for the sedate set, in as lavish a setting as the famous Rainbow Room next door, and with just as dazzling a view of the city's lights. Yesteryear's headliners put on high-style shows to upstage the scenery. The type of place you can take your mother.

The Russian Tea Room, 150 West 57th St. Tel: 265 0947. This classic New York restaurant now has an upstairs cabaret, with some of the city's top performers. Shows twice nightly.

UPPER EAST SIDE

Comic Strip, 1568 Second Ave at 82nd St. Tel: 861 9386. A casual and popular proving ground for young stand-up kamikazes, both known and unknown. Open seven days a week, with three shows nightly on weekends.

CHELSEA/GREENWICH VILLAGE/SOHO

The Comedy Cellar, 117 MacDougal St, tel: 254 3480. A cramped basement room where the tables are packed so close together that even if you don't get the jokes, you may make some new friends. Show starts at 9pm.

The Duplex, 61 Christopher St. Tel: 255 5438. A landmark of the gay West Village, attracting a friendly and mixed audience.

Shopping

Shopping Areas

Even more so than in most American cities, shopping is a major pastime in New York, but it is not easy to point to specialties. New York's distinction is its variety; there isn't much to be found anywhere that can't be found here, and usually more of it. Art, of course, is a good bet; apart from the major auctioneers, **Sotheby's** and **Christies**, where world-record prices are set for world-famous works, there are hundreds of art galleries in which to browse (if not to buy) and antiques can be found in indoor "malls" (such as **Manhattan Art & Antiques Center**, 1050 Second Ave, tel: 355 4400; Metropolitan Art & Antiques Pavilion, 110 West 19th St, tel: 463 0200) as well as Greenwich Village around University Place, around Hudson Street and the Midtown area around Third Avenue.

The famous department stores offer something for almost everyone but differ somewhat in their clientele, ranging from glittering **Bloomingdale's** (Lexington Ave at 59th St), and **Henri Bendel** (712 Fifth Ave); to **Macy's** (151 West 34th St). Other uptown stores are **Saks Fifth Avenue** (611 Fifth Ave); **Lord & Taylor** (Fifth Ave and 39th St); **Bergdorf Goodman** (754 Fifth Ave); and a branch of the Tokyo-based **Takashimaya** (693 Fifth Ave) nearby.

The Upper East Side is where the highest proportion of classy shops can be found, with Madison and Lexington Avenues in the 60s and 70s thick with possibilities, most of them expensive. There's another stretch of elegance along Fifth Avenue between Rockefeller Center and the Plaza Hotel, interrupted by a burst of mass merchandising at 57th Street (where the huge and immensely successful Warner Bros. Studio Store has paved the way for similar mall-like ventures).

Electronic and photographic suppliers have blossomed around Times Square, along West 42nd Street and down Seventh Avenue in the garment district (mostly wholesale) but most of these outlets are directed at tourists and you'll find few bargains. A better bet might be in the downtown financial district or along Lexington Avenue around Grand Central Station.

The real bargains are to be found downtown in such places as Orchard Street, Canal Street between Sixth and Third Avenues, and Greenwich Village, particularly along 8th Street west of Sixth Avenue and on 9th Street, between First and Second avenues. Savvy New York shoppers also flock to Manhattan's **flea markets**, including the eclectic weekend antiques market on Sixth Avenue between 25th and 27th Streets and the smaller new wave clothing market that takes place weekends on lower Broadway between 4th and Great Jones Streets.

There are a few antiquarian and second-hand bookstores just north of Cooper Union, especially the **Strand Book Store**, 828 Broadway, tel: 473 1452, which claims to have two million volumes in stock and is a wonderful place to browse. The transformation of SoHo from a pioneering art colony to a trendy area of fancy shops and galleries has injected new life into lower Broadway, a few blocks to the east, and this is now packed with shoppers, especially at weekends. A similar thing has happened on Columbus Avenue, around 86th Street, where gentrification inspired dozens of smart, new boutiques at the cost of longtime neighborhood businesses. One of Manhattan's best-known gourmet delicatessens, **Zabar's**, is up here at 2245 Broadway, tel: 787 2000, this being the sole upper West Side bastion of a category more commonly found in SoHo (**Dean & DeLuca**, 560 Broadway), the Village (**Balducci's**, 424 Sixth Ave) or in Midtown East (**Maison Glass**, 111 East 58th St).

Major crosstown arteries (8th, 14th, 23rd, 34th, 42nd, 57th, 86th, 125th) are usually good for shopping and 86th Street has two bites of the apple, the eastern segment (on the other side of Central Park) being Yorktown with a distinctly Germanic tinge. In the final analysis, of course, that special little something that you didn't know you were looking for is liable to turn up just when you were least expecting it in some out-of-the-way shop that you discovered quite serendipitously. Rest assured, it's somewhere awaiting you.

What to Buy
Books

Books & Co., 939 Madison Ave. Tel: 737 1450.
Brentano's, 597 Fifth Ave. Tel: 826 2450.
Traveller's Bookstore, 75 Rockefeller Plaza.Tel: 664 0995.
Complete Traveller Bookstore, 199 Madison Ave. Tel: 685 9007.
Drama Bookshop, 723 Seventh Ave. Tel: 944 0595.
Endicott Booksellers, 450 Columbus Ave. Tel: 787 6300.
Gotham Book Mart, 41 West 47th St. Tel: 719 4448.
Science Fiction Bookshop, 163 Bleecker St. Tel: 437 3010.
Murder Ink, 2486 Broadway. Tel: 362 8905.
Rizzoli, 31 West 57th St. Tel: 759 2424.
St Mark's Bookshop, 31 Third Ave. Tel: 260 7853.
Samuel Weiser, 132 East 24th St. Tel: 777 6363.
New York Bound, 50 Rockefeller Plaza. Tel: 245 8503.
The huge Tower Books, 383 Lafayette St. Tel: 228 5100.

Women's clothes

Agnès B, 1063 Madison Ave. Tel: 570 9333.
Ann Taylor, 645 Madison Ave. Tel: 765 2343.
Betsy Bunki Nini, 980 Lexington Ave. Tel; 744 6716.
Capezio, 177 MacDougal St. Tel: 477 5634.
Chelsea Designers, 128 West 23rd St. Tel: 255 8803.

Emporio Armani, 110 Fifth Ave. Tel: 727 3240.

Hanae Mori, 27 East 79th St. Tel: 472 2352.

OMO-Norma Kamali, 11 West 56th St. Tel: 957 9797.

Harriet Love, 126 Prince St. Tel: 966 2280.

Putumayo, 857 Lexington Ave. Tel: 734 3111.

Saint Laurent, 855 Madison Ave. Tel: 988 3821.

Men's clothes

Barney's, 106 Seventh Ave. Tel: 929 9000; 660 Madison Ave. Tel: 826 8900.

Brooks Brothers, 346 Madison Ave. Tel: 682 8800.

Countess Mara, 445 Park Ave. Tel: 751 5322.

J. Press, 16 East 44th St. Tel: 687 7642.

Mano a Mano, 580 Broadway. Tel: 219 9602.

Orvis, 355 Madison Ave. Tel: 697 3133.

Paul Stuart, Madison Ave at 45th St. Tel: 682 0320.

Men's and women's clothes

Armani Exchange, 568 Broadway. Tel: 431 6000.

Barney's, 106 Seventh Ave. Tel: 929 9000; 660 Madison Ave. Tel: 826 8900.

Brooks Brothers, 346 Madison Ave. Tel: 682 8800.

Burberry's, 9 East 57th St. Tel: 371 5010.

Calvin Klein, 654 Madison Ave. Tel: 292 9000.

Charivari, 257 Columbus Ave. Tel: 787 7272.

Polo-Ralph Lauren, 867 Madison Ave. Tel: 606 2100.

For men's designer discounts, try Pan Am, 50 Orchard St. Tel: 925 7032; for women's try Loehmann's, 5746 Broadway in the Bronx. Tel: 718-543 6420; for both, Century Twenty One, 22 Cortlandt St in lower Manhattan. Tel: 227 9092; Daffy's, 111 Fifth Ave. Tel: 529 4477 and branches.

Cameras & photography

Willoughby's, 110 West 32nd St. Tel: 564 1600.

47th Street Photo, 67 West 47th St. Tel: 921 1287.

Hirsch Photo, 699 Third Ave. Tel: 557 1150.

Electronic equipment

47th Street Photo, 67 West 47th St and 115 West 45th St. Tel: 921 1287.

SoHo Electronics, 530 Broadway. Tel: 941 8533.

The Sharper Image, 4 West 57th St. Tel: 265 2550 (and branches).

Music stores

House of Oldies, 35 Carmine St. Tel: 243 0500.

Jazz Record Center, 236 West 26th St. Tel: 675 4480.

Tower Records, 692 Broadway (and branches). Tel: 505 1500.

HMV has three gigantic record stores, including one at 86th and Lexington, (supposedly the largest music store in the US), and one at 72nd and Broadway. Tel: 721 5900.

Sports equipment

Herman's, 845 Third Ave. Tel: 688 4603.

Scandinavian Ski & Sports, 40 West 57th St. Tel: 757 8524

Paragon, 867 Broadway. Tel: 255 8036.

Toys

FAO Schwarz, Fifth Ave and 58th St. Tel: 644 9400.

Penny Whistle, 448 Columbus Ave. Tel: 873 9090.

Tenzing & Pema, 956 Madison Ave. Tel: 288 8780.

The Enchanted Forest, 85 Mercer St. Tel: 925 6677.

One-stop shopping

And don't overlook one-stop centers like the Manhattan Mall, Sixth Ave and 33rd St; South Street Seaport, Fulton and Water Streets; the World Financial Center, Battery Park City; and the World Trade Center, West and Vesey Streets.

CLOTHING SIZES

The table below gives a comparison of American, Continental and British clothing sizes. It is always best to try on any article before buying it, however, as sizes can vary.

Women's Dresses/Suits

American	Continental	British
6	38/34N	8/30
8	40/36N	10/32
10	42/38N	12/34
12	44/40N	14/36
14	46/42N	16/38
16	48/44N	18/40

Women's Shoes

American	Continental	British
4 1/2	36	3
5 1/2	37	4
6 1/2	38	5
7 1/2	39	6
8 1/2	40	7
9 1/2	41	8
10 1/2	42	9

Men's Suits

American	Continental	British
34	44	34
—	46	36
38	48	38
—	50	40
42	52	42
—	54	44
46	56	46

Men's Shirts

American	Continental	British
14	36	14
14 1/2	37	14 1/2
15	38	15
15 1/2	39	15 1/2
16	40	16
16 1/2	41	16 1/2
17	42	17

Men's Shoes

American	Continental	British
6 1/2	—	6
7 1/2	40	7
8 1/2	41	8
9 1/2	42	9
10 1/2	43	10
11 1/2	44	11

Sports and Leisure

Participant Sports

New York's parks offer varied facilities for the sports or athletically-minded with, of course, Central Park offering the most attractions, including traffic-free roads for the benefit of cyclists all weekends and lunchtimes during the summer.

Rowboats can be hired at Central Park Lake (also at lakes in Kissena Park, Queens; Prospect Park, Brooklyn; and Van Cortlandt Park in the Bronx).

Tennis can be played on courts at 96th Street and Central Park West.

Horses can be hired at the Claremont Riding Academy, 175 West 89th St, tel: 724 5100, to ride on park trails.

There is ice skating at both the Wollman and Lasker Rinks, between October and April (also at the Rivergate Ice Skating Rink, 401 East 34th St, tel: 689 0035 and year-round, at Sky Rink, 450 West 33rd St, tel: 695 6555)

More than a dozen **baseball** or **softball** diamonds are open to park visitors, as well as a variety of **jogging** tracks. The New York Road Runners Club maintains a running center at 9 East 89th St, tel: 860 4455.

A dozen public **golf courses** are distributed among the parks of the five boroughs, including Pelham Bay Park and Staten Island's Latourette Park. For details call the Parks Department at 360 8217 or 1-800-201 7275.

The new Chelsea Pier complex, along the Hudson River between 17th and 23rd streets, features a golf driving range and everything from roller skating to swimming and rock climbing. Tel: 336 6666.

Several hotels have **swimming pools**, including the Skyline Hotel, Parker Meridien, UN Plaza, Sheraton Manhattan and New York Vista. There are also several public indoor and out-door pools around the city, including one at Carmine Street and Seventh Avenue South that's open all year, as are those in the ymcas at 206 West 24th St. Tel: 741 9226; 224 East 47th St. Tel: 755 2410 and 5 West 63rd St. Tel: 787 1301.

Private health clubs and **spas** with pools are also listed in the *Yellow Pages* of the telephone book.

In addition to the courts in various public parks, **tennis** is also available at the Midtown Tennis Club, 341 Eighth Ave. Tel: 989 8572; the Manhattan Plaza Racquet Club, 450 West 43rd St. Tel: 594 0554 and the Wall Street Racquet Club, Piers 13 and 14. Tel: 422 9300.

Spectator Sports

New York is understandably proud of its top-rated teams, the Mets and Yankees, who play **baseball** from April to October at (respectively) Shea Stadium in Flushing, tel: 718-507 8499 and Yankee Stadium in the Bronx, tel: 718-293 6000; also the Knickerbockers and the Nets who play basketball between October and May at (respectively) Madison Square Garden, tel: 465 6741, and the Meadowlands Arena in East Rutherford, New Jersey, tel: 201-935 8500. College team schedules are listed in the sports sections of daily papers.

Football takes place from September to December, with both the New York Giants and New York Jets playing at Giants Stadium situated in the Meadowlands.

Madison Square Garden is also the main site for major sporting events in **boxing**, **ice hockey** (the New York Rangers play here; the Islanders play at Nassau Coliseum on Long Island, tel: 516-794 9300) and **tennis**. (More tennis can be seen at the West Side Tennis Club, Forest Hills, tel: 718-268 2300; and the National Tennis Center, Flushing Meadows, Queens, tel: 718-271 5100, where the US Open Championships take place every year in September).

Soccer, increasingly popular since the 1994 World Cup, which was hosted by the United States, takes place at the Meadowlands between April and October. Cricket matches are played on summer Sunday afternoons in Van Cortlandt Park, as well as on Randall's Island and in various parks in Brooklyn.

The closest thoroughbred **horse-racing** tracks are at Aqueduct in Queens. Tel: 718-641 4700 (Subway from Eighth Ave and 42nd St); and Belmont Park, Elmont, Long Island. Tel: 718-641 4700 (Long Island railroad from Pennsylvania Station). Standardbred tracks include Yonkers Raceway, Yonkers and Central Avenue. Tel: 914-968 4200; the Meadowlands Racetrack. Tel: 201-935 8500 (Buses from Port Authority terminal).

Further Reading

General

The Age of Innocence by Edith Wharton. Scribner, 1983.
AIA Guide to New York City by Elliot Willinsky and Norval White. Harcourt Bace Jovanovich, 1988.
A Natural History of New York City by John Kiernan. Fordham University Press, 1982.
Another Country by James Baldwin. Dell, 1988.
A Tree Grows in Brooklyn by Betty Smith. Harper & Row, 1968.
The Beautiful Bronx: 1920–1950 by Lloyd Ultan. Crown, 1982.
Bonfire of the Vanities by Tom Wolfe. Farrar, Straus, Giroux, 1987.
Broadway by Brooks Atkinson. Macmillan Publishing Co.
At The Theatre: An Informal History of New York's Legitimate Theatres. Dodd Mead & Company, 1984.
George Balanchine, Ballet Master by Richard Buckle. In collaboration with John Taras. New York: Random House, 1988.
Here is New York by E.B. White. Warner Books, 1988.
History Preserved: A Guide to New York City Landmarks and Historic Districts by Harmon H. Goldstone and Martha Dalrymple. Schocken Books, 1976.
The Lincoln Center Story by Alan Rich. New York: American Heritage, 1984.
Literary Neighborhoods of New York by Marcia Leisner. Starhill Press, 1989.
Manhattan '45 by Jan Morris. Oxford University Press, 1987.
The Movie Lover's Guide to New York

by Richard Alleman. Perennial Library/ Harper & Row, 1988.

New York Art Guide by Deborah Jane Gardner. Robert Silver Associates, 1987.

The New Chinatown by Peter Kwong. Hill & Wang, 1987.

New York by Djuna Barnes. Sun and Moon Press, 1989.

New York: Heart of the City by J.P. MacBean. Mallard Press, 1990.

New York's Nooks and Crannies: Unusual Walking Tours in all Five Boroughs by David Yeadon. New York: Charles Scribner & Sons, 1986.

New York Times Guide to Restaurants in New York City by Bryan Miller. Times Books, 1990.

New York Times World of New York by A.M. Rosenthal and Arthur Gelb. Times Books, 1985.

On Broadway: A Journey Uptown Over Time by David W. Dunlop. Rizzoli International Publications, 1990.

Poet in New York by Federico Garcia Lorca. Farrar, Straus, Giroux, 1988.

Slaves of New York by Tama Janowitz. Pocket Books, 1988.

Time and Again by Jack Finney. Simon & Schuster, 1970.

Uptown & Downtown: A Trip Through Time on New York Subways by Stan Fischler. E.P. Dutton.

You Must Remember This. An Oral History of Manhattan from the 1890s to World War II by Jeff Kisseloff. Harcourt Brace Jovanovich.

Washington Square by Henry James. Penguin, 1984.

When Brooklyn Was the World: 1920– 1957 by Elliot Willensky. Crown, 1986.

When Harlem Was in Vogue by David Levering Lewis. Oxford University Press, 1983.

Winter's Tale by Mark Helprin. Harcourt Brace Jovanovich, 1983.

The WPA Guide to New York City, Federal Writers Project Guide to 1930s New York. Pantheon, 1982.

Other Insight Guides

The 190 books in the *Insight Guides* series cover every continent and include 40 titles devoted to the United States, from Alaska to Florida, from Seattle to New Orleans. Destinations in the region include:

Insight Guide: Washington DC is essential reading that conveys the power and the story of America's capital.

Insight Guide: Boston. An excellent team of writers and photographers celebrates Boston, one of America's most intriguing cities.

Insight Guide: Philadelphia. The cream of Philly's writers and photographers document the City of Brotherly Love in comprehensive detail.

Insight Guides have two newer series for visitors in a hurry. *Insight Pocket Guides* act as a "substitute host" to a destination and present a selection of full-day, morning or afternoon itineraries. They also include a large, fold-out map. *Insight Compact Guides* are miniature travel encyclopedias, carry-along guidebooks for on-the-spot reference.

Insight Pocket Guide: New York City. In the town of a thousand choices, personal recommendations and sightseeing routes take the big angst out of the Big Apple.

Insight Pocket Guide: Boston. This slim volume offers personalized itineraries for a short stay in this beautiful, historic city.

Insight Compact Guide: New York. The definitive quick-reference travel guide to the city, both readable and reliable.

Index